JOHN HENRY JOWETT,

C.H., M.A., D.D.

John Henry Jowett

C.H., M.A., D.D.

BY

ARTHUR PORRITT

WITH A FOREWORD BY
THE ARCHBISHOP OF CANTERBURY

"A man not only wins his character largely, but
reveals his character largely, through his work."
GEORGE A. GORDON.

HODDER AND STOUGHTON
LIMITED · LONDON

MADE AND PRINTED IN GREAT BRITAIN
RICHARD CLAY & SONS, LIMITED,
PRINTERS, BUNGAY, SUFFOLK.

TO

MRS. JOWETT

FOREWORD
By His Grace the Archbishop of Canterbury

I complied readily with the request made to me
by the author of this book that I should provide it
with a short Foreword.

It is eminently right that such a Biography should
be written. I hope it will be widely read. And I
gratefully take the opportunity of expressing my own
regret that I was not more persistent in an endeavour
to secure closer intimacy with a contemporary
Christian teacher whose words have rightly carried so
wide an influence. Preachers belonging to the front
rank are rare in the England of to-day; rarer, I am
afraid, than they used to be. Of that small number
Dr. Jowett was pre-eminently one. More than once
I listened with admiration and profit to his speeches,
and although I never actually heard him preach I
used regularly to read some of his contributions to the
religious press and not a few of his published Sermons.
His eloquence was nobly used for giving to his hearers
in a stirring and thoughtful way the straightforward
message of the " good news of Jesus Christ the Son of
God," and I have no doubt that thousands in Birmingham, in New York, in Westminster can testify to-day
to what his presentment of that Gospel has meant to
their souls' health.

My knowledge of him was confined to some conversations, important but infrequent, during his
Ministry in Carr's Lane, and some ampler intercourse

during the last years of his life. We had abundant talk and fellowship during the anxious war-months of 1918, and again in what was known as the Peace Campaign of 1922. In regard to that effort some of his eager proposals proved—as he came fully to admit—to be unworkable, but we owed a great debt to his fervent appeal. " I am more of a bugler than a captain " he said to me in, I think, the last of our many talks upon the subject, and beyond doubt his clear bugle-note rang far. It has reverberated powerfully in a good many conferences since he has passed to " where beyond these voices there is peace."

In the steady " movements " for Reunion which, during the last two years have so often drawn to Lambeth the Free Church leaders who were his friends, his counsel would have been invaluable and his outside call far-reaching, for his keen spirit had already been pointing him thitherward.

It would be unreal not to say that there were, in his many-sided life, incidents, utterances, attitudes which I found it difficult to appreciate or perhaps to understand aright, but I am conscious that the fault or failure may have been largely my own. At all events I am increasingly convinced, after reading this record of the fine output of his strenuous years, that to me at least, and possibly to him, an earlier and closer intercourse between us would have been of abiding service in the activities of our common life.

RANDALL CANTUAR

Lambeth,
    August, 1924.

PREFACE

DR. JOWETT kept no diary. He preserved very few letters. He made no systematic collection of newspaper cuttings about himself, or his work. He left no notes or memoranda of a personal character. He forbade the publication of his unpublished sermon manuscripts. In fact, with the ingrained modesty which was one of his outstanding and most attractive characteristics, he seems never to have imagined that his life would ever engage the attention of a biographer.

Happily, scattered over Dr. Jowett's published sermons and books and in newspaper reports of his speeches, there are generous fragments of autobiography, ingenuous, self-revealing and often lit up by playful humour. From these fitful glimpses into himself, an outline autobiography, mosaic in construction, might almost be compiled, and the reader of this biography will discover that no opportunity has been lost to make use of " Jowett testifying as to Jowett."

Dr. Jowett cannot be accused of allowing the art of letter writing to die out. But he confined his letter writing to a small group of intimate friends with whom he communed through the post, writing generally with his own hand in a script that never grew slovenly, and transmitting to them the very secrets of his soul. I am deeply indebted therefore to Rev. John Loosmore, Rev. David Young, Rev. Edgar Todd, Rev. Thomas Towers, Mr. John G. Hurst, K.C., Mr. John Pells,

Mr. H. F. Keep, Miss Alice Slater and Rev. and Mrs. Hugh P. Young for their kindness in permitting me to read these sacred missives of friendship and for allowing me to make extracts for publication.

I am indebted, too, to Mrs. Jowett, at whose request I have written this biography—from which responsibility, but for her desire, I should certainly have shrunk—for her confidence and help.

I gladly acknowledge assistance in the form of valuable material, and of painstaking efforts to verify facts and to clear up obscurities from Dr. Archibald Duff, Mr. Thomas Feather (Dr. Jowett's friend in childhood and boyhood, now a London journalist), Mr. Arthur Birnage, Dr. Griffith-Jones, Rev. T. H. Martin, M.A., Rev. James Mursell, Rev. E. Johnson Saxton, Rev. J. G. Henderson, The Dean of Worcester (Dr. Moore Ede), Principal Hywel Hughes, and Mr. David Williamson.

My own personal association with Dr. Jowett dated from the year 1894 and grew through the years into a friendship which was, I would fain hope, based on his side on genuine regard and confidence as it assuredly was on mine. So, the writing of this story of his life has been less of a literary task than a labour of love— the weaving of a garland of friendship.

13 *Fleet Street*,
    London, E.C.

CONTENTS

xi

CONTENTS

CHAPTER I

THE baby boy born into the humble home of Josiah and Hannah Jowett at Halifax on August 25th, 1863, was their fourth child and their third son. And since " the first baby is a great event, the second an episode, and the others merely incidents," it is possible that the birth of John Henry Jowett occasioned no tempestuous flutterings in the family circle. Sixty years later the news of the death of this fourth child of Josiah and Hannah Jowett was flashed by cable all over the world, and wherever the English language is spoken and " the Name that is above every name " is honoured, there was sorrow over the passing of a Christian preacher from whose lips comfort and stimulus had radiated to the uttermost parts of the earth. The Eastern prayer, found on the walls of an ancient mosque, that " you came into the world crying while all around you were smiling; so live that you may go out of the world smiling while all around you are weeping " had been fulfilled in his case. This memoir is the story of " The Years Between."

The industrial towns of Yorkshire, drab as they are, have shown an amazing faculty for producing prophets, priests and kings. All these towns have

B

their curious external resemblances, yet each seems to possess some subtle individuality, a temper, a mentality, an ethos of its own; and each in its own way seems to have made some special contribution to our island story. One may boast of having given birth to a political giant or a spiritual seer. Another may claim to have harboured a little Dissenting Academy where the lamp of learning was kept burning brightly even when the great Universities were sunk in somnolence. Still another may have presented a field for some bold pioneer in industrial processes, while yet another may have provided a pulpit for a far-reaching prophet of God—some Dissenting minister whose lips have been touched with a live coal from the altar. A sturdy race of men not far remote from the soil inhabits these Yorkshire towns—men of gritty independence and fearless outthrust, with a fierce integrity as if it were bitten into them that honesty is its own reward.

Trace back the pedigree of almost any family in these towns—mushroom growths of the industrial revolution—and in a generation or two you are back among the tillers of the soil. The pedigrees have an odd similarity. Josiah and Hannah Jowett both sprang from farming folk who, when steam power was applied to spinning and weaving, were drawn into Halifax by the resistless suction of the towns. The surname Jowett is not uncommon in Pennine Yorkshire. It is pronounced there with the hard vowel sound (as in cow) as distinguished from the long soft O (as in the " know-it " of the familiar Limerick) in the name of Dr. Benjamin Jowett, the famous Master of Balliol. The name is an old one. Professor Ernest Weekley in " The Romance of Names " gives a list from the Hundred Rolls of cottagers resident in

the village of Steeple Claydon, Bucks, in 1273 which
includes persons named " Joyet," of which Jowett
and Jewett are modern equivalents. It is suggested
by Professor Weekley that Joyet was a diminutive of
Joy.

In 1863, when John Henry Jowett was born, his
father and mother lived in a hill-slope region called
Claremount, on one of the ridges of Beacon Hill,—
the highest point of the Pennines in that district,—
and about a mile out of the centre of Halifax. The
house was at once the family home and the place of
business of Josiah Jowett, who carried on his trade
as a tailor and draper on an upper floor. Mr. William
Nicholl of Sheffield, who was apprenticed to Josiah
Jowett by indenture in 1865, has described the Jowett
home " as a nice double house with nine rooms, a
fine garden in front and a large open space at the
back." Mr. Nicholl, who lived with his parents in
the next house, often nursed John Henry Jowett as
a baby, and frequently took him out in the perambu-
lator to his paternal grandfather's farm at Shibden
just outside the town. One of Jowett's own earliest
recollections was of driving in a mourning carriage to
his grandmother's funeral. Through the window he
saw one of his little playmates on the pavement and
he remembered thinking that no doubt he, too, would
like to be driving in a carriage to his grandmother's
funeral. Jowett was still a small boy when the home
was removed to Godley Road—to a home which
provided ampler accommodation for both the enlarged
family and the expanding business. It was of this
home that Jowett, speaking forty years later and in
justification of his almost immoderate love of his
garden, said he lived through his boyhood years in a
house that was one of a row in a long unlovely street

in which not a tree, nor a flower, nor even a blade of grass grew.

Godley Road was a thoroughfare cut through the side of the hill slope on which Halifax is built. The front door of the eight-roomed Jowett home opened directly on to the street pavement, while the back windows looked down over a thickly peopled hill-side and valley. There was another quite independent house under the back ground-floor rooms of the Jowett house, which was thus without garden or yard of any kind. Until he left Halifax for College this was Jowett's home environment—simple and modest but serenely happy. " I was blessed," he said, " with the priceless privilege of a Christian home."

Great men owe much to heredity and environment, but they owe most, perhaps, to spiritual impacts received, almost unconsciously, in their early years. Most of all, they are usually life-debtors to the influence in their earliest years of a strong womanly mother. Olive Schreiner went so far as to claim that there was never a great man who had not a great mother. At all events Jowett went through his life chanting the praises of his mother. To the end of her life she was the object of his solicitous care. He never wearied of acknowledging the immensity of his indebtedness to her. " At my mother's knee," he said once, " I gained my sweetest inspirations." To a friend who once asked him whence came his gift for felicitous illustration he replied, " From my mother ! It was she who taught me to see—she taught me to see things, and the things within things." " From my earliest days," he said at his ordination, " everything around me was made to point heavenwards. Every material structure seemed to be completed by a spire which indicated the spiritual aspiration to which it ought to be allied. And yet in all this abounding suggestiveness there was nothing to frighten even a child. Fortunately our parents knew nothing of those long theological names in which learned men sought to enshrine the interpretation of God's ways. ' Jesus ' was about the longest and the hardest word they knew, and Jesus found its interpretation in the shorter word ' Love.' So it happened we were brought up not to fear a monster described by an unpronounceable name but to love a friend who kept us while we slept, and smiled upon us when we were good. In the days of our infancy, around our mother's knee, in the little evening prayer, we were taught that Heaven was a happy land, far, far away, where all good people lived, and that even we might live in the portal of that beautiful land. And the parents who taught the doctrine lived the truth."

A plain, simple-spoken Yorkshire woman, humbly placed but proudly independent, Hannah Jowett mothered her boys and girls with a firm but gentle hand. Her supreme interests were her Home and her Chapel—the latter being Square Congregational Church, to whose history her son's life and work added imperishable lustre. Hannah Jowett shrewdly realised the value of education, and she encouraged her children to treasure knowledge and to use it for the fashioning of character.

Immersed in his growing business, Josiah Jowett entrusted the care of his family to his capable and godly wife. In some senses she was the stronger individuality. He belonged to a gentle type, rare in Yorkshire—a quiet unassuming man with delicately cut features, a slight though rather tall physique and a manner that was courteous and gracious without a shade of obsequiousness. " Whenever I wish to

think of a Christian man," said Jowett once at Newcastle, " I think of my father. In all our home life
I never heard him speak an impatient or an unkind
word."

While there was no favouritism in the Jowett
home—where the boys and girls had their little household duties to do and did them; for no servant was
kept—the third boy, John Henry (following the Yorkshire habit he was always given the benefit of both
his Christian names), who " moved and spoke in quiet
grown-up wise," had a peculiar place in the family
circle. His elder brothers went into the tailoring
business; but Josiah Jowett always had other ambitions for his third boy—this " lad of pairts."

Jowett's first school, which he attended when the
family home was in Claremount, was known as St.
Thomas's. It was a mixed National school of an
old-fashioned type, but it was practically the only
school then available in the locality. With his elder
brothers he went to this school; but he was never
happy there. He complained of the harshness and
injustice of the master, and finally he went home one
day, when he was about ten, with an ultimatum—
he was not going again to St. Thomas's School, he
announced. The boyish revolt was not regarded
seriously by his parents, and nearly a week passed
before his father discovered that Jowett had been
playing truant of set purpose, in order to be removed
to another school. This led to his becoming a day
pupil at Hipperholme (locally pronounced Hipperum)
Grammar School—an old educational foundation with
classical traditions, just outside Halifax, and about a
mile and a half away from the Jowett home. There
Jowett was perfectly happy and he made rapid progress in his studies, though, as he said, he never won

a prize at school. When just under fourteen years of age he left Hipperholme School to become a pupil teacher at Victoria Street Board School. Mr. James Littlewood, the Headmaster under whom he worked, was a good disciplinarian and a conscientious educationist. Jowett cherished his memory fondly and once said of him, " He aided me in warring a way through the intellectual difficulties of youth." At the same time Mr. Littlewood found an earnest student in the young pupil teacher. Every morning at 7.45 he held a study class for his pupil teachers. Jowett was always there, and always there punctually. In 1911 Mr. Littlewood recalled, after thirty years, that Jowett was thorough and able as a teacher. Another testimony to his efficiency came from a severer judge, Mr. Mark Pole, H.M. Inspector of Schools, before whom Jowett, when in his "fourth year," gave a " criticism " lesson. " You have given a very good lesson," said the Inspector, " but it is rather too deep." Jowett earned the " Excellent " grant from the Board of Education on the completion of his pupil-teacher course, and his English composition was adjudged to be by far the best in the country that year. He also won a prize, the gift of a local committee, and selected Brown Jamieson and Fausset's " Portable Bible Commentary." " While absolutely devoid of egotism," said Mr. Littlewood, " he was a youth of considerable self-esteem, conscious of purposeful power and uplifting ambition."

From early boyhood Jowett combined a studious disposition with an overflowing sense of humour inherited, he said, from his mother. He loved to tell merry stories and he was an expert in droll mimicry. As a lad he did not mind telling a story in which the joke told against himself. When his youngest brother was born, the maternity nurse (it was before the days of professional trained nurses) not only attended to the mother and baby, but did the household work. With childish curiosity Jowett watched her coming and going about her duties, and made naïve comments on her way of doing things. " My mother does not do that," he observed. This observation was repeated three or four times until the woman, losing patience, gave the boy a sharp box on the ears, observing, " There, does thi mother do that? " Another story which Jowett told against himself concerned his early love of drawing. While his mother was about her housework Jowett, a very little boy at the time, drew pictures on a slate with a pencil. It was always the same picture—a cow. And as he finished a new picture he rushed off to his mother to get her never-failing commendation. One day, in a mood of daring innovation, he broke his own convention and drew a house on his slate. Off he went with it to his mother. Busy over her work she gave her usual meed of praise without glancing at the drawing. " There," she said, " you have drawn a beautiful cow, John Henry! " His love of drawing survived this discouragement, and at later stages in life as school teacher and as Biblical expositor, Jowett used his chalk and blackboard to advantage. Another memory of his boyhood which, he said, never lost its colour or its strength was the memory of his mother reproving him in tears. " Punishment might have been bearable, but I could have faced it. But tears, they vanquished me. A mother's suffering for a son's disloyalty to truth—that was something that made my act repulsive, and at the same time revealed to me a heart of love and reconciliation and peace."

If Jowett had any early zest for sports and pastimes

J. H. JOWETT (AGED FIVE).

[To face p. 8.

he was denied the opportunity for their pursuit. Facilities for outdoor games did not exist in Halifax in those days. No recreation ground was within his reach. Cricket was in its infancy even in Yorkshire, and football had not then taken its exalted place in school curricula. Just outside Halifax there was the wild moorland country of the Brontë novels, and Jowett occasionally explored these uplands. But his recreations were chiefly followed indoors.

I had no adventures (he wrote in some memories of his boyhood) no hairbreadth escapes by flood or field. My life ran very evenly along comparatively commonplace ways. But I had some interesting passions. At the time of the Russo-Turkish War I had a war-fever in a very pronounced degree. I used to watch for the coming of the *Daily News* that I might read the marvellous letters sent by Archibald Forbes from the seat of war. I bought a large quantity of toy soldiers and day by day arranged them in the order of the strife that was proceeding in the Near East. I overturned them wholesale with a couple of spring guns. But this was altogether too tame, so I bought a real cannon and charged it with real powder and fired. The result both upon my tin soldiers and the furniture in the room, was such as to bring my Russo-Turkish War to a stern conclusion.

Jowett's playground was the cutting-out room behind his father's shop in Godley Road. There, with his special chum, Thomas Feather, he exercised his ingenuity in adapting a box for the purpose of giving shadow representations of " Pepper's Ghost." Jowett's real passion was for printing. A corner in the same cutting-out room, with the connivance no doubt of his father, provided a printing office. Jowett bought a small printing press with a large assortment of type. His ambitious idea was to issue a little paper among his school friends. Jowett and Feather wrote, edited, printed and published the paper. Its title was *The Telephone* and it was about the size of a sheet of small notepaper. The contents, limited by space, but varied to taste, were notes, news, extracts from favourite authors and even verses. Jowett, recalling the boyish venture, claimed that, anyway, " it was edited with magnificent dogmatism." Published weekly, its circulation rose to about twenty-five copies. Jowett and Feather made it a habit to take a few copies of *The Telephone* to the Mechanics' Institute news room and scatter them judiciously over the reading tables. Then they hung about, open-eyed, to see what impression *The Telephone* made on readers. They had two degrees of jubilation —quiet elation when anyone read it on the spot and riotous exhilaration when any reader put a copy in his pocket to take home with him. Jowett's ambition soon vaulted higher. He determined to illustrate *The Telephone* with woodcuts of his own engraving. These turned out ghastly failures. Years afterwards Jowett found one print that had survived the wreck of his hopes. It was a grotesque representation of Disraeli in the character of a fox. Those were Jowett's politics.

The Mechanics' Institute was a boon and a blessing to Jowett. Its library first opened the wide world of literature before him. When a pupil teacher, he spent his evening hours night after night poring over the books to which it gave him access. To ensure a clear evening's reading at the news room he rose early and did his Grammar School " prep " and his pupil teacher studies in the early morning. How he acquired the regular habit of early rising he explained to an American audience.

I used to hear the factory operatives (he told the Divinity School at Yale) passing my house on the way to the mills, where work began at six o'clock. The sound of their iron clogs ringing through the street fetched me out of bed and took me to my work.

He made early rising a matter of conscience then, and this precocious sense of duty became to him an inexorable law. Until his last year of life he began his working day in the ministry at six o'clock.*

Some of his schoolboy friends in Halifax were incredulous about his early rising, and to put matters to the test two of them knocked at the Jowett home door about half-past five one morning. The door was promptly opened by Jowett—dressed and evidently already at work on his home lessons. Sheepishly the incredulous boys owned up that they only wanted to make sure that he really did rise with the lark.

What books Jowett actually read during those long evenings in the Mechanics' Institute I have not been able to ascertain. Poetry, history, English literature and politics were, however, his favourite reading as a young man. Later in life he sometimes commented in tones of dismay on the sloppy literature read by boys of our own time, and he would recall that at their age he was devouring books of travel, biography and science. A little incident occurred one night in the Mechanics' Institute news room which was possibly pivotal in his life. As he was poring over a book an elderly gentleman, whom he had never seen before and never saw again, paused and looked over Jowett's shoulder to see, no doubt, what the boy was reading

* " I can no longer hear the Yorkshire clogs," he explained, " but I see and hear my business men as they start off early to earn their daily bread, and shall their minister be behind them in his quest for the Bread of Life ! "

so assiduously. Then touching Jowett gently on the back he said, " My boy, you must make your way to the University." He passed out of the room and out of Jowett's life; but the words rang in the boy's ears and thrilled his soul. They breathed into him a new hope and vision. When he got home Jowett told his mother of the little episode. " Oh," she said, " but I don't think we could ever afford to send you to the University." Jowett possibly never dreamed that they could; but the train was laid by the stranger's stimulating words, and Jowett won his own way at last to the Universities of Edinburgh and Oxford.

A few lessons from a Pianoforte teacher quickened Jowett's natural love of music—which is inbred in a Yorkshireman. Though he did not carry his musical studies far his love of music was a passion all his life.

Square Church and its minister, Dr. Enoch Mellor, bulked largely in the lives and thoughts of Josiah and Hannah Jowett. Both were members of the Church : but they were not in any way prominent in its affairs. Their family pew in the front gallery was always occupied, for they were faithful in attendance at the sanctuary and they held Dr. Mellor in a reverence amounting to awe. Dr. Mellor was a man of outstanding power and a personality of distinction. He was a great natural orator—Jowett always said he was the finest platform orator it was ever his fortune to hear. He exercised a tremendous influence on Halifax, and not on Halifax alone but on the whole West Riding and on all English Congregationalism. Jowett described him as " imposing in presence, possessed of a magnificent voice." He was one of the " giants of those days." Dr. Mellor came of a well-to-do Yorkshire family and had been a Gold Medallist at Huddersfield College before going to Edinburgh

University, where he won high distinction in Philosophy. He became minister of Square Church, Halifax, in 1848 and quickly gathered round him an overflowing and extremely influential congregation. Halifax people, irrespective of creed, looked upon him as a man whose presence in their midst lent distinction to the borough. His own Church was composed of merchants and manufacturers—men of wealth, character and generosity—as well as a large element of humble, earnest working people—of whom the Jowetts were types—who gave him their heartfelt devotion. The old square, squat, brick church in which Dr. Mellor started his ministry was replaced by a costly and dignified Gothic building which was, and still is, an ornament to the town. Terse, vigorous and spirited in his manner of speech, he was patently honest and sincere. After thirteen years at Square Church (i.e. in 1861) he was enticed away to Great George Street Church, Liverpool, but six years later (i.e. in 1867— when Jowett was a child of four) he returned to Halifax and resumed his powerful sway as preacher and platform orator. This influence remained undiminished, if indeed it did not expand, year by year, until his death in 1881.

This mighty preacher, with his almost magnetic presence, force of character and concentration of spiritual gaze, must, all unconsciously, have deeply impressed the sensitive spirit of the boy Jowett, listening half understandingly, perhaps, in the family pew in the gallery.

While Dr. Mellor * was a man of independent mind and of utter fearlessness in expression, he loved Evangelical truth, and delighted to proclaim it.

* Obituary : Congregational Year Book 1882, pp. 316–318.

He felt that the life, the growth, the stability of
the Christian Church were inseparable from it, and
in his advancing years resolved to make it the
burden of his message, the substance of his ministry.
He could sympathise with the difficulties of the
thoughtful, none more so; for his own mind had
wrestled with them, but he took his stand with a
firm foot on the revealed truth of God, the redemption which is in Jesus Christ. With a voice
at once powerful and mellow combined with the
charm of a graceful delivery he delighted to proclaim " Christ, the same yesterday, to-day and for
ever."

Up to his nineteenth year Jowett listened Sunday
by Sunday to Dr. Mellor's enlightened and inspiring
Evangelical preaching, assimilating his splendid ideal-
ism and catching his great accents.

Never (wrote Jowett) shall I forget a sermon
he (Dr. Mellor) preached one Sunday night when I
was a boy. A racecourse had been established in
Halifax, which he regarded as an imported iniquity,
and he raised his voice in passionate denunciation.
On the night on which he preached the sermon the
great church was crowded in every part. He
announced his text "Have no fellowship with the
unfruitful works of darkness, but rather reprove
them." The sermon that followed laid hold of my
young mind and heart, and I felt my life throbbing
with the moral purpose which possessed the preacher.
That sermon so raised the moral sentiment of the
town that the races were doomed and Halifax is
to-day freed of the pestilence.

Dr. Mellor was the moral idol of Jowett's boyhood
dreams. But they never met, never shook hands,
never exchanged a word. This seems strange and
almost inexplicable; but it is the truth, and it has
to be recorded. Of course Dr. Mellor was the minister

of a very large church and his congregations ranged
from a thousand to twelve hundred people. The
Jowett family were quiet, obscure, reticent people,
not in the least likely to push themselves forward.
They lived a mile away from Square Church on one
side of Halifax, and Dr. Mellor lived a mile away from
his Church on the other side of the town. Though
he visited his people systematically, Dr. Mellor, burdened
with public engagements in, and outside of, Halifax,
took two or three years to make the round of his
congregation. And even when he made his pastoral
calls on the Jowett family, it would be on a week day
when John Henry Jowett, who was not actually a
member of the Church until 1882, would naturally be
at school. So the circumstance that the famous
Halifax preacher and his young disciple, who in turn
eclipsed the older man's fame as a preacher, made no
personal contact in those early days, may be accepted
as more curious than significant. It is noteworthy,
however, that more than once Jowett heard Dr. Mellor
lament that Square Church had sent no young men
into the Christian ministry. So it was at least Jowett's
proud privilege to fulfil one of the deepest wishes of
his old minister's heart and to carry on the torch of
cultured ministry as it fell from the hands of a " gentleman who had helped to raise the standard of God's
truth." Thirty-five years after Dr. Mellor's death
Jowett confided to a fellow voyager on an Atlantic
liner that he had always modelled himself as a preacher
upon Dr. Enoch Mellor." * " Square Church was to
me," he said, " a very fountain of life, and I owe to
its spiritual training more than I can ever express."
From very early childhood Jowett was a scholar in

* Rev. Dugald Macfadyen: " Reminiscences of Dr. Jowett,"
The Christian World, March 12, 1924.

Square Church Sunday School, which gathered in the original brick chapel. In Dr. Mellor's time it had about 800 scholars and teachers. One-third of the scholars were above the age of fourteen, and some of them were over sixty years of age. Mr. Edward Crossley was the Superintendent of the School in Jowett's time and his early teacher was Sir Frederick Whitley-Thomson, cousin of Mr. J. H. Whitley, the Speaker of the House of Commons. Two of his teachers, Mr. James M. Todd and Mr. J. W. T. Dewhirst, exercised more immediate influence over Jowett's boyhood than, perhaps, anyone outside his home circle. Of Mr. Dewhirst Jowett, at his ordination, said :

It was through his influence that I entered the ministry. He made the Sabbath the sunniest day of my week, a day looked for, longed for, loved. Well do I remember one Sabbath afternoon when we were expecting to meet him, a message came that he was very ill and, spontaneously, the little class was turned into a prayer meeting and the scholars pleaded with God for the teacher who was sick.

Not that Jowett was always a pattern Sunday School-boy. Friends and relations in recalling the days of his youth rather delight in recording stories of his healthy fondness for boyish mischief. He never denied the soft impeachment. All the facts point to his having been a very human boy with a lively sense of fun and a normal boy's capacity for getting into scrapes, and wriggling out of them. One escapade with his friend Feather caused them to be threatened with expulsion. They escaped by requesting to be removed to other classes whose teachers had a better understanding of the ways of the adolescent boy.

Jowett looked back on his Sunday School days with a sense of personal obligation.

Mine is a debt too big for words (he said). I can never in my manhood turn to the Twenty-third Psalm, either in public ministry or in private devotion, without the figure of a humble carpenter appearing upon the illumined page, for it was he who first led my feet into its green pastures and by its still waters and who showed me something of the audacious fearlessness of the friends of God. And neither can I turn to the fourth chapter of John without a lowly porter standing upon its threshold, for on one never-to-be-forgotten day he stood with me by the well, and he spoke to my soul of its vitalising properties and of the rare medicinal qualities of its waters " springing up into Eternal Life." And when I turn to the greatest of the Old Testament prophets I find, standing among the cultured crowd of college professors who have helped me and enriched my discernment, an unordained wayfarer from the Sunday School whose personal enthusiasm first made me realise the stature of Isaiah.

Another institution connected with Square Church which laid its formative hand on Jowett was the Young Men's Society. Founded in the 'fifties, this was one of the first (if not actually the first) discussion classes for young men established in Yorkshire : and it had had a vigorous life for over forty years. Though its total membership never exceeded fifty and the average attendance was never much above twenty, the Society provided a training school for the best speakers in Halifax public life. Jowett was constant in his attendance, and took part frequently in the debates. This regular practice in speaking developed his natural gift of oratory rapidly. It was at one of

c

the annual meetings of the Young Men's Society—
which were always made "open occasions"—that he
made his first public speech. By that time he was
one of the best speakers within the Society's membership. His studious temper of mind and his early
acquired habit of newspaper reading equipped him
for the purposes of debate. He soon attained facility
in extemporaneous speech (an art he sadly neglected
later, and almost lost as the years went by) and he
rarely intervened in a discussion without marked
effect. This aptitude for speech led to Jowett being
invited by his Sunday School teacher to take part in
some mission services that were started by workers
from Square Church in a common lodging-house in
Halifax. He agreed and threw himself whole-heartedly
into this evangelistic work, and his first religious
address was to the inmates in the lodging-house.

Jowett's first sermon followed quickly after his first
religious address, and many years later he unearthed
the faded manuscript of that first sermon from a
bundle of buried papers. Turning over its soiled and
ragged pages awakened in him many a sleeping memory
and recalled " the lost flavour of a very high day."
Of its fifteen pages quite a third were occupied with
lengthy poetical quotations. The thought, he confessed, straggled over a considerable area and the
route taken was somewhat zigzag in its tendency.
The text of that first sermon was " And Samuel grew,
and the Lord was with him " (1 Sam. iii. 19).

The sermon (said Jowett) was written when I
was seventeen years of age and was preached several
times to my mother, with most splendid and re-
assuring results, before it was delivered to the
general public. If I were to write here the words
of loving surprise uttered by my mother when I

had solemnly said the " Amen "—well, every minister who might read them would marvel at the great similarity between them and the words spoken by his own mother when he declaimed to her *his* first discourse.

A " kindly dispositioned " congregation of homely people in Range Bank Chapel—a little branch of Square Church—listened to Jowett's first discourse.

> My Sunday School teacher (wrote Jowett) accompanied me, along with several members of his class. This class was cemented together by the most unselfish of bonds, and what concerned one of the members gained the interest of all. Their presence was a source of much strength and inspiration. . . . My greatest fear concerned itself, not with the sermon but with the acts of devotion. I wondered if I should be able to lead the congregation in prayer. That was the burden of the service—a burden which remains to this day. Seated in the front row was a white-haired old man, one of the regular worshippers at the branch Church. In the prayer with which I opened the service I heard a quiet response. It was from the old man. That response gave me comparative confidence. It was like the strengthening breath of the Holy Spirit. Why not say it was the breath of the Holy Spirit? I can feel it now across the years. At a moment of great timidity I entered into the gracious strength of fellowship, and the expressed spiritual sympathy of an unknown brother created an influence in the young preacher which I remember still with thankfulness and joy.

Jowett himself described his first sermon as preeminently practical—if by practical is meant the harnessing of truth to the heavy, burdensome tasks of common life.

When Jowett preached his first sermon his thoughts

had not begun to turn to the Christian ministry as his vocation. Nor, though he was nearing the end of his period as a pupil teacher, did he feel himself definitely committed to the teaching profession as a career. He was happy and successful at Victoria Street Board School, and discovered that he had the qualifications necessary for an effectual teacher. Eagerly he sought, and tried, new methods for investing his lessons with the charm of freshness and the lure of novelty. The boys liked him and he won their affection. But somehow his heart was not in schoolmastering, and as his period of apprenticeship drew near to its close he was full of misgivings and hesitations. A political career attracted him strongly and ideas of the law as a profession, with Parliament as a distant goal, captured his imagination. In cherishing this ambition he found his father ready with encouragement. Whenever a renowned politician came within fifty miles of Halifax his father always arranged for Jowett to go and hear him. So he journeyed to hear Gladstone, Disraeli and John Bright. Next day he would get a newspaper giving a verbatim report of the speech and in the privacy of his bedroom he would declaim it, reproducing, if he could, the very accents and emphases of the orator. His first visit to London was to hear a debate in the House of Commons. On this occasion Josiah Jowett only agreed to his son making the journey on condition that he could find an older companion to go along with him. Happily one was found, and two eager youths left Halifax at twelve o'clock on Sunday night, arrived in London early on the Monday morning, sought out their Parliamentary member and obtained his good offices in securing admission to the House in the afternoon. "It was a wonderful night!"

Possibly it was that gala night at Westminster—John Bright made one of his great speeches during the debate—that strengthened Jowett's inclination to become a lawyer. At all events a few weeks later his father had virtually completed all the arrangements for him to enter a Halifax firm of solicitors as an articled clerk. On the day before the articles were to be signed Jowett met his Sunday School teacher, by accident, in the street and told him what he was about to do. Mr. Dewhirst looked grieved. " I had always hoped," he said, " that you would go into the ministry." Jowett, with his profound affection for his Sunday School teacher, was taken aback. He thought seriously over the suggestion and going home anxiously considered his whole future. He was strongly drawn to the ministry, but was he divinely called? Years afterwards recalling this crucial moment in his life, he said " the grip " came to him as he stood by the harmonium in the parlour at home. From that moment he had no hesitation. His course was clear. " It was the result," he said, " of no urgent argument, nor the issue of any calculation of profit and loss : it was a gracious constraint, an inclination born of love, a decision shaped by the worship of Jesus Christ." The first communication of his decision was made, as might be expected, to his mother. He knew, no doubt, that her assent was sure. Both his parents gave ready approval to his resolve which, they knew, had not been reached without deep searching of heart. His father had always hoped that Jowett would be a public speaker, but he had never made any suggestion that this implied the ministry. A few weeks later Jowett had been accepted by the Governors of Airedale College as a candidate for the Congregational ministry, and a new chapter in his life had opened.

CHAPTER II

(*Æt.* 19–26)

AIREDALE COLLEGE, to which Jowett was admitted
as a probationer in September 1882 for a course of
theological training for the Congregational ministry,
exists no longer under that name. When Jowett
entered the College it was housed in a large, new
building near Manningham Park, Bradford—only a
few miles away from his native town. Airedale
had an honourable record as one of the Dissenting
Academies. In the 'eighties of the nineteenth century
it was enjoying a period of almost unexampled prosperity and influence. Dr. Andrew M. Fairbairn had
assumed its Principalship in 1877, and his far-spread
reputation as a scholar, preacher and teacher attracted
students from all over the North of England, and even
from Scotland. Jowett had just passed his nineteenth
birthday when he came under Dr. Fairbairn's tutelage.
His education, even during his years as a pupil teacher,
had gone on uninterruptedly and he was well prepared
for at least the preliminary Arts work of a Theological
College. Dr. Fairbairn, under whose influence Jowett
came with his entry into Airedale, was a massive
personality. An erudite scholar and a profound
thinker, he swept the ages in his historical perspective
and was a living synthesis of philosophical and

22

theological thought. Though the gentlest of men, Dr. Fairbairn had an authoritative manner, calculated to set up feelings of awe in a young student. Jowett possibly had this experience in his early days at Airedale, but it gave place to a mingled admiration and affection, as he discovered a tender side in the Scottish philosopher's nature. He never forgot, and often repeated, one remark of Dr. Fairbairn's. He had preached in the sermon class, with Dr. Fairbairn presiding. In sermon class criticism the young lions at theological colleges have " leave and liking " to roar, and Jowett's sermon was severely handled by some of his fellow students. Dr. Fairbairn listened to the criticisms and then closed the discussion by saying, " I will tell you, gentlemen, what I have observed this morning. Behind that sermon there is a man." Another of Dr. Fairbairn's criticisms of Jowett in sermon class gave him lifelong amusement. When Jowett had finished, Dr. Fairbairn (who had himself, very pronouncedly, the curious habit of wringing his hands when he preached) descended on the young preacher with the observation, " Mr. Jowett, your gestures are most ungraceful. It seems as if you have a semicircular row of lighted candles in front of you which you proceed to extinguish, moving your hand from the candle at one end to the candle at the other. Mr. Jowett, we must strive to avoid all mannerisms." As an example of Satan reproving sin Jowett always thought this episode unequalled. Altogether Jowett spent seven years in college and at the University, in his preparation for the ministry ; but by a series of mischances it was only in two of the seven years that he had Dr. Fairbairn as his Gamaliel. He was ever ready, however, to say how deeply Dr. Fairbairn impressed him.

Only his students (he said) know Dr. Fairbairn's power.   He is great in the pulpit and on the platform, but he is not less great in the class room.   Some of the most inspiring utterances I have heard from Dr. Fairbairn have been delivered extempore in the class room on sermon day.

On another occasion Jowett spoke humorously of the peril there was when he was at Airedale of turning out a species of dwarfed or miniature Fairbairns :

We could so easily (he said) acquire the trick of his style—that strange antithetical sentence doubling back upon itself and which we fashioned like standardised pieces of machinery cast in a foundry. I believe I became rather an expert in the process, and for some time I carried the Fairbairn moulds about with me; only unfortunately there was nothing in them.

More than to Dr. Fairbairn, Jowett, in his early College days, owed the incentive to study hard and open-mindedly to Dr. Archibald Duff, then one of the two Professors at Airedale and now Professor at Yorkshire United College.   Dr. Duff is an ecstatically enthusiastic Hebraist and a ripe Old Testament scholar.   A tradition among his old students credits him with chanting the Psalms, in the original Hebrew, in his sleep.   He has inoculated several generations of theological students with his own passion for Old Testament studies, and few men have left his College unpledged to a lifelong affection for this inspiring teacher.   Jowett himself always declared that Dr. Duff was one of the deepest influences that came into his life.   He felt he could never repay the debt he owed him.   Between the Hebrew scholar and the young theologue working together in the College class room a strong mutual affection grew rapidly.   The comradeship grew into a friendship that never wilted. A year before his death Jowett spoke of Dr. Duff as " My beloved professor." Dr. Duff's own description of Jowett is " My beloved pupil." As an act of devotion to his dead friend, Dr. Duff has analysed his class registers, now forty years old, to discover Jowett's College record at Airedale. The extracts form an illuminating summary.

(1) In session 1882–3 (writes Dr. Duff) the loved Jowett's name is on my class books for Mathematics and German. He used to gain 80 to 100 per cent. of maximum marks.

(2) In sessions 1883–4: 1884–5: 1885–6 and 1886–7 Jowett's name is not on the class rolls. That means that he was away at Edinburgh during those four sessions, taking his University course there for the M.A. degree.

(3) In session 1887–8 he reappears marked as M.A. and in his first Theological Year : i.e. the first of our regular course of three years. In this session (1887–8) he attended my classes in (a) German authors, reading Harnack on " Luther," (b) Hebrew " Grammar Elements "—taking 80 to 90 per cent. (of maximum marks), (c) History of " Hebrew Religion " and (d) History of Christian " Monasticism,"—taking up to 97 per cent. (of maximum marks).

(4) In session 1888–9 he is entered on the books as second year's student in Theology, but he accepted the pastorate at Newcastle-on-Tyne that Autumn and went to Oxford to attend lectures there. Of course that ended his study with us, but he joined no other college and, in fact, remained an Airedale student.

In his first year at Airedale Jowett devoted himself to the study of the Greek and Latin classics, with

English literature, under Professor W. C. Shearer, and to Mathematics and German under Professor Duff.

About five years previously Dr. Fairbairn, with the full approval of the Governors of the College, had instituted a plan for sending Airedale students to one of the British Universities for a full undergraduate course in Arts as a preliminary to a three years' course of purely theological study. Three Bursaries (known as Brown scholarships) of the value of £60 a year were established to facilitate this policy. Before the end of the first year Jowett was awarded one of these scholarships and was free to choose the University at which he should study. His first preference was for Glasgow, but on consulting Dr. Fairbairn he found his Principal distinctly hostile. " No," said Dr. Fairbairn, " you must go to Edinburgh. You want polishing up. If you go to Glasgow you will come back just a raw Yorkshire lad." Jowett told the story with evident relish in his later years, but to those who knew the later Jowett as the perfectly polished Christian gentleman, Dr. Fairbairn's description will seem almost incredible. At all events Jowett proceeded to Edinburgh.

" Passing rich " on a £60 scholarship,* Jowett entered Edinburgh University in October 1883 for a four years' course in Philosophy and general Arts. The exercise of very little imagination is required to conjecture what impression Edinburgh made on this Yorkshire boy fresh from life in industrial towns.

---

* His financial resources were supplemented by Square Church and by Mr. John Whitley of Halifax. " No one knows," Jowett said years afterwards, " the encouragement Mr. Whitley gave me when I was passing through days of struggle. I wonder how often he wrote to me in my University days and gave me inspiration." To Jowett's credit it must be recorded that the financial help he received from Square Church was refunded by him early in his ministry.

Who, indeed, does ever forget his first glimpse of this stately queen of cities—" East-windy-West-endy place " though John McNeill called it ? Universities have their golden ages,—periods when they throb with intellectual vitality and are vibrant with spiritual pulsations. Jowett was fortunate. He struck Edinburgh in one of the glorious patches of her modern history. Two wholly dissimilar books—Sir James Barrie's " An Edinburgh Eleven " and Sir George Adam Smith's " Life of Henry Drummond "—help us to realise the atmosphere Jowett breathed in his University days. Fresh from the little cloistral Academy at Airedale—stimulating though he had found the intellectual life there—Jowett was plunged into a rarer and ampler air. He basked in the sunny glow of University life, enriching his mind and expanding his soul in the process.

Another ministerial student, Rev. James Mursell, one of a family that has given many distinguished sons to the Baptist ministry, had arrived in Edinburgh for his graduation course a day or two before Jowett. Mr. Mursell has vivaciously described their early association:

After securing lodgings three flights up at 17 Livingstone Place, The Meadows, and gaining the consent of Mrs. Bell, my landlady, to find a companion, I hunted up some " Airedale " men who, I heard, were on the lookout for quarters. I found three of them named Brayshaw,* Vaughan † and Jowett. The last of the three, tallish, slight, pale-faced, with a slightly Yorkshire accent, had something about him that attracted me. In a few minutes he and I paired off. An inspection of my

* Rev. H. H. Brayshaw, minister of Zion Congregational Church, Hulme, since 1885.
† D. W. Vaughan, M.A., afterwards Congregational minister at Cheetham Hill, Kentish Town and Haverhill : died July 19th, 1910.

rooms and the discovery that my landlady and her
husband, David Bell,* were Congregationalists sealed
the compact, and little dreaming what the future
held for him, my junior by something like three
years, we roomed and even slept together all that
winter.   The bedfellowship arose from the refusal
of us both to occupy a " bed closet " off the sitting
room—a refusal which amazed Mrs. Bell, who told
us that her previous " young gentlemen," who had
been medicals, preferred it because it enabled them
to dress and undress by the fire.   But to sleep in a
cupboard was more than either Jowett or I could
stand, so we used the " bed closet " for newspapers
and fruit, the fruit mostly mine and the newspapers
mostly Jowett's.

Edinburgh has always been a sermon taster's
paradise, and Jowett, bent on fashioning his preaching
on the best models, enjoyed to the utmost the privilege
of wandering round the churches.   The choice was
varied enough to satisfy every passing mood.   Dr.
Alexander Whyte, then in his majestic prime, was at
Free St. George's.   Dr. Matheson, the blind preacher
who " traced the rainbow through the rain " and saw
spiritual truth in brilliant flashes of insight, was
preaching regularly at St. Bernard's, while Dr. Walter
Smith, the poet-preacher, was at the Free High Church.
At Albany Street Congregational Chapel Dr. John
Pulsford, mystic, and author of " Quiet Hours,"
gathered his congregation of select souls.   Dr. Landels
was drawing crowds to Dublin Street Baptist Church.
What a galaxy !   Edinburgh in those days was a
veritable University of preaching, as well as of arts
and sciences.   Jowett drank deep of these Pierian

---

* Jowett never lost sight of the Bells until their death.   He
always visited them whenever he was in Edinburgh, and the author
has reason to believe that he helped them financially in their old age.

springs. Throughout his first winter in Edinburgh he was faithful in his attendance on Dr. Pulsford's ministry, but in course of time he " sampled " all the Edinburgh preachers in turn, with a catholicity of spirit that soared high above all denominational predilections. Beyond all doubt, however, his favourite Edinburgh preacher was Dr. Alexander Whyte, who held his reverence through all his days. " Few preachers," he said, " brought home to their audience the sense of sin so deeply as Dr. Whyte. One could not listen to him without feeling the pressing need of a Gospel."

Though Jowett's primary purpose at Edinburgh was to study Philosophy and take his degree in that subject, his tastes were eclectic and the study of general literature absorbed a large proportion of his energy and time. Professor David Masson's lectures on literature were a perpetual feast of nectared sweets to the young Yorkshire student. He was fascinated by the man. Like Sir James Barrie, Jowett could almost say, " I seem to remember everything Masson said, and the way he said it." It was to Masson's influence that, in after years, Jowett attributed his own lifelong joy in etymological study and in delicate literary nuances. But Masson's impact on the young man from Halifax did far more than that. He opened vast vistas into literature, quickened his critical perceptions and kindled into a flame that never died down an admiration for the great English classics, especially Milton and Bunyan. About the Professor, who was Carlyle's friend and Milton's biographer, there was a suggestion of an Olympian. Sir James Barrie, in " An Edinburgh Eleven," says that Masson always comes to his memory first knocking nails into his desk, or trying to tear the gas bracket from its socket.

It was when his (Masson's) mind groped for an image that he clutched the bracket. He seemed to tear his good things out of it. Silence overcame the class. Some were fascinated by the man, others trembled for the bracket. It shook, groaned and yielded. Masson said another of the things that made his lectures literature; the crisis was passed and everybody breathed again.

It was an Edinburgh tradition that the janitor in the corridor always glued his ear to the keyhole when Masson was lecturing.

Of Professor Masson Jowett had one precious memory which he often recalled in conversation. An impious undergraduate in his day smuggled a street dog into Masson's class room, and when the Professor's lecture was under weigh the student gently pinched the dog to make it whine. Masson stopped his lecture. " If the student," he said, " who has brought in that dog will take it out I will close my eyes while he does so, and keep them closed till he is back at his desk." The undergraduate took out the dog and returned looking like a whipped cur. Then Masson, who had kept his head bent low, with his hand over his eyes, resumed his lecture, without a word of reproach about the incident.

Everything (said Jowett) in the personality of the man (Masson) was interesting. I well remember how he would turn from his brown and faded manuscript, and recall some reminiscence of his intercourse with a great man, such as Carlyle. In his teaching there was a constant element of surprise, and he knew how to give his pupils a deep and abiding love of literature.

Professor Calderwood was another Edinburgh mentor to whom Jowett made acknowledgments of lifelong obligation. Under him Jowett studied Moral Philosophy. " Calderwood," he told me in Copenhagen in 1922, " fixed my philosophy for life ; I have never had to readjust it."

It was my inestimable privilege in my University days (said Jowett) to enjoy the enlightened leadership of Professor Calderwood, and what he imparted to me has been of incomparable service in my personal life and public ministry."

The ancient tradition among Scottish students of poverty, porridge and catechism had not, in Jowett's time, been destroyed by Carnegie Trust subventions. Edinburgh students were poor, and proud of it. With his Brown Bursary of £60 a year Jowett, in his University course, did not suffer any hardships.* One of his mild extravagances was upon newspapers. Another was an occasional visit to the theatre. Rev. James Mursell in his recollections of his year at Edinburgh with Jowett reminds us that those were the spacious days of the Fourth Party and the baiting of Gladstone in the House of Commons by Mr. Arthur J. Balfour, Lord Randolph Churchill, Sir Henry Drummond Wolff and Mr. John Gorst.

Jowett (writes Mr. Mursell) was keen on politics, and had promised to speak during the Christmas vacation at some society connected with Square Church, Halifax, of which he was a member. So almost every afternoon we walked round the Queen's Drive to the Waverley Station where he would buy three or four London papers off the train that reached the Scottish capital at half-past three. These he would devour with immense gusto when we got back. Randolph Churchill was his peculiar

* Jowett and Mr. Mursell pooled their expenses during that first year and the cost worked out at £41 each.

detestation and delight, and as in later years he would seize some vivid sentence from Isaiah and hold it like a jewel to the light and let its facets flash their truth on you, so then he loved to catch some clever phrase of " Randy's " and hold it up to show that it was paste, a flashy imitation of the truth. He was already in those student days fashioning the method he was to use so skilfully and so effectively all through his life.

The visits to the theatre were forsworn by Jowett during that first winter in Edinburgh. Mr. Mursell and he had fallen in with the student custom of spending Friday evenings at the theatre as a little relaxation after long days and sometimes late nights spent on grinding at classics and mathematics.

Jowett (Mr. Mursell recalls) had never been inside a theatre till I took him there, and he possessed even more than I the feeling that theatres stood a long way down the broad road that leadeth to destruction. One evening we were in the pit stalls of the Lyceum, whither we had gone to see Ristori play Elizabeth. During one of the intervals I pointed out some women in the upper circle who were quite obviously of bad character. Jowett was horrified. He was as innocent and clean-minded as a child, and he was so upset that the evening was quite spoiled for me as well as for him. On the way home we talked things over, with the result that we resolved never to go to theatres again.

While the academic influences of Edinburgh and the *genius loci* of the University were exerting their sway on Jowett's mind, another gracious influence played upon his spirit and set an indelible imprint upon his soul. This was Henry Drummond. On hundreds of occasions in after life Jowett, by voice and by pen, bore testimony to Drummond's moulding influence upon him in his

University days. The magic power Henry Drummond wielded swayed Jowett till the end of his days, and his name was always fragrant on his lips. It was in 1884 that Drummond began those meetings for students at the Oddfellows' Hall at Edinburgh that were at once the passion of his life and the crowning glory of his all too short career. Though he was barely thirty-three Drummond had already won international repute. Eleven years before D. L. Moody had laid on his young shoulders the responsibility of following up the Moody and Sankey evangelistic campaign in the great cities of Great Britain and Ireland, and the young shoulders had not bent under the strain. At thirty he had written " Natural Law in the Spiritual World " to reconcile the new evolutionary conclusions of science with the fundamental truths of evangelical Christianity, and the book had made a sensation in two continents. This had been followed by his appointment to a new Lectureship in Natural Science at the Free Church College at Glasgow, and later to a full Professorship there. By this time Drummond was a famous man—as an evangelist, a scientist and a traveller. The world was at his feet. Duchesses and other titled personages flocked to Grosvenor House in West London to hear Drummond talk to them about their immortal souls. He was pressed to enter Parliament and deluged with tempting offers of posts of honour and distinction. But Drummond's paramount interest was the spiritual welfare of students. He felt that his life work was among them. There his genius lay, and—though he was utterly devoid of conceit—he knew it. Sir George Adam Smith says that perhaps the most conspicuous service Drummond rendered to his generation was to show them a Christianity which was perfectly natural. There was an " ease and

D

conversations with him, have I ever discovered evidences of any intellectual crises in Jowett's life. He escaped vicissitudes. He seems, in fact, to have passed through none of those soul-searching phases of doubt and difficulty that occur in the intellectual experiences of most men who lived through the last two decades of the nineteenth and the beginning of the twentieth century. It had been his good fortune in early childhood not to be indoctrinated with any of the hard, semi-Calvinistic conceptions of God, judgment and the future which haunted the childhood of so many of his contemporaries. His religion, like Drummond's, was sunny because it was rooted and grounded in the Love of God and the redeeming Grace of the Lord Jesus Christ. Those were his fundamentals —the rocks of his faith that were never shaken.

Drummond devised a plan for sending out Edinburgh students, who had come under his religious influence, as missionary bands to conduct extensive campaigns all over Scotland, England and the Continent. His instructions were that they were not to preach, but just to tell people what Jesus Christ had done for them. Jowett went, in 1885, on one of these crusades with Dr. D. Anderson Moxey, and six or seven other students from Edinburgh. They held a week's mission in Bradford. No preparations had been made, locally, for their efforts, and they had to beat up their own audiences. They succeeded, for the congregations in the Mechanics' Institute and the Y.M.C.A. grew night by night. On one evening Jowett prayed and spoke and strongly impressed the audience.

The Airedale students who were contemporary with him at Edinburgh occasionally met, as a group, after the usual (Drummond) meeting on Sunday evenings. Some of these small gatherings were of great spiritual value.

One of them (wrote Rev. Alexander Mann, will never be forgotten by the writer. It was held in " Jowett's digs," and there were only four present. Two hymns were sung, and four prayers were offered in succession. The simple meeting occupied scarcely forty-five minutes, yet its results have refused to be effaced from the heart by the wear and tear of the years which have followed. It was a time of genuine sincerity and down-right reality.

While studying at Edinburgh Jowett on two occasions gave the Sunday evening addresses at the Gilmour Street Mission of Augustine Church where Rev. E. Johnson Saxton, then a student at the Edinburgh Theological Hall, was acting as student-pastor. Mr. Saxton remembers still how well Jowett adapted himself to an audience of poor working people and how responsive they were to his message.

In order to exercise some supervision over the Airedale undergraduates at the Scottish Universities it was the practice of the Governors of the College to send one of the Professors once a year, or oftener, to visit their students at Edinburgh, Glasgow and Aberdeen.

It was my privilege (writes Prof. Duff) to do this repeatedly, especially during Jowett's years at Edinburgh. Of course there would be personal interviews with each student, and some devotional engagements during the hours of day-time. And then Rev. A. B. Morris, the co-pastor of Albany Street Church, who was a noble helper, would bid us all, students and visiting professors, with, occasionally, other friends, to his house for a happy evening of reunion. There we had merry converse; we sang student songs and we had recitations. Usually there would be some brief addresses, perhaps by Edinburgh ministers.

The Airedale students at Edinburgh (continues

of its teaching faculty, the creation of an adequate
library and the planning of ambitious College buildings
engaged all Dr. Fairbairn's skill as an administrator.
Necessarily he had, even before the actual transfer was
made to Oxford, withdrawn from his duties as Principal
at Airedale. Jowett, who had been eager to pursue
his remaining theological studies under the profoundly
learned Principal, was acutely disappointed.

But (writes Dr. Duff) he nobly accepted the situation in the lamed United College for one year. It
was a wonderful deed of loving trust in the school
which had sent him to Edinburgh and which was
moreover the school and child of his own native
West Riding. He studied on with Professor Shearer
and me and went through that session although
other students left us to follow Dr. Fairbairn to
Oxford. How gracious were the hours in my dear
little old corner class room! It was to us all one
happy summer day of growth and harvesting through
all those ten months. How we read! How we
conferred! How lights gleamed in upon us all the
way! We sought together, first and foremost, and
indeed altogether and only, to see in the utterances
of those wonderful Hebrew and Jewish preachers,
narrators, philosophers and singers the marvellous
story of how their faith and works resulted at last
in the coming of Jesus. To do that we tried to grasp
the genius of their language and then to understand
their noble literature. Then we linked into one chain
the whole upward progress from the men of lowest
cruelty to the missionary ideals of Jeremiah and
Isaiah. Then we watched how the poor little people
left in Judah rose in generation by generation till
there dawned upon them the " Christ " idea of the
" Solomon " Psalms. But in one year how little of
this could we cover! Nevertheless Jowett entered
entirely into the spirit of it all. He became
enthusiastic—a very joy to watch.

Jowett left on record his own vivid picture of the inspiring days spent with Professor Duff in that little corner class room. " Dr. Duff," he said ten years afterwards, " made Hebrew literature as fascinating as a romance," and twenty years later, speaking at a College reunion, he revived his memories of the Old Testament class at Airedale, in words that went straight to his old Professor-friend's heart.

> Dr. Duff (said Jowett) did not show me any new things : they were, and are, there always in Hebrew and Jewish literature. He showed me how to study them, *i.e.* not to read in anything that does not belong there, and not to leave out anything that does belong there.

On still another occasion Jowett, speaking with " reverent gratitude for the inspiration and illumination of his College days," said, " there were class rooms in which an apocalypse was an almost daily experience and in which mind and heart were held in constant surprise."

Long summer vacations, extending through July and August and even into September, gave Airedale students an excellent opportunity for gaining practical experience by undertaking village pastorates. They were encouraged so to spend part at least of the vacation. As many students as possible were appointed to the temporary charge of village churches in the scattered villages of Yorkshire and Durham. Jowett, eager to preach and full of zest for pastoral experience, allowed no possible opportunity of this kind to slip away. During his first summer vacation he ministered to a little Church at Cotherstone, a tiny but picturesque village on the borders of Yorkshire and Durham, and a few miles away from Barnard Castle. The life of this little church was feeble and flickering when Jowett was of his methods of securing a congregation and the excellence of his preaching spread abroad and reached the ears of the Congregationalists at Barnard Castle. The church there was without a minister, but the deacons had decided to go through the summer with " supplies " for the pulpit. They asked Jowett to preach on two Sundays during his vacation of 1886 and then to serve the church as student pastor for five weeks in 1887. Barnard Castle, one of the beauty spots of the Teesdale country, was much appreciated as a holiday resort by Newcastle people possessed with a taste for the quiet of the uplands rather than the garish attractions of popular seaside resorts. The little town provides the scene for Jessie Fothergill's romantic story " Borderland." The castle, perched on a rocky eminence overlooking the Tees, excited the admiration of Sir Walter Scott as he saw it from Balliol's Tower. Among the Newcastle visitors in the summer of 1887 were Congregationalists associated with St. James's Church, which was then seeking a minister. Jowett's preaching at Barnard Castle interested them, and they brought his name before the Deacons. The ultimate result was that his first settled pastorate was at Newcastle.

Jowett's acceptance of the pastorate at Newcastle transgressed one of the laws common to Theological Colleges, and no doubt essential to their discipline, that a student should not enter into definite arrangements with a church without consultation with the Principal. The Governors of the United College did not relish being faced with a *fait accompli*, especially as Jowett, at the same time, was requesting permission to spend his next, and last, session as an Airedale student at Mansfield College. However, as he had completed six years of uninterrupted and successful study in connection with Airedale—which was one year more than the period for which he had originally entered—and as the engagement into which he had entered with the church at St. James's, Newcastle, could not then be altered or postponed, the College Governors acceded to his request. Jowett's determination to go to Oxford for his final year arose out of his desire for a change of scene for the last phase of his preparation for the ministry. He wished, too, to have the benefit of Dr. Fairbairn's lectures at Oxford, while retaining his connection with Airedale as a student of that College. The link with the Yorkshire College was never severed, though he may have felt some soreness at the grudging consent given by the Governors to his appeal for freedom to go to Oxford. Any momentary resentment, however, passed away in time and he subscribed generously, when he was in America, to the £10,000 scholarship Fund which Principal Griffith-Jones raised just before the war, and he was a regular contributor to the College Funds year by year till he died. In his last year he expressed a verbal wish that £1,000 should be set aside out of his estate to establish a Jowett scholarship at his old College. This wish has been honoured by Mrs. Jowett, and the Memorial Scholarship is now in being.

Only two terms were spent by Jowett in Oxford (1888–9), and even they were not perhaps so profitable as he had hoped. While the new building for Mansfield College was being erected the lectures were given in rooms in the High Street. The Mansfield men were in scattered lodgings, and the community life of the College with its stimulating intellectual friction had scarcely come, influentially, into existence. Jowett was not, strictly speaking, a regular Mansfield student

CHAPTER III

(Æt. 26–32)

BEFORE Jowett left Airedale College for his final
terms under Dr. Fairbairn at Mansfield College, more
than one influential Congregational Church in the North
of England, seeking a minister, had turned its eyes
in his direction and made overtures, either direct or
through the College Principal, with a view to securing
his services. His settlement at Newcastle-on-Tyne,
as has been shown, came about almost fortuitously
through his holiday student-pastorate at Barnard
Castle. The story of his first settlement has some
points of peculiar interest. When the attention of the
deacons of St. James's Congregational Church had been
called to the promising young student-preacher who
was temporarily ministering at Barnard Castle, they
invited him to occupy the Newcastle pulpit for one
Sunday at the end of November 1887.

> A most vivid impression was made on all who
> heard him (said Mr. Robert Rowell, Chairman of
> the Church Committee) : everyone was struck with
> his grasp of the word of God, his keen insight into
> the spiritual meaning, the freshness of his thoughts,
> his facility of expression and the deep human
> sympathy which brought him into touch at once
> with his audience, while the whole service was
> pervaded by an earnestness which seemed to promise
> the most blessed results from his ministry.

J. H. JOWETT (AGED TWENTY-ONE).

[*To face p.* 48.

It might have been imagined that an invitation to the vacant pastorate would have followed promptly. But in those days Congregational Churches were leisurely in their action in so momentous a matter as the selection of their minister. Jowett was invited to pay a second visit. He did this three months later, *i.e.* at the beginning of March, and the first favourable impression was revived, even deepened. Even yet, however, the church was not to be rushed into an invitation. The officers were urged to give the congregation further opportunities of hearing the promising young preacher. So on the first Sunday in May Jowett paid a third visit to St. James's. This time the feeling he created was described as " so strong that it was determined to bring matters to a final issue." Even this was not a definite invitation. Jowett was asked to occupy the pulpit for five consecutive Sundays in June and July (1888). So it was only after eight hearings that a formal and unanimous invitation was sent to him. When it was given, the " call " was given with enthusiasm, for attached to it were the signatures of all the church members and seat-holders with their families, with hardly a single exception. No impetuous haste was shown by Jowett in his response to the call : he took full time for consideration, and his letter of acceptance was not sent until August 7th, 1888.

The prolonged and seemingly tedious processes which preceded the invitation were no doubt due to the fact that it was thought to be a highly venturesome experiment to call a ministerial student fresh from College to the pastorate of so large and influential a church as St. James's, Newcastle. Almost synchronously another great and historical Congregational church at Kensington was making what was looked upon as a daring innovation in inviting Mr. C. Silvester Horne, a fellow

E

collegian with Jowett at Oxford, to its pulpit. In both instances there was a suggestion of audacity, a defiance of tradition, in calling young, inexperienced men to the pastorates of churches involving heavy responsibilities, and calling for the exercise of many gifts quite apart from eloquence and power in the pulpit. At Kensington, as at Newcastle, the office bearers thought that a large measure of risk was being run. Subsequent events justified the adventure of faith in both cases.

Congregationalism has never been quite indigenous to Newcastle. Possibly owing to geographical proximity to Scotland, Presbyterianism had a predominating influence in the city throughout the early part of the nineteenth century, and Congregationalism came late into the field. St. James's Congregational Church had its origin in a schism in a Presbyterian Church from which a disaffected minority had gone forth and built an independent church in Blackett Street. This building was in time bought by a small body of Congregationalists who had started a " cause," and who, on acquiring the building, were joined by the " split " Presbyterian community which had worshipped within its walls. The Congregational community was formed into a " Church " in 1833, and a few years later Rev. James Guinness Rogers became its minister. Meanwhile the congregations had grown in numbers and influence, and to meet their needs the present church, which ranks among the finest buildings in the city, was erected at a cost of £18,000. The building seats over a thousand people and lends itself both to reverent worship and the ministry of the pulpit.

The words and phrases in which Jowett accepted the call have an interest still :—

Four weeks ago (he wrote) there seemed to be many roads opening before me ; now all roads are closed save one, and this I regard as conclusive indication of the Master's will. I therefore cheerfully accept the invitation you have so heartly extended to me. I will rest assured of being remembered in prayer at your family altars and be convinced of this, that if the home fire be kept burning the enthusiasm of the larger sanctuary will indeed be permanent. I am not about to make any elaborate promises. One promise only will I make, and it is this : in God's strength I will labour with both hands and try to do my duty.

After a sympathetic reference to the signatures of the young people appended to the " call " and an expression of his hope to " make their love for Christ deep and permanent " Jowett added :

I would invoke the divine blessing upon the union thus established. I rest in Him, and though youth and inexperience dim the vision and limit my outlook, these lackings are abundantly compensated by the glad consciousness of the leadership of Christ.

Settled in mind as to his immediate future, Jowett devoted a few months more to theological study, and especially to sermon preparation, closing his student life with the end of the Oxford Hilary term. In the early days of October he moved to Newcastle, took lodgings in St. Mary's Terrace quite close to St. James's Church, and on the first Sunday of the month assumed the responsibilities of his first pastorate.

Jowett's first sermon as minister of St. James's Church was in the nature of a manifesto of his faith. It was preached from the text, " I am determined not to know anything among you, save Jesus Christ, and Him crucified." " By God's grace," he said in the very first sentence of his first sermon in his first pastorate, " I want to make that the keynote of my ministry." The morning was rainy, but *The New-castle Chronicle*, which devoted three-quarters of a column to the young preacher's inaugural service, states that the congregation was " very large " and adds that there was " evidently a fair proportion of strangers." Even the abbreviated report enables one to see that thus early in his ministry Jowett had acquired some of the characteristics that marked his maturity. In what *The Newcastle Chronicle* reporter describes as " a very able sermon " Jowett showed his facility for illustration and imagery. Æstheticism and the love of the beautiful might be a magnificent endowment, he was arguing, but it might be a snare and a very power of darkness. " The sculptor might chisel out an angel and yet be a fiend. The painter might exquisitely paint the Lord's Supper and be a very Judas himself. The poet might sing of love and heaven and yet be the victim of appetite and passion." How familiar and how Jowett-like these phrases ring. " They must turn from the crucifix to the Cross, and against the æstheticism which made the Cross a mere decoration they must lift up the stern reality and build up the Gospel of the Son of Man, of the Son of God, Christ Jesus and Him crucified." " Let them live to Him and He would impart to them His own love and enable them to conquer sin." " That was the Gospel that he wished to preach and his prayer was that all the members of that congregation might not merely be saved from hell, but that they might have the love of Christ shed abroad in their hearts." Thus in his first message from his first pulpit, Jowett struck the note of Evangelical assurance which ran through all his ministry.

At a social meeting held the following week to welcome him to the pastorate Jowett warned his people not to deceive themselves with regard to the large congregations on his first Sunday. They were, he said, largely composed of strangers from other churches who came mainly through curiosity, and nothing had such a short life as curiosity. In a few weeks those congregations would melt down as the novelty wore off and they would be left with a hard nucleus. Jowett's prophecy went wildly astray. It never was fulfilled. From that first Sunday at New-castle in October 1889 until his last Sunday at West-minster Chapel in December 1922 he never knew what it was to preach save to crowds.

Ordination has a significance of its own to the Christian people who call themselves Congregation-alists. Just as they believe—and this is a very High Church doctrine—that wherever two or three are gathered together in the name of the Lord and redeemed by their faith in Him, Christ is in their midst and His presence makes a Church, so they believe that when the voice of God calls to a man to minister in His name, he is already ordained and no act of man can add to, or detract from, the validity of his minis-terial acts. No ecclesiastical organisation is needed to recognise his ministry: no laying-on of hands can impart any fresh grace or add to his authoritative ministry. In practice, however, Congregationalists do solemnly set apart their minister by an ordination service, though in reality this service is an act of recognition rather than an act of ordination. The procedure is simple, but not without dignity. After a short devotional service, some honoured and experi-enced minister gives an exposition of Congregational principles designed to remind the old, and to instruct the young, in the polity and faith of their order. An official of the church to which the young minister has been called to minister, then makes a statement as to the steps by which the Church has been led to invite the minister to its pastorate—the purpose being to show that God's will has been sought and His guidance followed. The young minister is then called upon to state his grounds for believing that he has been divinely called to the ministry and to give, too, some outline of his fundamental beliefs. Sometimes, but not invariably, he then kneels down and two, three or four of his ministerial brethren lay their hands upon him while a prayer of ordination is offered by another minister of the same faith and order. The Principal, or it may be one of the Professors, of the College in which he has received theological training then addresses the young minister, "charging" him to fulfil before God the sacred responsibilities of the ministerial office. Another "charge" is addressed to the Church emphasizing the Church's obligation to the minister. In Congregational theory all members of the Church are equal (under the principle of the Priesthood of all Believers) in spiritual standing—a layman, *e.g.* may administer the sacraments—but in a large measure this theory is now in abeyance, and the minister by virtue of his special divine call to ministry and his call to minister to the Church, is in fact endowed by his own people with spiritual prerogatives,—or as Dr. Dale once put it "delegation of powers to ministers from the general body of the faithful."

At Jowett's ordination, which took place at St. James's Church on November 19th, 1889, these fundamental Congregational principles were clearly affirmed. Dr. Falding (by this time the Principal of Yorkshire

United College) gave an address in which he said explicitly that " if the minister to be ordained to-day is not already a minister of Jesus Christ we cannot make him one. He is called not by us but by the Lord and Master, by the inward sense of conscience and sense of duty." All the distinguished men who took a prominent part in this ordination service at Newcastle have since passed away, and only very few of those present either as friends or ministerial neighbours are now surviving. Professor W. C. Shearer, who had been one of Jowett's tutors at Airedale, gave the exposition of Congregational principles. Dr. Fairbairn, his Principal in his first year at Airedale and in his last year at Oxford, addressed the newly ordained minister who " that day by act of God, by the choice of his own soul, by fond approval of Fathers and Brethren had entered upon the work of the ministry." Later in the day Dr. Charles Albert Berry of Wolverhampton, who had just resisted a tempting invitation to succeed Henry Ward Beecher as minister of the Plymouth Church, Brooklyn, U.S.A., preached the ordination sermon or " charge " to the Church.

Wise and weighty as were the utterances at his ordination service, Jowett's own words, his declaration of his faith and his hopes are all that have any surviving interest to-day. One of his observations was strangely self-revealing and affords a key to many things in his subsequent career. " May I confess," said Jowett, " that my greatest difficulty in College has been to combine the study of theology with the maintenance of a spiritual life."

Though he declined to attempt to express his faith " in a creed of one hundred words," and refused to fix any cast-iron fence within which his mental move-

ments would be confined, Jowett took pains to make
daylight clear his own Evangelical views :—

> God is love (he said) ; when we have measured a
> mother's love, when we have laid our fingers on its
> outermost limits, then we may begin to build a creed
> in which to enclose the whole love of God.   And so
> I regard God's truth as progressive revelation, as an
> ever-expanding and ever-brightening light.   I believe
> that God lets in more light as the eyes of men are
> able to bear it, and that the true attitude is one of
> expectancy, a striving for a purity of vision which
> is able to " bear the burning bliss " and to under-
> stand the larger truth.

Another illuminating passage in Jowett's declaration
of faith showed the elasticity of his mind :—

> To-day men are busy (he said) restoring the old
> cathedral of doctrine, removing a crumbling stone
> here, and an unsafe parapet there : my prayer is
> that their demeanour may be characterised by an
> intense reverence, in the remembrance that the
> ancient pile has been the resting place of many a
> soul who has had sweet visions of his God and that
> the place whereon they stand is holy ground.   If
> to the old organism of ecclesiastical beliefs there are
> clinging any parasites which need to be removed,
> well, let the operation be performed with the delicate
> instrument of reverence and not with the tomahawk
> and scalpel of a ruthless love of novelty and change.
> This is the spirit in which I would like to go about
> my work, and in seeking to remove any excrescences
> I will be prayerfully careful lest I sever the arteries
> of any man's life.   My prayer is that the teaching
> of this pulpit may be constructive and not merely
> destructive.   And if the Master has any new life
> for us to-day, as I joyfully and gratefully believe
> He has, then our work is not that of going about
> ruthlessly smiting off the old leaves; our work is

lovingly to insert the new sap into the old trunk and
the old leaves will quietly fall away, urged by the
sweet constraint of the new ones.

A phrase that often fell from his lips in subsequent
years, " we are saved not by a dead faith but by a
living hope," occurs in Jowett's ordination declaration
of faith.

Soon after his ordination at St. James's Jowett paid
a visit to London which drew much public attention
to him. He went to preach at the Lyndhurst Road
Church at Hampstead where Dr. R. F. Horton was
beginning his work. *The Christian World* and *The
Nonconformist and Independent* published laudatory
articles on Jowett.

> Mr. Jowett (said *The Christian World*) is a very
> young man, but there is in his utterances a marvellous
> ripeness of thought, set off by unusual felicity of
> language. . . . The preacher, slight in form, in
> appearance a true heir of our Anglo-Saxon fore-
> fathers, at once made it felt that he is a new force
> entering into the circle of Church leaders. . . . Mr.
> Jowett is a true son of his time. He is penetrated
> with a sense of the needs of the long-neglected and
> despised classes. Religion in his view needs to be
> socialised, and it is to be socialised by making every
> man and every woman realise their individual
> responsibility.

The article in *The Nonconformist and Independent*,
which was given the title " A Country Minister at
Hampstead " and bore traces of having been written
by a Mansfield College man, referred to Jowett's
" originality of thought and rhetorical power," adding—

> Mr. Jowett has an unaffected, manly bearing, a
> clear, outspoken, unconventional style, and a power-
> ful resonant voice that adds greatly to the effect

of his utterances, and we predict for him a useful
and honoured place in the Congregational ministry.
. . . We shall watch his career with much interest
and trust that the ministry of the Congregational
Churches may speedily be enriched by the presence
of many more young men of the sterling type and
powerful calibre of this young Yorkshireman.

Success and influence attended Jowett's ministry at
St. James's Church from the very outset. He came,
he saw, he conquered. For him there was no agonising
and chilling experience of waiting for a hearing from
a reluctant people.

His preaching power (writes Rev. David Young
of Whitley Bay, a revered veteran in Northumberland Congregationalism) arrested the attention of
Newcastle and the neighbourhood immediately.
The Sunday services were soon talked about on the
Monday morning, down on the Quayside and in the
places where people met for business. The church
filled to the doors, and in the evening was crowded.
Even more remarkable, perhaps, were the gatherings
on week evenings. Pulpit celebrities with a national
reputation the growth of many years could not
have achieved more in this way than the new
beginner.

Some of the sermons of those days were especially
talked about. I often used to hear of one on the
City with the Twelve Gates. Like all preachers
who have made an impression with a particular
sermon, he would be asked to preach it a second
time. He generally replied that " hash " was a
poor substitute for fresh meat, or, as they describe
it in Scotland, " cauld kail het again." My impression is that he developed very much in those six
years of his Newcastle ministry. When I knew
him first, Emerson used to be much on his lips and
probably counted for something in his preaching.
But as he settled down to the inevitable daily

experience and came in frequent contact with the sick, the dying and the bereaved, the struggling people of every sort, and especially those harassed by the personal problems of the soul, he found the only resource and solution in the appeal for an accepted Christ. At all events, as it seemed to me, Emerson and writers of that class receded into the background, and the Christ of the New Testament occupied the foreground commandingly. I am reminded of what Mr. Augustine Birrell says in his brief but impressive biography of his friend Sir Frank Lockwood in the days when Lockwood became seriously out of health and questioned his ultimate recovery. Says Mr. Birrell, " He knew enough about human nature to know it was deeply wounded somewhere and sorely stood in need of a healer." And so, ever more and more Jowett became the preacher pointing with no doubtful finger to the only one who could be called the Great Physician.

Newcastle outstretched its welcoming arms to the new young minister at St. James's, and almost before he realised it, Jowett found himself drawn into the larger life of the city. The Sunday night congregations at St. James's almost immediately taxed the accommodation of the church. His preaching attracted young people in large numbers and his influence upon young men was almost phenomenal. The church membership, which was about 230 when he began his ministry, rose steadily, and every branch of the church's activities felt the quickening touch of his enthusiasm and driving force. He revealed unsuspected gifts of leadership and of cautious judgment. One of his first innovations was to make visits to common lodging-houses—as in his boyhood he had done in Halifax—and address the tramps there, as well as organise the distribution of magazines and

papers among them. From the first he proclaimed his
strong convictions on the Temperance question, both
by his utterances and by active association with the
Band of Hope Union, to whose Presidency he was
elected. A story he told many years afterwards
indicates the tenacity with which he pursued his
temperance crusade.

I had heard on excellent authority that one of my
people was " giving way to drink." He was a man
of some standing in the church and he was possessed
of considerable wealth. I had already preached
more than one Temperance Sermon, but these had
been general messages addressed to the congregation. I was now ordered by my Master to carry
the message to an individual and tactfully to with-
stand him to his face because he stood condemned !
How I wriggled under the commission ! How I
shrank from it ! How I dallied with it ! And, even
when I had fought my way almost to the door I
lingered in the street in further fruitless loitering.
But at length courage conquered fear. I faced my
man, tremblingly gave him my message, and by the
Grace of God he heard the voice of God and was
saved from a horrible pit and the miry clay.

An ardent politician from boyhood and an un-
swerving Liberal by conviction, Jowett stood out
boldly for his political faith from the very beginning
of his ministry at Newcastle. At that time Mr. John
Morley sat in Parliament as member for Newcastle,
and, says Jowett, " no member of Parliament ever
had a more devoted, loyal and enthusiastic constituent
than I was to Mr. Morley." He stood on political
platforms side by side with Mr. Morley and on one
occasion moved a vote of confidence in " Honest
John " at a meeting in Newcastle Town Hall.

Six months after his settlement at Newcastle Jowett was married in the pretty little Congregational Church at Barnard Castle, which had been the scene of his summer student ministries, to Miss Lizzie A. Winpenny, younger daughter of Mr. Francis Winpenny, an honoured figure in Northern Congregationalism, and for fifty years a consistent and zealous office-bearer in Barnard Castle Church. The wedding service was conducted by Dr. Archibald Duff, Jowett's most deeply beloved Professor in his Airedale College days. Another lifelong friend, Rev. John Loosmore, was the best man. Both parents of both bride and bridegroom were present. The honeymoon was spent in North Wales. Their first home was in St. George's Terrace, Jesmond, with open country, long since built over, stretching away over the wide expanse of Town Moor. The married life of Dr. and Mrs. Jowett was from their wedding day an idyll. Mrs. Jowett not only made Jowett's home a temple of peace and a refuge from care, but in multitudinous ways helped and sustained her husband in his public and Church work. Her vigilant care extended his life and his influence. Only those who were privileged to enjoy Jowett's intimate friendship were able fully to appreciate what his serene and happy home-life meant for him. Ten years after their marriage, having no children of their own, Jowett and Mrs. Jowett adopted a little girl, and a new joy came with the advent of this daughter into their home. In his mother, wife and daughter Jowett was richly blessed, and upon all three he poured the wealth of his affection.

During this first pastorate Jowett formed habits of work from which he never deviated far in his later ministries. Bible studies occupied his freshest and best morning hours—especially the study of Isaiah, the Gospels and Paul's Epistles. His method was to paste the whole text of a book of Scripture on one side of a large manuscript book, and then make marginal notes and reflections on the other side. Later he often made pictorial sketches of the environment of a theme—as a help to his historical imagination.

No part of Jowett's Newcastle ministry cost him more painstaking thought, nor gave him more undiluted joy, than his work among young people. From the beginning of his ministry at St. James's he set himself to capture the children and the young men and women. With the help of Mrs. Jowett he started a series of regular services especially intended for children, and he succeeded in gathering them together in large numbers. Almost at once he had the boys and girls in the hollow of his hand. It was at one of the earliest of these special children's services that an amusing incident occurred, which provided him with a platform story. He had just started his address when some boys who had surreptitiously crept into a seat at the back of the hall began a shrill obbligato on penny whistles. A steward caught them and led them to the vestry. Four of them with hangdog countenances and downcast eyes were standing in a row when Jowett entered. He was told that they were the dire offenders. But Jowett had not worked alongside Henry Drummond in his spiritual clinics at Edinburgh without learning the art of dealing with bad lads. He strode towards them and with contempt in his tone asked, " Can't you fellows play on tin whistles better than that? If you can't I shall have to get Mrs. Jowett to give you some lessons." Trepidation fled from the boys' faces. Their eyes beamed back. The upshot of the incident was that a few weeks later four boys trooped on the platform at the children's service and played a quartette on tin whistles to Mrs. Jowett's accompaniment on the pianoforte. Jowett had them enslaved after that.

The preponderance of young people in the Sunday evening congregations at St. James's gave Jowett opportunities which he eagerly seized for appealing directly to young men and women. They heard him gladly, captivated by his manly sincerity and the wholesome, natural fashion in which he presented Christianity to their minds, hearts and souls. In direct, urgent language he appealed to " you young fellows "—as he had heard Drummond appeal to the Edinburgh students—to seek the Kingdom of God and His righteousness. The " wooing " note was present in those earnest evangelical appeals, from which, however, every suggestion of sensationalism or mere emotionalism was absent, and many a young man and woman—as he learned later—quietly registered a decision for the Lordship of Christ over their lives. He never despised the old-fashioned word " conversion " : avowedly he preached for conversions, and his boundless faith in the transforming power of Christ and His grace winged his words.

In all our preaching (he declared) we must preach for verdicts. We must present our case, we must seek a verdict, and we must ask for an immediate execution of the verdict. We are not in the pulpit to please the fancy. We are not there even to inform the mind, or to disturb the emotions, or to sway the judgment. . . . Our ultimate object is to move the will, to set it in another course, to increase its pace and to make it sing in the ways of God's commandments.

Six years, fruitful and formative, were spent by Jowett in his first pastorate at Newcastle. Each suc-

ceeding year added evidence of his increasing and
expanding influence. Only the size of St. James's
Church fixed limits to the congregations that flocked
to hear him. Mission branches, Sunday Schools and
many new channels of activity, which he opened out,
grew in numerical strength and spiritual influence
under his inspiring leadership and sagacious direction.
His people responded loyally to his every call. He
supplied the dynamic impulse; they, with lavish
devotion, poured out their energies, their thought and
their financial resources at his call. Between Jowett
and his Church officers at St. James's a tender and
affectionate relationship based on mutual regard and
confidence subsisted from the first. In every respect
it was a happy ministry to which Jowett never looked
back except in cheerful retrospect.

While at Newcastle Jowett's reputation spread
throughout his own denomination and among the
Free Churches generally. He attained the distinction
of having his name linked with his city. " Jowett of
Newcastle." Though always in peril of breakdown—
all his life he had to do his work on a very slender
margin of physical and nervous strength—he under-
took a full measure of public work outside his own
Church and City. He served for a time on the Newcastle School Board. The Durham and Northumberland Congregational Association elected him to its
chair. As his popularity as a preacher spread—and
it spread almost with suddenness—he became in constant demand as a " special occasion " preacher. Many
temptations to transfer his ministry to other churches,
both famous and influential, came to him, but he
quietly resisted all such blandishments. In his own
mind he had fixed ten years as the probable duration
of his ministry in Newcastle, and his people at St.

James's also entertained some such expectation. But on March 13th, 1895, an event occurred, two hundred miles away, that brought the shadow of separation over Jowett and his Church. On that day Dr. R. W. Dale died, after a lingering illness, and the pastorate of Carr's Lane Church, Birmingham, became vacant. To those who knew both Carr's Lane and Jowett, he seemed predestinated to be Dr. Dale's successor. No time was wasted by the Birmingham Church before moving in his direction. Jowett having preached there twice, a special statutory meeting held on June 23rd received from the deacons a unanimous recommendation that he should be invited. This recommendation was adopted with absolute unanimity and marked enthusiasm by the members of the Church. Then, as prescribed by the Carr's Lane Trust Deed (since modernised), it was submitted to a vote of the male members. A valid election required a two-thirds majority of the total male members on the register. For the call to Jowett over 200 out of the total male membership of 260 voted, and then, following the curious custom, also prescribed by the Trust Deed, the male members wrote their names in indelible ink upon cards provided for the purpose. To the people at St. James's Church, Newcastle, this news, though anticipated, brought sorrow amounting even to dismay. Before the formal invitation to Birmingham had reached Jowett a special meeting of the Church and Congregation at St. James's had been summoned and a resolution was unanimously passed urging that " the necessities and possibilities that are in our midst and lie around us on every hand call louder and plead more truly than even the voice from a great Midland town."

We think it is our duty (ran the resolution of St.

F

James's Church) very respectfully to place before you our deliberate opinion that your removal from St. James's at the present time will have a serious influence upon the results of your work in our midst during the last few years—results which have, especially among the young people, so evidently secured the Divine blessing. We are convinced that the work of years is, at this moment, hastening on to a remarkable fruition and we fear exceedingly that the removal of a spiritual leader and the necessary unsettlement which attends a vacant pastorate, will tend to check and may-be quench much of the young life which is just beginning to rejoice in the conscious friendship of a Divine Saviour and Lord. We almost fear that, in some way, you may scarcely be aware of the extent to which the young people look to you for guidance and inspiration, and while we are far from having a desire to put any undue pressure upon you, or to magnify the effect of your removal, we cannot refrain from putting these things before you.

An appeal so moving, and with so adroit an emphasis on the possible effect of his severance from the young people whose spiritual well-being had been a concern very close to his heart, was not lost on Jowett. He was torn by conflicting emotions and by the clash of what seemed a double imperative—the love he bore his first church and the unbounded opportunity at Birmingham. He asked his people at Newcastle for their sympathy, forbearance and prayers at this solemn crisis in his life. A fortnight later Jowett's mind was clear of all doubt and misgiving. After the morning sermon he announced his acceptance of the Carr's Lane pastorate. His statement was long and entered into detail as to the issues that he had had to face and the motives that had led to his decision.

To be called (he said) to stand in succession to Dr. Dale, while it may fill the heart with the healthiest of fears, is calculated to stir the deepest springs in a young man's soul. No man, whoever he be, could lightly dismiss a call coming from a Church of such proportions and influence. And yet, had I considered my feelings only, I should have immediately declined the call. . . . Here I have had a ministry of unclouded happiness. . . . Our work has been singularly blessed. . . . Six years ago I came to you from College to assume the leadership of this Church. The demands of the pastorate have been heavy, not because the people have been unreasonable but because of its many-sided and ever extending life. I have had little marginal time beyond the actual preparation of my weekly work for any refurnishing of my resources and for the quiet and studious maturing of my own thought. . . . And now when the whole matter is before me in its well-considered details I have the clearest conviction that I have no option but to accept the call. My dear friends, when I came to be your minister I came because I felt it my duty to come. You will believe me when I say that an equal sense of duty inclines me now to go to Birmingham.

Jowett's impending departure from Newcastle was made the occasion for many demonstrations of affection and respect, but perhaps the crowning tribute paid to his ministry was the editorial declaration of *The Newcastle Daily Chronicle* that his preaching " had purified and sweetened the business life of the Tyneside."

On his last Sunday in Newcastle (July 28th, 1895) hundreds were unable to gain admittance to St. James's Church for the farewell service, though every foot of standing room inside the building was occupied. In his closing words Jowett said :—

What has my ministry in Newcastle taught me? I have learned this lesson—that sin is mighty but that God is mightier; I have learned that man is impotent to redeem himself; I have learned that no man need be regarded as beyond redemption; I have learned that for the ruined life there is a power and a peace and a joy unspeakable; I have learned that the care and the misery of this Church are in the homes where Christ is absent; I have learned that the happiest and most beautiful homes connected with this congregation are the homes of the redeemed. These are the lessons of my ministry, and standing upon the experience of these severe years of labour I declare with a glad and a confident heart that Jesus has power and willingness to redeem everybody.

A Communion service was held after the evening service, and in the quiet solemn moments spent in commemorating Christ's farewell to his disciples the pastoral bond between Jowett and his first Church was severed.

CHAPTER IV

(*Æt.* 32–48)

A CONGREGATIONAL Church which is financially independent, *i.e.* drawing no money grants from County Union or Central Funds, need consult no denominational authority when it is choosing a minister. But a subtle pressure of what may be called denominational sentiment exercises an undefinable measure of influence when the church occupies so commanding a place in Congregationalism as Carr's Lane Church, Birmingham, and is the trustee of traditions and associations which are the treasured possessions of the whole denomination. Behind the call of Jowett to Carr's Lane there was consensus of Congregational opinion that he was the man pre-eminently marked out for the succession to Dr. Dale. Though he was conscious of his rapidly developing power as a preacher, Jowett was too modest to assume the mantle of Dr. Dale without genuine trepidation of heart. His first thought was that " the thing was altogether too big " and too crushing for him, and the fear that he would not be able to face the work made him inclined to decline the call. Carr's Lane is a church which demands all a strong man's consecrated energies and gifts, and he was afraid the duties involved would overwhelm him. His acceptance was a venture humbly but hopefully made.

The position occupied by Carr's Lane Church in the

life of Birmingham has perhaps no parallel in any other English city. Birmingham traces its rise to greatness both commercially and politically, to the influx of Nonconformists into the town after the Restoration. For two centuries onwards the borough enjoyed unbounded prosperity owing largely to the business enterprise of a group of Nonconformist families who developed its industries and expanded its boundaries. The political importance of the borough sprang from the influence of men like the famous Dr. Joseph Priestley, who carried on his scientific investigations in Birmingham, and as a stalwart Unitarian gave the political thought of the town its radical bent. Carr's Lane Church came into being as a secession from the Old Meeting House and as a protest against the pronounced Unitarianism preached from the pulpit there. The Church takes its name from a *cul-de-sac* off Bull Street in which the original chapel was built and which was formerly called " Godde's Cart Lane," because in Popish times the holy carriage used for displaying the sacred articles in Roman Catholic street processions was housed in a hovel in this passage. In course of time it was abbreviated to Cart Lane, then to Car Lane, and finally it became Carr's Lane. Early in its history the Church acquired an important status in English Congregationalism. One of its ministers, Dr. Williams, was a pioneer in the foreign mission enterprise and indirectly a founder of the London Missionary Society. During the ministry of John Angell James, which began in 1804, Carr's Lane Chapel was a stronghold of Evangelicalism and a centre of missionary zeal. Dr. Dale's historic ministry confirmed and broadened this influence and authority.

Nevertheless there had for many years been some

valid ground for doubting whether Carr's Lane Church would for any long period maintain its authority and influence. Its geographical location, downtown and somewhat inaccessible, was against it. Moreover the centrifugal tendency had for years been thrusting the resident population of Birmingham to the outer fringes of the city. Other Congregational Churches had sprung up in the suburbs, and their existence and progress seemed to menace the old chapel in the business centre. As long ago as 1850 Dr. Dale had predicted that Carr's Lane Chapel would " go to pieces as soon as John Angell James goes to heaven." Dr. Dale's own ministry belied his gloomy prophecy, but the idea that Carr's Lane would collapse when Dr. Dale died remained in some quarters. No successor modelled on Dr. Dale's massive mental and spiritual scale appeared to be on the horizon, and by some people it was felt that only a man cast in a similarly titanic mould could be expected to maintain the traditions of the Church. The dispensability of any man, however eminent, is an unpalatable fact that the human mind is always loth to accept, and Dr. Dale's pre-eminence blinded men's eyes to the truth that each generation produces the man needed for the continuance of the work. Jowett was not another Dale, and it may even be doubted whether another Dale would have met the new needs of the swiftly changing times.

Dr. Dale had exercised an extraordinary influence on Birmingham as a preacher, but he was far more than a preacher. His political authority was tremendous. When taunted, once, in Parliament with being " the member for Dr. Dale " Mr. Joseph Chamberlain retorted that he was proud to represent such a constituency. Until Dr. Dale's divergence from Gladstonian Liberalism on the Home Rule question no

limits could be set to his political influence on English
Nonconformity. He was an educationalist, a member
of the Birmingham School Board, a governor of the
Grammar School, a member of the Royal Commission
on Secondary Education, a governor of Spring Hill
College and the originator of Mansfield College, Oxford.
He had accustomed his people at Carr's Lane Chapel
to exercise all their mental powers in listening to
massive doctrinal sermons, often an hour long, based
upon elaborated argument and abstruse thought. "I
hear you are preaching doctrinal sermons to the congregation at Carr's Lane," said a friend to him once,
"and they will not stand it." "They will have to
stand it," answered Dr. Dale with what he, himself,
called "the insolent self-confidence of youth." But
Dr. Dale persisted and he made his people listen.
In spite of the heavy doctrinal sermons Carr's Lane
prospered and Dr. Dale's congregation went undiminished. So at Carr's Lane the tradition of scholarly
preaching was firmly established.

The responsibility of succeeding Dr. Dale braced
Jowett to the exercise of his fullest powers. There is
a sense in which it made him. He confessed to a friend
that he had been in peril of mere prettiness in preaching,
but carrying on Dr. Dale's work proved his deliverance.
"He read (writes his friend) everything his mighty
predecessor had written, he assimilated Dale's profound
evangelicalism with eager zest, he began to preach on
the great texts and the great themes, and it was from
this period that his insistence on the doctrine of Grace
began to dominate his preaching." Jowett's own
testimony to Dr. Dale's influence upon him was
publicly given.

There is no man (he said) better qualified than I am
to appreciate the true and enduring greatness of

Dr. Dale . . . and I confess that I am filled with a growingly reverent admiration at the marvellous deposit of liberalising truth and spirit and temper which he left in the Church to which he had consecrated the strength of his life. . . . For what did I find in the church when I came? I succeeded a great man who made it easy for his successor to labour. I succeeded a very great saint and a very great teacher and preacher who by the greatness of his personality had created a liberal spirit at Carr's Lane—a broadly liberal spirit which made it quite easy in certain senses for his successor.

In his first sermon as minister of Carr's Lane, preached on October 6th, 1895, Jowett gave expression to his fears and hopes.

I stand to-day (he said) in the line of an illustrious succession. I have to take up the work of a man who moved with rare and reverent intimacy among the greatest truths of the Christian religion. This pulpit has never been belittled by the petty treatment of small and vulgar themes. The familiarities of this pulpit have been sublime. If the stones of these buildings could be made to speak, I think that all their utterances would gather round about the redemption wrought for us in Christ. The secret and the hidden things of God have here been opened and revealed. But a man who is to know the secrets of the Lord must live in the secret place, and in that secret place my sainted predecessor made his home. It is the thought of his spiritual intimacy that humbles me as I now assume to sustain his work. I feel my poverty most when I remember the purity and the altitude of spirit which gave possibility to his profound spiritual discernment. Such rare vision required a rare holiness. To be able to enter into the bliss of the eternal life required a consecrated and a thrice purified soul. . . . But, then, it is my joy and my encouragement to know that I serve

When I first came to Carr's Lane (wrote Jowett in 1908) my one fear gathered about the church's traditions. I knew that the church had been great for 100 years, and I wondered whether its traditions would fit me like an easy and familiar garment, or whether they would bind me like a coat of mail. Should I inherit multitudinous rules or liberalising principles? Should I be oppressed with fixity of method or inspired with freedom of spirit? I am now in my thirteenth year, and most gladly do I testify that I inherited a magnificent spiritual deposit, a vast reservoir of spiritual energy, which was at my disposal for my own appointed work. Whatever else Dr. Dale did, he was instrumental in forming a church with a gloriously free spirit; a church which, while it reveres its noble traditions, has never been fettered nor embarrassed by them.

In this congenial atmosphere Jowett mellowed and deepened. As a preacher he reached his zenith at Carr's Lane, for though, in his later years, he figured far more prominently before the world, it was at Birmingham that he came to be recognised as " the greatest living master of the homiletic art." Sir William Robertson Nicoll, writing upon a visit to Carr's Lane, said * :—

The great simplicity, reality, sympathy and tenderness of the prayers moved one strangely. . . . Of the startling wealth and beauty of Dr. Jowett's diction, the incisiveness of his contrasts, the overwhelming power of his appeals it is impossible for me to write adequately. Excellent and inspiring as are his published sermons, one has to hear him in order to understand the greatness, and I had almost said, the uniqueness, of his influence. In Dr. Jowett everything preaches. The voice preaches, and it is a voice of great range and compass, always

* *The British Weekly*, Dec. 22, 1910.

sweet and clear through every variety of intonation.
The eyes preach, for though Dr. Jowett apparently
writes every word of his sermons, he is extraordinarily independent of his manuscript. The body
preaches, for Dr. Jowett has many gestures, and not
one ungraceful. But, above all, the heart preaches.
I have heard many great sermons, but never one at
any time which so completely seized and held from
start to finish a great audience. . . . Above all
preachers I have heard Dr. Jowett has the power of
appeal. That the appeal very deeply moved many
who were listening was obvious, and no doubt it
moved many who gave no sign. At times the
tension of listening, the silence, and the eagerness
of the crowd were almost oppressive. It was all
very wonderful and very uplifting.

Jowett's own modest and simple description of his
Carr's Lane ministry was that he tried to preach the
good news of salvation and tried to urge those who
had the good news to express it in good deeds and
especially in social enterprise for the redemption of
the dwellers in the slums of the city.

Throughout his Birmingham ministry, which he
might well have pleaded was more than sufficient for
his strength, Jowett gave himself lavishly in service
to the Free Churches at large. He drew no denominational distinctions in accepting invitations to preach
up and down the country, and he was ever ready to
respond to calls made upon him by other Birmingham
churches. Invitations to preach poured upon him—
sometimes as many as thirty such requests reached
him in a single day. His secretary often spent a
whole afternoon answering them. Frequently he wore
away his physical reserves by travelling to fulfil
preaching engagements. Wherever he went people
crowded to hear him. Whether it was in London or

Edinburgh, in a great provincial city or an industrial centre, in an agricultural market town or even a remote village, his unvarying experience was that a crowded congregation was there, of rich and poor, cultured and simple, eager to listen and respond to his evangelical message. To begin a service half an hour before the announced hour, because the church was already crowded, was nothing unusual in his experience. Only his cloistered home life and Mrs. Jowett's unremitting care enabled him to meet the demands made upon him in those strenuous days.

When Jowett went to Carr's Lane he found in use there a Hymnal compiled by Dr. Dale and published in 1874 under the title of the " English Hymn Book." Dr. Dale had endeavoured to include only those hymns which seemed to him to be in harmony with the characteristic life of English piety—hymns, as he said, distinguished by a certain manly simplicity, expressing the religious thought and emotion of ordinary Englishmen. It was a catholic collection, but, as might be expected, from the period of its compilation, it was marked by extreme individualism and a somewhat rigid theology. At the request of the deacons of Carr's Lane, Jowett, with the aid of a small committee, carried through the revision of the " English Hymn Book " and in 1908 the " Carr's Lane Hymn Book " was published. Even a cursory comparison of the two Hymnals reveals how far Jowett had travelled beyond Dr. Dale in certain aspects of thought and sentiment. Jowett felt that the ideal hymn in public worship is one in which the congregation moves together as a fellowship, bearing one another's sins, sharing one another's conquests, " weeping with them that weep and rejoicing with them that rejoice." He avoided " any sacrilegious suppression of hymns which have become entwined about the minds and hearts of our people," but he took care to omit hymns of a lugubrious type—substituting others which reflected his own sense of joy in Christian living and adding a collection of hymns of service. In the selection of his hymns for public worship Jowett was punctilious to the last degree. He chose them long before the actual service, carefully weighing each hymn " to be a positive ministry in constraining the congregation to intimate fellowship with God," while taking care that the hymns used in each service met the varying moods of the heavy hearted, the joyful, the old and the young, the spiritually experienced and the neophyte in religious experience. " Many of the hymns we sing," he said " are artificial, they are superficial and unreal," and he did his best to eliminate this type of hymn from the new hymnal.

Congregations crowding Carr's Lane Chapel—which seats 1500 people—gathered Sunday by Sunday throughout the sixteen years, drawn together by Jowett's uplifting evangelical preaching. The prosperity and power of the church grew and solidified with the years. Men eminent in the commercial and civic life of the city rallied round him and gave him their absolute loyalty. Carr's Lane in Dr. Dale's time had always an artizan element in its membership, and Jowett was happy in retaining this allegiance. The young life of the church was Jowett's pride and joy. As at Newcastle, he paid particular attention to young men and women. The four large Sunday Schools were always close to his heart. He made the Anniversary a red-letter day in the lives of the scholars. For the Anniversary Sunday the Town Hall was engaged, and Jowett's sermon-address was one of the

great events of the year. He began his preparations
months beforehand. His early experience as a school-
teacher served him well on these occasions. Generally
he gave an object lesson with some carefully collected
" exhibits " to illustrate his message to the children.

Jowett was firm in his faith that the week-night
service is neither out of date nor obsolescent. To his
own service at Carr's Lane he devoted constant care
in preparation, and his Thursday evening meditations
were scarcely less finished in style than his Sunday
sermons. They were delivered in the church, and the
area of the building was often full. Numbers were
drawn from towns within the Birmingham area. A
Sunday School Teachers' preparation class was another
feature of his Birmingham ministry which spread his
influence over the Midlands. Sunday School teachers
flocked to hear him expound the lesson for the following
Sunday. Jowett, who did nothing perfunctorily, took
great care over these " lessons on the lessons." He
used the blackboard freely and he prepared a type-
written syllabus of each lesson with the utmost
attention to detail—as will be seen from a specimen,
which reveals a good deal of his own working theology
as well as a wealth of suggestive teaching material.

The Last Judgment

Matt. xxv. 31–46.

A. Warnings to the Teacher.

   (1) Don't be so literal as to be untrue.

   (2) Remember that Christ has many things to
       say to children but ' they cannot bear them
       now.'

   (3) Don't teach so that Christ the Judge ousts
       Christ the gracious friend.

JOSIAH JOWETT (FATHER OF DR. J. H. JOWETT).

[*To face p.* 80.

B. The Lesson.

1. The Judge of our life will be Christ.
   (1) The Son of Man shall come in His glory (v. 31). Mark this tremendous claim. No one ever spoke like this.

   Put some other name for Son of Man and read the words.

   (2) If Jesus was good He was God : If he wasn't God He wasn't good.

2. He will make no mistakes in His judgments.
   (1) He cannot be deceived. He never mistakes a goat for a sheep. Never mistakes ' profession' for 'piety,' 'show' for 'reality;' the sheep's skin never deludes Him.
   (2) There are only two classes. The division is vertical, not horizontal; it runs through all classes. Sheep—goats !

3. How will He judge us?
   In examinations we wonder what the examiner will ' fix on.'
   (1) What we ' fix on.'
   Profession of creed; membership in the Church; attendance at God's house; 'never done anybody any harm.'
   (2) How the Lord will judge us. He fixes on common kindnesses.
       (a) To those who are in want of necessaries, food, drink, clothing.
       (b) To those who are in want of friends.
       (c) To those who are in want of health.
       (d) To those who are in want of freedom.
   (3) He regards all kindnesses as done to Him.
   He regards all unkindnesses as done to Him.

4. The results of the Lord's Judgments.
   (a) Separation.
   (1) The Christlike.
       (a) To intimate friendship with God— ' Come, ye blessed of my Father.'

G

(*b*) To glorious Kingliness—Inherit the Kingdom. Kings and Queens in power and joy and peace.

(2) The Unchristlike.

    (*a*) To loss of intimacy with God—Depart.

    (*b*) To the fellowship of those they most resemble—'The devil and his angels.'

Foreign missions, Home Missionary efforts, denominational funds, the Hospitals and other philanthropies, especially the Salvation Army—all these found in the Carr's Lane Church generous and even munificent support. Jowett interested himself in Congregational extension in the Birmingham area, and had a hand in starting new churches at Hay Mills, Sparkhill and Kings Norton. He laid stress constantly upon the Christian duty of sacrificial giving. This idea was in the very warp and woof of his thinking.

> I have come to believe (he wrote) that if a spiritual presence can tenant a material body it is not incredible that a spiritual influence can accompany a material gift. In these realms the character of the giver determines the momentum of his gift. If there be sacrifice in the giver there will be spiritual power in the gift. I believe that all our offerings—of strength or time or money—have their virtue conditioned by the sacrifice that gave them birth. . . . We begin to operate with vital forces when we cross the border into the land of sacrifice.

As long as the Digbeth Institute stands in what Jowett called "one of the most oppressive and least advantaged districts in the entire Kingdom" Jowett needs no other monument in Birmingham. He dreamed it into existence, and he saw his dream take shape in wood, brick and stone. Perhaps the very proudest moment in his life, rich as it was in great moments, was when Mrs. Jowett, on Thursday, January 16th, 1908, turned with a golden key the lock of the Digbeth Institute and declared it open.

If Jowett rarely preached what is called the Social Gospel he was always insistent that spiritual energy should be harnessed to practical purposes. Carr's Lane had a mission in Moseley Street and another at Balsall Heath, but neither, nor both, offered an outlet for all the missionary energy generated by Jowett's preaching. Moreover they were small missions and he had reached the conclusion that small missions are both expensive and inefficient. Their day, he felt, was past, and the time had come when Carr's Lane had outgrown its short equipment and must launch out into the deep. To some degree he was influenced by a movement, led by his friend Rev. C. Silvester Horne, for establishing what were called " Institutional Churches " in the heart of the great cities from which the middle classes had migrated, leaving behind them a stratum of population of working people and assistants " living in " at the larger shops. It had become a tradition, against which some of the younger social enthusiasts in the Congregational ministry were revolting, that Congregationalism could only minister effectively to the middle classes, or, as Dr. Dale once said, to an " intellectual aristocracy." This revolt against a tyrannous tradition had found expression in the creation of the Mansfield House University Settlement at Canning Town and the Robert Browning Settlement at Walworth as well as the Institutional Missions at Claremont in Pentonville, Crossway in Southwark, and Whitefields (which Rev. Silvester Horne designed to be the cleanest, brightest and lightest mission in the world) in the Tottenham Court Road Similar movements had been started at Leeds, Man-

chester and Bradford.   Jowett, who had made manifest his sympathy with all these endeavours, determined
that Carr's Lane should do similar work on an heroic
scale in inner Birmingham.   The need was palpable
enough.   Almost within a stone's throw of the doors
of Carr's Lane there were slums so grimy and unsavoury
that they were a standing reproach to the Midland
city.   The Floodgate area—composed of the Deritend
and St. Bartholomew's wards—was a desert of dreary
streets from which branched numerous narrow courts
still more dreary and forbidding.   In this area the
death rate was 24 to the thousand, and there was a
public house for every 250 people.   The appalling
housing conditions startled social investigators.
Squalor, vice, disease and crime rioted.   Into this
noisome region Jowett asked Carr's Lane to plunge.
As he told a friend, he was afraid that his people might
get " fatty degeneration of the soul " unless they
adventured into some chivalrous social crusade.

So (wrote Jowett) I raised the question among my
deacons.   It was a somewhat unillumined gathering
which met in my house that night.   I rather suspect
that some of my brethren thought that I had lost my
judgment and had become " a bit dotty."   It was
suggested that the scheme might cost £15,000, and
there was a silence in the room like death.   It was
as though we were meeting in the dim morning
twilight when the mists were on the ground, and we
could see no highways across the wastes.   But we
all determined to go among the mists, and see if we
could not find a road.   And the scouts returned
with more hope in their faces, and it was determined
to lay the matter before the Church.   And what a
meeting that was which we called together—large,
enthusiastic, confident !   Within two hours £10,000
had been promised, and we sang the doxology with

jubilant assurance. And then the scheme began to grow and grow until our £15,000 had become £25,000 and my wondering people retained both life and hope.

When the foundation stone of the Digbeth Institute was laid on June 30th, 1906, nearly £17,000 had been raised. One of the stones was laid by the Lord Mayor; the other by Jowett, who spoke of the Digbeth scheme as the consummation of a long-nursed ideal. It was not, he emphatically declared, the product of any feverish sentimental impulse or frenzied, spasmodic emotion, but " in an exceedingly oppressive sense of the need of the dingy neighbourhood in which there was nothing calculated to foster and sustain the higher life of the people, and everything calculated to destroy it." " The people in this district," Jowett said, " have scarcely any chance to live healthy and decent lives, and we are coming here to give them the chance." " We propose," he continued, " to bring into this area a distinctly human ministry, and to carry to the people a sympathy so tactful that it will never be obtrusive. It would be a comprehensive ministry, with nothing narrow or impoverishing in its spirit. They would address themselves to every side of the people's lives —to their minds, their bodies and their souls. In and about the Institute everything would be bright and light and beautiful. No single wall would have anything so mean as an almanack, and art exhibitions for the people would be arranged."

Between the Foundation Stone laying in June 1906 and the opening in January 1908 Jowett took upon his shoulders the personal responsibility of raising the remainder of the cost. Begging was a new experience for him, and he squirmed over the duty, but he carried it through manfully. " I was such a poor hand at begging," he said, " that the men I called upon took pity upon me and gave me their donations to put me out of my misery."

Before the end of 1907 the whole £25,000 was in hand and in addition he had secured promises of three billiard tables, the furniture, and crockery for the café, the tables and the trestles for " times of festivity " and multitudinous gifts of pictures and smaller furnishings. Meanwhile Jowett watched the Digbeth building rise stone by stone with consuming joy. He literally haunted the place, interesting himself in every detail and rejoicing in the Ruskinian thoroughness with which architect and builder strove to carry out their work. Digbeth was designed to serve as a church for worship, as a hall for concerts and cinematograph displays and as a palace of recreation. Flooded with sunshine by day and brilliantly illuminated by electric light by night, the entire building was planned to give an impression of brightness and warmth. Jowett's aim was to erect the finest equipped mission in England, and he realised it.

The culminating moment of the opening day was reached when Jowett declared that " I feel I can grow old in this town now, with a place like this." Tumultuous applause burst out from the crowded meeting, quick to seize the implied hint that he would give the remainder of his life to Carr's Lane. As Rev. Silvester Horne said later, they thought they had " built him in." Jowett's speech, reflecting the gaiety of his spirits, was in his happiest vein. Digbeth stood, he declared, for pure living, for clean hearts, clean lips, clean ears, clean hands, clean reading, clean lectures, clean amusement, clean recreation and clean billiards. Dr. Alexander McLaren had recently said to him in tones of warning, " It will take a lot of billiards to make a

Christian." "I accept that," said Jowett. "I accept the warning from our very venerable friend. But then it takes a lot of golf to make a Christian." Laughingly he confessed that after his own first very poor attempt to play golf he had almost resigned his pastorate at Carr's Lane. In his congregation at Newcastle there was a very canny Scot who carried round with him an old golf club which he could hurl freely on the grass when he had made a mis-hit. Jowett's defence of billiards had more than passing significance. Many Free Church people had frowned on the Institutional Church movement from an old-fashioned prejudice against the games permitted on the premises. Jowett's defence of them was whole-hearted.

We do not make Christians by billiards (he said), but we do expect to teach them to play a clean game. Whatever of devilry there is in billiards the Son of Man is here to destroy. We want billiards at Digbeth minus devilry. Billiards will not make a Christian, but a man whose foundation in life is the name of Jesus Christ may in the billiard-room enrich and fortify his consecration vows by recreation under conditions such as we shall offer here.

Jowett also said that Digbeth stood for a cheerful disposition. "Laugh and grow fat is," he said, "a physiological fact," and "if every room in this place resounds with laughter I will come down here for physiological diet. I shall think I have done God's business when, by some unpolluted merriment I have brought some laughter into the drab lives of the poor people around here. We stand here for clean laughter, which is not only physiologically good but morally and spiritually good." Then, said Jowett, Digbeth would stand for chivalrous service.

The Lord (he said) has put us down in a terrible district. An experienced journalist says there is no worse in New York, in Manchester or in East London. And we are in this place as knights and ladies of King Jesus, and I tell you in the King's name that before twelve months are up we shall see many of the people of this terrible district living in the light of God.

All Jowett's sanguine expectations concerning Digbeth were realised. He had found in Rev. William Jones a Superintendent for the Mission whom he believed to be a God-sent colleague. From the first the Institute was immensely popular with the people of the Digbeth district. It was crowded out seven days a week. Jowett never had any reason to fear that the purely recreational side of Digbeth would overwhelm the religious work. Carr's Lane responded gloriously to his challenge. Workers came forward to man all the societies and organisations, and the heavy financial burden of maintenance was cheerfully borne. An endowment fund of £3,000 was raised to pay the ground rent, and a recreation ground was acquired for the clubs. The Lord Mayor of Birmingham, presiding at the Anniversary in 1917, said that " to the efforts of the earnest band of workers at the Digbeth Institute was largely due the fact that the character of the neighbourhood had changed, crime and drunkenness having decreased "—a testimony of the utmost significance coming from so authoritative a source. An instrument for moral reformation in sordid slums, Digbeth stands commemorating a famous ministry and enshrining the name of Jowett through the years to come.

Jowett's own interest in Digbeth never wavered throughout the rest of his life, and in a letter written from New York three years after the Institute was opened he declared that some of his hardest work and some of the purest joy of his life were associated with it.

There is nothing (he wrote to Mr. H. F. Keep) in the whole of my ministry which has given me such sacred pleasure. Every stone of the building is dear to me, and I watched it rising with the enchantment of a great hope. My unceasing experience in life is teaching me more and more that no abiding work can be done unless it is intimately associated with Christ. Everything else is transient and in the long run impotent. The only way in which to help men and women vitally is to introduce them to the friendship of the Lord. We have always tried to keep this in mind at Digbeth, and I hope that this sacred end will always be kept in view. Every institution is only a kind of side-room leading into the secret place, and if the door of the secret place is always closed the full work of that department is never done. . . . Such work has to be done with the most delicate and gracious tact. A worker in the gymnasium must not always be naming the name of Christ or he will become a very ill-advised friend of his Lord, and he can easily do more harm than good. But a worker in a gymnasium should keep his Lord in view, and even though he rarely names Him he will be leading his men in the direction of His gaze. And so it is with every room of the place.

Civic patriotism is a very intense thing in Birmingham and Jowett was too good a citizen not to foster and enrich it by his influence. He was one of the men whose presence was regarded as a *sine qua non* at any special function in the life of the City. The pronounced Unionism of Birmingham was certainly not to his taste. While maintaining his Liberal views, he refrained from purely party activity. When he thought it right and dutiful to do so he spoke out boldly on affairs of State—particularly upon the Education question and the House of Lords. Yet he was able to say at the close of his sixteen years' ministry that he never received a single letter or heard a single word from any member of his congregation calling him to task for exercising the duties of a large national citizenship, though probably the majority of the members of his congregation did not share his political opinions. This perfect freedom to express himself was a priceless privilege which Jowett never abused, but which gave Carr's Lane an unshakable hold upon his affection. He was always proud to quote a dictum of Dr. A. T. Pierson that Carr's Lane was the finest Church in the world. What Birmingham came to think of Jowett was succinctly expressed by *The Birmingham Daily Post* when it declared that he was one of the intellectual and moral assets of the City.

CHAPTER V

THE CHAIR OF THE UNION

Two honours are at the disposal of the Congregational Union of England and Wales. It can invite a minister to preach the " Union Sermon " before its autumnal assembly, which is usually held in some large provincial centre; and it can elect a minister (or a layman) to be the Chairman of the Union for a year. The invitation to preach the " Union Sermon " is an honour conferred by the Committee : the election to the chair is by the vote, through the ballot box, of the ministers and delegates of all the constituent churches of the Union. The first honour almost invariably precedes the second. Jowett was invited to preach the " Union Sermon " in 1900. He was thirty-seven at the time and had been eleven years in the ministry. The distinction coming to him at an unusually early age was a recognition of the high place he had so swiftly won for himself among the preachers of his time. The Congregational Union's autumnal assembly in the year 1900 was held in Newcastle-on-Tyne, a circumstance that lent additional *éclat* to the occasion, since Newcastle claimed a sort of proprietary interest in Jowett. His ministry there was still fresh in people's minds. Though Brunswick Wesleyan Methodist Chapel, lent for the occasion, is the largest Free Church building in Newcastle, its seating accommodation proved pitiably unequal to the demands of that day. Even the choir seats were invaded, so disorganising the choristers that an anthem specially prepared for the service had to be abandoned.

Jowett's " Union Sermon " was notably brief for such a special occasion. He based it on Romans xii. 12—" Rejoicing in Hope." This he interpreted as a characteristic of the fine genial optimism of Paul, who always, he said, " moved with the mien of a conqueror " and " never lost the kingly posture."

> This apostolic optimism was not born (said Jowett) of shallow thinking or of idle and shallow observations. . . . It is the man who, when he has surveyed the dimensions of evil and misery and contempt, merges his dark indictment in a cheery and expansive dawn, in an optimistic evangel in which he counsels his fellow disciples to maintain the confident attitude of a rejoicing hope.

Jowett traced Paul's radiant optimism to its secret springs in the Apostle's vivid sense of the reality of the redemptive work of Christ. The central argument of the sermon was that the Church to-day must draw on the same source for courageous and energetic optimism and that in the glory of redemption—" By Christ redeemed "—all relationships are to be assorted and arranged, and the common lives of men vitalised and energised.

It has often happened that the " Union Sermon " of the Congregational Union has given the keynote to the Autumn assemblies to which it serves as a prelude. Jowett's optimistic utterance rang in the ears of ministers and delegates throughout the ensuing week. The circumstances of the hour contributed to the effect and timeliness of the sermon. The Boer

War in its final phases had been dragging wearily and sorely depressing earnest minds. Then a General Election snapped on the " Khaki " issue, bitterly fought, had just been won by the Party from whom the Free Churches had—as events proved—nothing to hope and everything to fear. Congregationalists were conscious that many difficulties were facing them. The atmosphere in which the ministers and delegates of English Congregationalism had assembled at Newcastle might quite legitimately be described as depressing and debilitating. Upon this mood Jowett broke with his " Union Sermon " sounding the apostolic confidence that made Paul a sunny optimist rejoicing in hope because of his sense of the reality of redemption, because of his wealthy consciousness of Divine resources, and because of his impressive sense of the reality of future glory. Jowett with his intuitive gift of insight " sensed " the mood of the hour, and spoke a word, " timely happy, timely wise."

An interval of five years elapsed between Jowett's delivery of the Congregational Union Sermon and his election to the Chair of the Congregational Union. Jowett, not yet forty-two, was the youngest chairman ever elected.

He entered on his Chairmanship at the May Meetings in 1906. Meanwhile events in the sphere of politics had gravely agitated all the Free Churches, and Congregationalists, perhaps, most of all. The long acrimonious controversy following the Balfour Education Acts had inflamed Nonconformist feeling to such a degree that passive resistance to the Education Law had been organised all over England and Wales. A Bill to amend the Education Acts had just been introduced into the new Parliament by Mr. Augustine Birrell, but the clerical supporters of sectarian education openly boasted that the House of Lords would give it short shrift. So there was " thunder in the air " when the Congregational Union assembled in London in May 1906. Jowett's preliminary remarks at the inaugural meeting raised the battle cry.

> One or two things (he said) were becoming painfully clear. In the first place it had become as clear as the noonday that the so-called National Church did not represent the nation . . . and that it was afraid of the people. . . . Some very ominous features were emerging. It was becoming very clear that the contending parties in the controversy would be classified under the descriptions " Churchmanship *v.* the Bible." In that contention he had no fear as to the issue. He must express his amazement at the violence, the unwisdom and the short-sightedness of the Anglican attack upon simple Bible-teaching. He stood amazed at the disparagement of the unexpounded ministry of the Word. Even the bare reading of the Word of God was not without moral and spiritual force. Was it not so in their family worship?

A fragment of autobiography gave point to his argument. For five years, he said, he was a teacher within the walls of a Board School, and he knew from his own experience that the Episcopal disparagements of the religious instruction given in the Board Schools were altogether unwarranted, and ought to be rescinded. Jowett called upon the Government to make no further concessions to the clamour emanating from palaces and deaneries and rectories, and to see to it that the already expressed will and judgment of the people was registered in legislation. The Congregational Union Assembly cheered to the echo Jowett's warning to the Established Church not to seek to find its defence behind the hoary bulwarks of the House of Lords—" a flimsy and a rotten defence."

Jowett was exactly half-way through his span of working life when he gave his two addresses from the chair—the first in May in London, the second in October in Wolverhampton. Seventeen years of preaching had brought him to ripe maturity; another seventeen years of noble service lay before him. " The prerogative of perfect freedom of speech "—to borrow a phrase of Dr. Dale's—is always granted by the Congregational Union to its chairmen : and the topics which each chairman chooses for his addresses are, in a measure, a key to his mind and soul, and a rough and ready index of the things that lie nearest his heart. Jowett chose two very practical, closely allied themes and deliberately left doctrinal and denominational issues out of his purview. In May his subject was " The Ministry of a Transfigured Church " and in October " The Ministry of a Transfigured Home." They were *ex cathedra* pronouncements, and as such embodied what he no doubt regarded as the kernel and core of his distinctive message and ministry.

The steady decline in attendance at public worship in all the Churches had been engaging the anxious consideration of all the Churches, and the startling figures of Mr. Richard Mudie Smith's systematic census of church attendance in London had come as a shock to Anglicans and Free Churchmen alike. The facts were all too fresh in the minds of Jowett's hearers to need recapitulation when he gave his May address from the chair. He drew his conclusions and stated them frankly. " I think even the most optimistic of us will be obliged to confess that the general tendency is undisturbed, that we do not generate force enough to stop the drift, and that the surrounding multitude

remains unmoved." Roughly he divided the classes
unattracted to, or alienated from, the Churches into
three primary groups : (1) Those who never think about
us at all, (2) Those who have thought about us, and,
as the result of their thinking, have determined to
ignore us, and (3) Those who think about us and who
are constrained by their thinking into the fiercest
and most determined opposition. To the warp and
woof of the daily life of the first group the Churches
contributed no thread—" to this particular class we
simply do not exist." To the second class, the Churches
were, for all simple, positive and progressive purposes,
no longer any good—" we are exhausted batteries."
To the third class the Church was a perverse, nefarious
and perverting influence, ministering to mental and
moral paralysis—" a foul fungus souring the common
soil." Jowett's preliminary analysis was a piece of
ruthless, exploratory surgery, and when he turned
from the general to the particular and asked " How
stands it with our beloved Congregational Church ? "
the candour of his answer left little room for self-
complacency in his audience. The Church, he said,
with all its loud and exuberant professions, was exceedingly like " the world." There was no clear line of
separation. " In place of the promised glories we
have a tolerable and unexciting dimness, in place of
superlative whiteness we have an uninteresting gray,
and in place of the spirit of an aggressive youthfulness
we have a loitering and time-serving expediency. . . .
The alluring wonder is largely absent from our
church. . . . What then do we need? We need the
return of the wonder, the arresting marvel of a transformed church, the phenomenon of a miraculous life."

Pursuing the examination of what he called the comparative poverty and impotence of corporate church

life, Jowett put his finger, unerringly, on some short-comings in " the manner of our fellowship." " We are not," he said, " subdued into the receptiveness of awe." He had seen flippant tourists on the Rigi at the dawn, missing by their noisy irreverence the very glory they had climbed the mountain to see. " That loud and irreverent tramp is far too obtrusive in our communion. . . . In our Nonconformist churches we are not sufficiently possessed by that spirit of reverence which is the ' open sesame ' into the realms of light and grace." In the " light and lilting, tripping strains " of some popular hymns—particularly " The Glory Song "—Jowett perceived a declension from the hymnody which possesses the " deepening ministry of awe."

We leave our places of worship, and no deep and inexpressible wonder sits upon our faces. We can sing these lilting melodies, and when we go out into the streets our faces are one with the faces of those who have left the theatres and the music halls. There is nothing about us to suggest that we have been looking at anything stupendous and overwhelming ! Far back in my boyhood I remember an old saint telling me that after some services he liked to make his way home alone, by quiet by-ways, so that the hush of the Almighty might remain on his awed and prostrate soul. That is the element we are losing, and its loss is one of the measures of our poverty, and the primary secret of inefficient life and service.

Pre-eminently it was our " impoverished conception of God " that explained the loss of awe which he was lamenting.

The popular God is not great and will not create a great race. . . . We have toyed with the light, but we

H

have forgotten the lightning. We have rejoiced
in the Fatherhood of our God, but too frequently the
Fatherhood we have proclaimed has been throneless
and effeminate. . . . My brethren, this mild, ener-
vating air of our modern Lutheranism needs to be
impregnated with something of the bracing salt
of Calvinism. Our very Evangelicalism would be
all the sturdier by the addition of a little " baptized
Stoicism." Our water has become too soft, and it
will no longer make bone for a race of giants.
Our Lutheranism has been diluted and weakened
by the expulsion of some of the sterner motive-
elements which it possesses at its source. If we
banish the conceptions which inspire awe, we of
necessity devitalise the very doctrines of grace, and
if grace is emasculated, then faith becomes anæmic,
and we take away the very tang and pang from the
sense of sin.

If our fellowship with God has been mean, Jowett
argued, our fellowship with man has been scanty.
The Church's riches were buried in the isolated lives
of individual members instead of all being pooled for
the endowment of the whole fraternity. " In lieu of
this broader and richer fellowship we have exalted
the ministry of one man, and out of the limited pool
of his experiences—and sometimes they are not even
experiences, but only fond and desirable assumptions—
the whole community has to drink, while the rest
of the many pools remain untapped. . . ."

This first address from the Chair, notwithstanding
its dominant note of searching criticism, ended in
a confident strain. Jowett was never pessimistic.
He looked facts straight in the face and weighed their
import : but his " apostolic optimism " never deserted
him. Not for a moment would he believe that the
alienation from the people is fundamental or ultimate.

Deep down (he said, in closing), beneath all the visible severances, there are living chords of kinship, ready to thrill and to respond to the royal note. Those living chords—buried if you will beneath the dead and deadening crust of formality and sin, buried, but buried alive—are to be found in Belgravia where Henry Drummond, that man of the high mountains and the broad plains, awoke them to response by the strong, tender, impact of a great evangel and a great experience. . . . And those living chords are also to be found at the pit's mouth, among the crooked and pathetic miners, and they become vibrant with devotion, as Keir Hardie has lately told us that his became vibrant, in answer to the awaking sweep of the strong, tender hands of the Nazarene! The multitude is not sick of Jesus; it is only sick of His feeble and bloodless representatives! When once again a great Church appears, a Church with the Lord's name in her forehead, a Church with fine, muscular limbs and face seamed with the marks of sacrifice, the multitude will turn their feet to the way of God's commandments.

The times might be disturbed—hopefully and fruitfully disturbed, by vast and stupendous problems, but " on every side the latch is lifting and the door of our opportunity stands ajar."

Jowett had an eager and receptive audience for his address. Whatever may be the architectural defects and the decorative barbarities of its interior, the City Temple, when crowded from the pulpit steps to the topmost galleries, presents to a sensitive speaker a strangely inspiring and inspiriting scene. Perhaps on no occasion in a career marked by great occasions was his peculiar genius more evident. Moving perfectly at ease in the gorgeous marble pulpit, his gestures, emphases, cadences and eloquent pauses added to the power and beauty of his words, and the earnestness

and solemnity of his thoughts. At a climacteric
moment in his life grace was given him to be, in all
respects, on the very summit of his resplendent power.

If Jowett's May address from the Chair dealt with
a grand theme in a majestic style, it may be said that
his Autumn address—delivered at Wolverhampton in
October 1906—dealt with a domestic issue in the
simple way. His subject was " The Ministry of a
Transfigured Home," and with a touch of humour he
conceded that there might be something apparently
antiquated in the very terminology of the title. But
he made no sort of apology for employing it. The
gracious term " home " was rapidly becoming an obsolete word, for while the church was aggressively
prominent and the school was never out of sight, the
home was somehow lost in the haze. Yet he felt
that the religious teaching in Sunday and day schools
was a very maimed and enfeebled substitute for
religious teaching—so shamefully neglected nowadays
—given in the home. Yet the natural and the appointed
place for children to make the acquaintance of God
was their own home, and the most powerful and per-
suasive lips for declaring the awful sanctities of religion
were " the priestly lips of the ordained parent."

I would prefer the early guidance of the illumined
father or mother to the instruction of all the State
teachers and official priests in Christendom ! . . .

Alive to actualities, he admitted that the restoration
of the religious ministry of the home seemed one of
the impossibilities stretching across the path of the
Church. He could not, he said, shake himself free
from the conviction that a most serious deterioration
was proceeding in our Christian homes. It was not
only that the home was no longer a school : it was

no longer a temple. The altar was overthrown. Parents provided their children with food, raiment, shelter, schooling, but in tens of thousands of Christian homes the apostolic duties of religion did not come within the recognised scope of parental responsibility. Jowett traced much of the baneful evasion of the deeper aspects of parental duty and privilege to a dull and even flippant conception of the solemn sacrament of marriage. In countless instances the marriage relationship was entered into as though life were a jaunty picnic and not a grave crusade.

Returning to the main current of his argument, he asked if the assumption was justified that ministers were competent to teach the parent how to instruct the child. " Do we ministers really know the child? " he asked. Have our studies led us to acquire a fine and serviceable knowledge of the child. What, for instance, had the ministerial training colleges to say about the child? Did they ever recognise its existence? What relation had the discipline of the class room to the needs of the nursery?

But I am not here to disparage the fruitfulness of college training, but rather to seek its increased fertility. I remember that a few years ago the great vine at Hampton Court began to give signs that its bearing energy was on the wane. . . . Careful investigation was made, and down among the roots of the vine were found the remains of ancient foundations, which were secretly obstructing its legitimate growth. The embedded obstacles were excavated, and the cavity filled with fifty to sixty tons of vine-earth, and the liberated tree revealed unprecedented fertility. Wild horses would not extract from me a detailed interpretation of this parable ! I will content myself by saying that there are flying rumours of more than one collegiate vine where an analogous excavation would be attended by most beneficent results. But mine is not now the advocacy of excavation with a view to greater force, but the advocacy of a more practical direction to force that already exists. It is not enough to make us accomplished grammarians, and expert theological theorists. . . . I do not disparage the value of Greek or Hebrew : it would be an exceedingly foolish disparagement : and how can I disparage them when they are ministers to me of daily discovery, for the enrichment of my own soul, and the profit of my people? I do not undervalue the virtue of dogmatics, the endless profit of exegesis, or the firm, steady stride that is gained from a sure knowledge of ecclesiastical history. But I would have the entire discipline taken a step further, and I would be taught its direct bearing upon actual sin and sorrow, upon moral health and moral degeneracy, upon spiritual atrophy and spiritual endeavour, upon the fears and pessimisms of the aged, and the opening wonder and curiosity of the child."

Jowett made three concrete suggestions with a view to the enrichment of ministerial training. He advised that far more attention should be given to the teaching of a definite psychology; he counselled the teaching of a more lucid and compact moral philosophy; and he advocated a more practical and usable pastoral theology, a theology in more vital and immediate touch with the necessities of spiritual hygiene and spiritual dietetics and spiritual pathology.

The second " address from the Chair " like the first was heard with obvious appreciation by the Union Assembly; and if the impression made by it was less abiding, that was no doubt due to the May address being on a larger theme and handled on a broader plane. "The Transfigured Home" came in a natural sequence to " The Transfigured Church," and in the two complementary addresses Jowett propounded his own fundamental belief that upon the purity and sanctity of the Christian home and the fidelity and consecration of the Christian Church the promotion of the Kingdom of Heaven is dependent. Neither address provoked any serious criticism, and, with his visitation of the churches in his representative capacity as Chairman, Jowett's year of office in the chair was a source of happiness to himself and of enrichment to British Congregationalism.

CHAPTER VI

FREE CHURCH PRESIDENCY

(*Æt.* 47-48)

THE Presidency of the National Council of the Evangelical Free Churches came inevitably to Jowett, and like his denominational honours it came at an almost unprecedentedly early age. His election took place in 1909 and he held the office from March 1910 to March 1911. The National Free Church Council is not strictly representative of the Nonconformist denominations. In most of the towns in England and Wales, and in many semi-urban areas, local councils composed of delegates appointed by the Free Churches have been established and these local Councils in turn elect delegates to the National Council which meets once a year. Provision is made for personal membership, apart from delegate-members. In this way the National Council resolves itself into a roughly representative Parliament of the Free Churches, with standing committees which meet regularly in London. As a ready means of focusing Free Church opinion, the National Council serves a valuable purpose and enjoys great prestige and influence, though it has no inherent authority over its constituency. In addition to serving as a mouthpiece of Free Church opinion, the National Council charges itself with the duties of promoting interdenominational evangelistic efforts and of quickening the spiritual vigour of the Free Churches throughout the land. From its President the Council expects a Presidential address at the National Council meeting and some sustained work in visitation of the local Councils during the year.

Jowett's election to the Presidency was immensely popular and his year of office was signalised by an attendance of nearly two thousand representatives at the annual Council meetings held in Hull. The address he gave on " The Ministry of the Word " impressed his hearers as much by his ruthless probing into the causes of the impoverishment of ministry as by his exaltation of the preacher's function in the life of the age.

> Everything is not right among us (he frankly avowed). We may be busy, but we are not impressive. We may interest, but we do not constrain. We may tickle men's palates, but we do not make them feel the bitterness of sin. We may offer them entertainment, but we do not amaze them with the overwhelming glory of God.

Seeking for root causes he suggested that their preaching might be deficient in dynamic. In all great preaching from the apostolic age down to Spurgeon or Newman, Binney or Dale there was a range, vastness, radiance and colour which seemed to have been lost. " We are not going to enrich our action by the impoverishment of our thought. A skimmed theology will not produce a more intimate philanthropy. You cannot drop the big themes and create great saints." The note of vastitude had to be recovered in modern preaching. Even when dealing with practical duties the preacher needed to emphasize their rootage in the Eternal. It was at the gravest peril that theology and ethics were dissociated.

All this (said Jowett) means that we must preach more upon the great texts of the Scriptures, the tremendous passages whose vastnesses almost terrify us as we approach them. Yes, we must grapple with the big things, the things about which our people will hear nowhere else—the deep, the abiding, the things that permanently matter. We are not appointed merely to give good advice, but to proclaim good news. Therefore must the Apostolic themes be our themes.

But there were certain things they had to avoid. " First of all we must avoid a fierce sensationalism." He warned ministers against *outre* sayings, startling advertisements, profane words and irreverent prayers.

There is no need to be vulgar in the attempt to be familiar. We never reach the innermost room in any man's soul by the expediences of the showman or the buffoon. The way of irreverence will never lead to the Holy Place. Let us be as homely as we please, but let it be the homeliness of simplicity which clothes itself in all things natural, chaste and refined; and, secondly, we must avoid a cold officialism. There is nothing more uncongenial to me as I move about amid the venerable stones and the subduing precincts of Westminster Abbey than to hear the cold, heartless, wonderless recitals of the official guides. Yes, there is one thing more uncongenial still—to hear the great Evangel of Redeeming Love recited with the metallic apathy of a gramophone, with the cold remoteness of an unappreciative machine. And that is our peril.

Signs of a revival of spiritual religion were discerned in the spring of 1910, and the Free Churches, which had been suffering from a long period of depression with an appreciable shrinkage in church membership and a startling decline in Sunday School attendance, gave clear evidences of reviving life. Encouraged by these happy omens the spirit of the Hull meetings of the National Council was high, and the idea of starting an aggressive campaign of evangelism was discussed. Jowett, however, as President, felt strongly that a well-devised campaign for stimulating the spiritual life within the Churches was an urgent necessity before any organised effort to reach the non-church-goer was undertaken. Consequently he resolved to devote his Presidential Year to a systematic and well-thought-out effort to that end. He felt he could best serve the Free Churches by holding a series of conventions in various provincial centres.

Upon the preparations for this series of conventions he lavished care and thought. All his organising powers—and they were remarkable—were brought into operation. No detail was left to chance. Jowett hated pietism and unreality, and he shrank from creating an atmosphere of spurious religiosity. He selected his coadjutors with cautious discrimination. As his first lieutenant he secured the aid of his old friend and neighbour, Rev. Edgar Todd of Acocks Green. Together they drew up all the plans, and worked over the general line of the series of addresses which Jowett proposed to deliver at each convention. Examination of the preliminary notes, now lying before me, display all Jowett's genius for taking pains. The skeleton notes of his addresses on Reconsecration exemplify his methodical care in preparation.

Reconsecration.

Our promised wealth. . . . Our actual poverty. The needed adjustments.

(1) Negative : an emptying : a putting off.

(a) Some things to be emptied out of self—

Bitterness, wrath, anger, clamour, evil-speaking, malice.

(b) Some things to be emptied out of the Church—The old leaven. The carnality of contention.

(2) Positive : A filling : a putting on of the Lord Jesus. How?

(a) By more common intimacy of fellowship with God—" Rejoice evermore."   " Pray without ceasing."   " In everything give thanks."   Psalm or hymn and spiritual songs. Drunk with the spirit. The whole armour of God.

(b) A new and more truthful fellowship with one another—In spiritual purpose. Likemindedness. In personal interest " Look not every man on his own things, but——" In community of gifts. " Ye are many, but one body." " Eye " and " hand." A glorious pooling.

(c) A more zealous crusade for the Salvation of the World—Our quest—the souls of the people. Our message—Jesus Christ and Him crucified. Our means—" all means to save some."

The first convention was held at Yarmouth at the end of May; the second at Bournemouth in mid-June. In each case the order of proceedings during the three days' meetings was identical—early morning prayer meeting at 7.30; morning session at 11, Tea Table Conference at 5. Public meeting (or sermon) at 7.30. At Bournemouth, where 350 delegates represented the South of England Free Church Councils, the average attendance at the early morning prayer meeting was 300, at the morning session from 1,000 to 1,200 and at the evening meetings about 1,250. Dr. J. D. Jones, describing the spirit of the convention, said he had attended many series of meetings, but for sustained spiritual power he could remember nothing to compare with the meetings at Bournemouth.

We were close to God all through.* The solemn hush and awe of the Divine Presence was upon us throughout; and at every session we sat down in the heavenly places in Jesus Christ. . . . Never did eternal things appear so vivid and so near and so real to me as they did during those memorable days. The prayer meetings . . . were gracious meetings with God. . . . They were vivid, alive and of absorbing interest.

Dr. Jowett led every prayer meeting with consummate wisdom and tact. . . . At each morning session Dr. Jowett delivered an address. . . . They were mighty addresses. . . . The evening meetings were called public meetings, but the religious note and the devotional spirit were never for an instant lost. . . . Here again Dr. Jowett was the dominating personality. For sheer overwhelming force I have never heard anything equal to the fifteen minutes' talk with which he brought the young people's meeting to a close. . . . The Convention was brought to a close with a sermon by Dr. Jowett. . . . I won't try to describe the sermon. But this I know, it was a mighty preaching. . . . There was one preacher at least listening to Dr. Jowett that night who felt he had not begun to preach as yet, and who went away resolved that preaching should be a more urgent and insistent business with him than ever it had been before. And many a preacher must have felt like that. . . . It was back to the sources of our power we were led, and verily we felt that the Kingdom of God was come nigh unto us.

The appeal everywhere was for Reconsecration; and he made it with compelling urgency, and sent a new impulse for service through the Churches. *The Blackpool Times*, commenting on the Lancashire Convention, declared that " Blackpool will be a sweeter, better, purer town in the coming days and the life of

* *The Christian World*, June 16, 1910.

the churches and of every spiritual and moral force of
the town will be enhanced and extended, improved
and enlarged, strengthened and increased by the breath
of the Pisgah air." Recalling his memories of association with Jowett in this enterprise, Rev. Edgar Todd
writes :—

   I shall always retain a very vivid memory of how
he faced my first reluctance to accompany him.
" I hear the call," he said, " like a great bell." He
was very full of his mission and spoke about nothing
else. An intimate sense of God and loyalty to Christ
were fundamental with him and always increasing.
Prayer and the word of God were for him like the
two sides of the same coin, and he spent himself in
both very freely. He had a wonderful intuition in
dealing with individuals and was father confessor
to hundreds. Men and women, entire strangers,
came to him and opened their hearts to him with
an astonishing unreserve. He was swiftly at the
essential centre of their business, whether they knew it
or not. A quiet question would come as a lightning
flash, and they knew his gaze was upon their most
jealously defended secret. When he was exercising
these high priestly prerogatives there was no remote
trace of priestliness about him. Although he had
an extraordinary power with crowds his thoughts
invariably crystallised about single persons. He
knew how the leaven must work and how the salt
must penetrate. He had no metaphysics, and
Forsyth, for example, puzzled him. He allowed
himself a strictly limited sphere for speculations
and had no use for " isms " that did not palpitate
with a vital spiritual purpose. He made dead bones
live. He was the Pygmalion of inarticulated truth.

Reconsecration Conventions with Jowett as leader and
inspirer were held at Yarmouth, Bournemouth, Llandrindod Wells, Swansea, Newport, Scarborough, New-

castle-upon-Tyne, Blackpool, Plymouth and Leicester. Each convention was designed to serve a wide area and the centres selected were all easy of access.   Jowett was the magnet, and although the Conventions were held in the months when holiday resorts are hibernating, eager crowds gathered from somewhere to hear him. In every place an early morning prayer meeting was held each day. " No one will come," he was told, " at seven o'clock in the morning." But events proved the contrary.

I well remember (writes Rev. Edgar Todd) setting off for one of those meetings at Plymouth. When we left the hotel the lamps were flaring and the snow was steadily falling in large flakes.   There were about one hundred people present at that meeting, about two hundred the next morning, and about four hundred and fifty the third morning. That is how it usually went in each place whatever the season of the year might be. Those early morning meetings were a revelation. Jowett was often at his best on these occasions, but the people were also at their best, and that best was a very astonishing and beautiful thing to behold.

Jowett's hand was on every detail in the arrangements. Sometimes the local authorities had everything neatly arranged beforehand.   They thought they knew precisely what was wanted, and were going to manage things for him. But that was not quite his way. Very courteously, but very firmly, he would set their arrangements aside, and carry out his own preconceived plans.   Solemn fussiness on the part of small officials distracted him and tended to make him keep things in his own hands.

Never (writes Mr. Todd) shall I forget the last of that wonderful series of meetings.   It was at

Leicester. The early morning prayer meeting was
at 7 a.m. Jowett was always about first and
knocked lightly at my door. That morning the
knock came as usual, and I called "Come in." The
maid came in and said, "Dr. Jowett wants to see
you." I went at once to his room. Immediately
I saw him I was assailed by a strange misgiving.
"Todd," he said faintly, "I cannot go this morning.
You and Gipsy (Smith) must see this through."
Lying there white and very weak, with a haggard
look in that alert eye, how loyally he had vindicated
his commission. It had been arranged that the
series of meetings should end in London, but there
could have been no finer ending than that in Leicester.

Necessarily the Conventions made heavy drafts
upon Jowett's already overdrawn banking account of
physical strength, and peremptory orders from his
doctor put a limit on his efforts during the remainder
of his days in England. But happy memories of the
Conventions remained with him in the years that
followed. He felt he had not laboured in vain. A
letter written two years afterwards reveals the spirit
of his retrospect.

New York,
Feby. 24, 1913.

To Rev. Edgar Todd.

What a fine glowing letter you have sent me.
It took me back to our eventful year when we
were running like fire over England. What a
time we had together! Sometimes it seems like
a dream, but it is one of those dreams which easily
become visions, and I suppose we shall never be
able to estimate what we did together that year.

HANNAH JOWETT (MOTHER OF DR. J. H. JOWETT).

[To face p. 112.

CHAPTER VII

PUBLIC LIFE

THE occasions on which Jowett became involved in controversy were very few, and very far between. Life ran placidly with him, though he filled it with hard work and conscientious effort. Temperamentally he disliked controversy and shrank from it, unless an imperative necessity arose for the defence of a principle or an assault upon an evil. He had not the polemical temper and he looked upon controversial triumphs as Pyrrhic victories—destructive of serenity of mind and human goodwill. A phrase of Emerson's, "nerve yourself on the affirmatives," was often on his lips, and his natural mental habit was to emphasize his own positive views rather than to antagonise the views of others. But when he was challenged upon some principle he held dear, he was a doughty fighter; and when goaded by an injustice or a misrepresentation he spoke with smashing emphasis.

On Dr. Gore's elevation to the Bishopric of Birmingham in 1905 the new Bishop was welcomed to his See at a meeting held in the Town Hall. Jowett was present, and spoke, as the representative of Nonconformity in the city. Dr. Gore dealt chiefly in his speech with the idea of Christian reunion, saying that he would like to bring together men of different kinds, and different points of view interested in religious questions to meet frankly face to face with one another,

and to get to know one another better. " In this
freedom and this fellowship of a common study of
what religion means," said Dr. Gore, " I see the great
forces of reunion in the future, and I believe Mr. Jowett
will agree with me in that." Jowett replied in a
genial and friendly spirit to Dr. Gore's overture,
expressing his belief that the Nonconformists of
Birmingham would feel the kindling of the new Bishop's
spiritual devotion, and that every section of the
community would feel his quickening and fertilising
influence.

But (said Jowett) I stand here as a Nonconformist,
a strong Nonconformist, as strong a Nonconformist
as the Bishop of London has just declared himself
a Churchman. I am a Nonconformist, convinced
and sincere, and I do not, in offering a courtesy
to-day, in any way disparage my own faith and
convictions. Courtesy that sacrifices principle is a
worthless, and, indeed, a very harmful thing. If a
courtesy is to be worth anything it must be genuine,
and have nothing about it that is counterfeit or
delusive. I do not suppose that this interchange of
courtesies will alter anybody's convictions, but it
may tend to sweeten and enrich our dispositions.
And perhaps the realms of conviction and disposition are not so divorced as at first sight they may
appear. It might be that our very convictions
would be modified, or rather that our conceptions
of one another's convictions would be modified, if
they were looked at through the correcting medium
of genial and mutual respect. . . . But if our
courtesies are to be effective, they must have two
characteristics. They must be sincere and they
must be reciprocal. Courtesy which is confined to
one side—whichever the side may be—is apt to
grow faint, and to be chilled in the atmosphere of
an unanswered approach. I feel very grateful to
you, therefore, my Lord Mayor, for arranging a

gathering where a Nonconformist can look upon a
live Bishop and discover that after all he does not
appear to be a monster, and where a Bishop can look
upon a representative Nonconformist and find that,
after all, his purpose appears to be set in pursuit
of truth and goodwill.

Nonconformists, who about this time were up in
arms against the Education Acts, were not altogether
pleased by this speech, and Jowett confessed himself
amazed at the number of remonstrances he received for
his action in taking part in the welcome of Dr. Gore.
" I would do it again gladly," he replied to his critics.
" Nonconformity cannot afford to lose its courtesy."

An opportunity to show that his expressed desire
for friendly relations with the Church of England did
not imply any weakening of his Free Church principles,
occurred at the National Free Church Council meetings
at Manchester a few days after his speech at Dr. Gore's
welcome to Birmingham. At Manchester Jowett
seconded a resolution moved by Dr. Clifford, con-
demning the Balfour Education Acts which placed
Sectarian Schools on the rates without placing them
under popular control and expressing sympathy with
passive resistance to the new education rates. In
asking Jowett to speak to this resolution, the Secretary
of the Free Church Council, Rev. Thomas Law, had
written saying it was desired that " someone not in the
fighting rank " should speak—" someone more associated with the devotional life of the Church." Jowett
made merry over this naïveté. " I refuse," he said, " to
be turned out of the fighting line, and still more I
refuse to dissociate Dr. Clifford and Mr. Silvester Horne
from the devotional side of our work." " This Act,"
he said, " is destroying the finest susceptibilities of
our people," and he referred scornfully to " the arma-

ments of a dominant Church." A General Election
with Free Trade or Tariff Reform as the issue was
approaching, and Jowett referred sadly to the readiness
with which moral and spiritual issues were brushed
aside by material interests. " Freedom of Trade,"
he said, " is important, but it is infinitely more important that we should have free communion with the
Highest without the intervention of any priest."
Jowett's " powerful and picturesque " speech completely
justified his claim to be in the " fighting rank " when a
great principle was in jeopardy.

The patience of Free Churchmen was strained to
an almost intolerable degree during the summer of
1906 by a new turn given to the Education controversy,
and the summer passed into an autumn of unrelieved
disappointment and chagrin. Early in April Mr.
Augustine Birrell unfolded the new Liberal Government's proposals for amending the Education Acts
and for redressing Nonconformist grievances under
the last Conservative Government's obnoxious Acts.
The fact, of which Mr. Birrell boasted, that the new
Secretary for Education was a Nonconformist born
and bred, nurtured in Nonconformist history and
Nonconformist tradition, and reared in the very library
of a Nonconformist minister had encouraged Free
Churchmen to believe that his Bill would both advance
the cause of elementary education and remove the heavy
hand of the priest from the elementary schools. But
the Birrell Bill totally disappointed them. Half-
heartedness was stamped all over it. Mr. Birrell is
credited with saying that he did not recognise his own
measure when it emerged from consideration in the
Cabinet. It is merely recording history to say that the
Bill carried compromise to a point which offended and
exasperated many stalwart Free Church Liberals.

Jowett, who had pleaded for a " Nonconformist attitude of magnanimity," confessed that the measure made him suspicious and uneasy. It was not the Bill he expected, nor the Bill for which Free Churchmen had been struggling. During its transit through the House of Commons, Free Church unrest was accentuated by the Government's unconcerned acceptance of amendments which, from the Free Church point of view, further weakened its vital provisions. Possibly Sir Henry Campbell-Bannerman and his Cabinet did not mind what happened to the Bill. In the form in which it was sent up to the House of Lords it certainly did not satisfy Nonconformity. But the Peers, aided and abetted by the Bishops, deliberately proceeded to tear it to ribbons. Their amendments ripped every vital principle out of the measure. They made optional concessions obligatory by substituting " shalls " for " mays " and, clause by clause, they transformed its character. As it emerged after its mangling by the Peers, the Birrell Bill, instead of removing, actually aggravated the grievances of Nonconformists.

Free Church indignation took shape in great demonstrations of protest all over the country. The Free Church Council Executive, exercising its rarely used power to summon an emergency meeting of the National Council, hastily convened an assembly in London. The delegates from every quarter of England and Wales met in fighting mood in the Holborn Restaurant—two thousand strong. Dr. Clifford, who had led the Nonconformist hosts throughout the Education controversy, moved a resolution declaring that the Peers' amendments stultified the verdict of the country at the General Election, destroyed the main principles of the Bill and rendered it worse than useless.

Jowett seconded this resolution. If there was any

occasion in his life when he spoke with a vehemence
distinctly tinged with bitterness it was in this speech.
It was just as well to know where they were. If there
was nothing of vital import that Nonconformists and
Anglicans could together teach the children, the
manifesto he had recently signed along with the Bishop
of Birmingham to foster the spirit of unity was not
worth the paper it was written upon. It was better
all pretence at union should cease and that they should
stand, as they had stood for centuries, in solid battle
array. It was, said Jowett, the Bishops they had to
fight, not the laity. They must tell the Bishops in
the House of Lords that no amount of Episcopal cooing
could make Free Churchmen forget the years of desola-
tion and deprivation from which they had been suffering. The King's Hall of the Holborn Restaurant rang
with cheers as Jowett, aflame with indignation, raised
his voice in this passionate protest against clerical
domination. The agitation availed the Free Churches
nothing. The Liberal Government bowed before the
House of Lords, dropped the Bill like a hot cake, and
troubled themselves very little more with Nonconformist grievances on Education.

In the Spring of 1909 Jowett found himself involved
in an ecclesiastical storm. It arose out of Canon Hensley
Henson's acceptance of an invitation to preach at the
first anniversary of the Digbeth Institute in defiance
of a formal inhibition by the Bishop of Birmingham
(Dr. Charles Gore). As soon as the Canon's acceptance
of the invitation was announced, the Vicar of St.
Gabriel's, in whose parish the Digbeth Institute is
situated, entered a protest against another clergyman
entering his parish to preach without his consent, and
appealed to his diocesan. The Bishop of Birmingham
—though in writing to Canon Henson he described the

whole affair as " a great bore "—felt compelled to intervene and exercise his veto. Canon Hensley Henson, brushing aside the pedantic legalism as obsolete, and expressing surprise that Bishop Gore should have thought the Vicar of St. Gabriel's protest deserving of notice, retorted that he was pledged to preach at the Institute and he should certainly endeavour to keep his engagement. In subsequent correspondence Canon Henson informed Bishop Gore that " if you send me any kind of formal inhibition, I may fairly tell you in advance that I shall hold it to be my plain duty to ignore it." Bishop Gore replied with a formal " inhibition," but sent with it a covering note saying, " I am very sorry to send a document which is to me extremely disagreeable to send. I still hope you will withdraw." To this Canon Henson replied that it was quite clear to him that it was his duty to ignore it, and he fulfilled his engagement. On the same day Bishop Gore wrote to the Birmingham newspapers intimating that this defiance of Incumbent and Bishop would have to be brought to a legal test. At this stage, Jowett, who had stood aloof from the controversy, intervened with a vigorous letter to *The Birmingham Daily Post*. After broadly hinting that Bishop Gore might wisely have restricted his action to episcopal counsel and warning against the endangering of weightier issues by clergymen unwisely claiming their ecclesiastical rights, Jowett wrote :

For myself, as I grow older, and life and work become more actual and solemn, I am less and less concerned with the smaller matters of formal etiquette which so often strangle and suffocate the liberty of Christian communion. . . . In every possible way I have sought to cultivate a close intimacy with the ministers of the Established Church, but the present action of the Bishop fills me with dismay. Ten days ago it would have seemed to me impossible; even now it appears incredible. How such action can serve the larger purpose of the Kingdom of God is to me inconceivable. It can only result in deeper alienations and divisions, in still further weakening our common campaign against wrong and in giving a further theme to the man who " sits in the seat of the scornful."

In a little while Jowett's high-minded letter was the only public memory of an ugly episode in Church relations.

In 1910, Edinburgh University, twenty-three years after Jowett's graduation, conferred its honorary degree of Doctor of Divinity upon him. The intimation that he was to be made a D.D. reached him in the early spring, and he received the news with undisguised satisfaction. The degree was conferred at the Arts Graduation Ceremonial in McEwan Hall. Dr. Patrick, the Dean of the Faculty of Divinity, who introduced Jowett to the distinguished assemblage, observed that it was manifest from the positions he had held, or was holding, that no name in English Nonconformity was held in higher honour than his.

Mr. Jowett (said Dr. Patrick) claims our regard as a preacher, an author and an administrator. . . . His writings enable us in some measure to understand his reputation as a preacher, characterised as they are by spiritual fire and insight, by a grace and distinction of style and by a wealth of imagery which " half reveals and half conceals " the thought but never interferes with the lucid and orderly development of the discourse. While pre-eminently a spiritual preacher, Mr. Jowett has realised that the Church, in pursuit of its highest aims, cannot ignore the necessary inter-relation of the spiritual and the material, but must claim for it the whole sphere of human thought and activity, and adapt itself to the social conditions and problems of to-day ; and by the foundation of the Digbeth Institute in harmony with a wide conception of Christian ethics, social and individual, has brought " sweetness and light " into the lives of thousands in a joyless and dull district of the city of Birmingham. By a record so honourable and so full of work Mr. Jowett has brought distinction upon the University of which he is a graduate, and I ask you to recognise that service by admitting him to the roll of our honorary graduates in Divinity.

After the " capping " ceremony a house-luncheon was given in the University Union in honour of the honorary graduates. Jowett proposed the toast of the University, and, as the occasion demanded, fell into a vein of happy reminiscence. He recalled an episode in his first week as an undergraduate at Edinburgh. In his lodgings, he said, his landlord came on Saturday night and locked up the piano but opened the harmonium. On Monday morning he came and reversed the order. That, he added, amid laughter, was his first experience of moral distinctions in Edinburgh.

Though a loyal Congregationalist and a staunch Free Churchman, Jowett had no patience with the frequent waste of energy for which mere denominationalism is responsible. When Dr. J. H. Shakespeare adumbrated a scheme for a United Free Church of England (at the Free Church Council Meetings at Hull in April, 1910) Jowett, who had just entered on his Presidential year, was one of the first to give the proposal his whole-souled support. But while eagerly welcoming the idea of a United Free Church, Jowett sagaciously warned Free Churchmen against imagining that they would attain to a noble union by everybody becoming lukewarm about his own particular church. He drew a subtle distinction :—

> It is a poor cosmopolitanism that is born of a withered patriotism. I do not think we should be any richer if every man became lukewarm towards any particular woman and professed a sort of diffused attachment to all of womankind. . . . No! in the ideal relationship we shall retain our particular loves and attachments, but our love will be wise and enlightened, and having many deep tendrils of communion we shall be sensitive to the general purposes of the Kingdom and we shall find our supreme joy in the common advance.

Another warning given by Jowett was against the notion that even if Dr. Shakespeare's Free Church unity proposals were adopted an immediate millennium would be ushered in. "Mere organisation will not make God's Kingdom come." Jowett often stressed this view. His faith in machinery was very faltering. He did not believe seriously, he said, that the impact and influence of the Established Church, notwithstanding her ordered unity, was so great as the influence of the Free Churches with all their lack of common aim and action. "But," he added, "if the ordered unity of the Established Church were deeply spiritualised and gloriously alive, its ministry would be tremendous." Free Church unity would ultimately come; but it would come slowly, a step at a time, by an evolutionary process, not a revolutionary coup.

From the one great theological controversy of his time—the New Theology furore of 1907—Jowett, if he did not hold aloof, kept studiously to re-emphasizing his own positive views without saying one word that wounded or embittered. Rev. R. J. Campbell, around

whom the controversy raged, and Jowett were on terms
of brotherly friendliness. He had preached at Mr.
Campbell's recognition at the City Temple, and turning
towards his friend had said, " We all recognise that the
Holy Father has made Mr. Campbell the Temple, of the
Holy Spirit : the perfume of the Master's presence in
him is felt by us all," and Mr. Campbell, in thanking
Jowett for his words, had replied, " I loved him before, I
love him more now. Humbly I promise in the presence
of this people I will obey the charge given by my
brother." When the New Theology storm burst its
bitterness distressed Jowett's spirit. He reasserted his
own firm Christology and left the professional theological
bruisers to wage their battle over Mr. Campbell and
his opinions. He re-affirmed his profound belief in
the Deity of Christ, denied that Jesus could have been
a product of evolution, and held firmly to His sinless-
ness. Later, with the then ex-Chairmen of the Congregational Union, he signed a manifesto setting forth in
positive terms the Congregational faith " as once for
all delivered unto the saints." His own personal
attitude towards the controversial issues was explained
to the members of Carr's Lane at a Church meeting
at the end of 1907.

People, he said, were mixing up Religion and
Theology—Doctrine and Experience. The one remains : but the other develops. Half the trouble is
caused by people criticising incomplete statements.

We are, he said, on the borders of great changes.
New ideas of the spiritual world are coming to light,
and a new conception of spiritual laws. God has
yet more light and more truth to break forth.
Especially we need some great mind to restate Paul's
teaching in modern terms. Nothing was more
urgently needed. We have to dress our thoughts in the
imagery and language of our day. We want to

grasp the central teaching of Christ and of Paul and clothe it in the imagery and symbolism of our time. Meanwhile we must exclude all personalities from the discussion, and our duty is to reaffirm the central verities of our faith.

All the Free Churches, accepting Jowett as the foremost preacher of his time, turned to him on their great special occasions. He was *par excellence* the " Centenary " and " Jubilee " preacher of Nonconformity and he found hosts of admiring friends in all the denominations. His broad sympathies overleapt denominational boundary walls, but outside Congregationalism his heart was warmest towards Methodists.

To Wesleyan Methodists he was friendly throughout his ministry. In the North of England (writes Rev. F. Luke Wiseman, ex-President of the Wesleyan Methodist Conference) I have been told of the ready help he gave to our churches there in his Newcastle days. I can speak from personal knowledge of his attitude after coming to Carr's Lane. Specially did he seem desirous to show his sympathy with the Methodist Forward Movement. His admiration of the Manchester Mission was unqualified : and he gave it the sincere flattery of imitation in the Digbeth Institute. For years he preached the noon sermon at the Manchester Mission Anniversary and his congregation filled the Free Trade Hall—a striking tribute to the power of the preacher and the regard in which Methodists held him. When we opened the New Central Hall in Birmingham I asked him to preach on the second Sunday evening. He instantly replied that he would be delighted to do so, if I would " supply " for him at Carr's Lane. For many years he attended the Anniversary meetings of the Birmingham Mission and received a tumultuous welcome. More recently the work at Cliff College appealed to him and he took part in the Whit Monday Anniversary—I believe he even hinted to Rev.

Samuel Chadwick that he would be glad to show his sympathy with that remarkable work. And what a reception he had from the thousands that throng Cliff grounds on the Anniversary day. " These are parts of his ways." And Methodists reciprocated his brotherly sympathy with whole-hearted admiration and affection.

The sturdy qualities of the " Primitives " commanded his admiration and he often gave expression to it. At a Centenary meeting in Birmingham Town Hall on July 10th, 1909, he made an exceedingly happy speech in eulogy of Primitive Methodism—its open-airness, its naturalness, its simplicity, its love of the highways and hedges and its fondness for the field. He prayed them to retain their early note of naturalness and simplicity in the pulpit, in worship and in private life. Modern life was becoming exceedingly complex and on every side there was danger of excessive and crippling elaboration. " We are becoming over-organised," he said, " over-mechanicalised, over-ritualised, and we are in very grave peril of forgetting the wind that ' bloweth where it listeth,' and whose vitalising breath could best be felt in the open country of the glorious liberty wherewith Christ has made us free."

The skilful and well-organised use of lay preaching in Primitive Methodism won Jowett's admiration, and on this occasion he reminded his friends of their " proud pre-eminence in the splendid roll of consecrated laymen."

More than in any other communion your laity are the ordained ministers of Grace, freely and joyfully recognised as the priests and kings and prophets of God. This has been one of your great glories. You have recognised the holy order of the grocer and the cobbler and the warehouseman and the miner and the clerk, and the blessed Lord has confirmed your recognition in a marvellous outpouring of redeeming Grace.

On three occasions Jowett was selected to be one of the Heckmondwike Lecturers. This Lectureship holds a peculiar place in the life of this West Riding Yorkshire town. Since the year 1762 it has been the custom of the Congregational Churches at Heckmondwike to hold a preaching convention (after the manner of a Welsh Cymanfa) in the week after the first Sunday in June, and the leading Free Church preachers of the day have always counted it an honour to be included in the panel of five preachers who in the course of two days preach these " Lectures." Jowett was among the very few who have, in the whole history of the Lectures, been invited to preach more than once. One of his sermons preached in 1894 is still remembered at Heckmondwike, and through its memory he " being dead, yet speaketh." He reached his high-water mark on that memorable day and swayed his native Yorkshire audience by his words. To this day Heckmondwike people quote Jowett. " Tha can't do it; no ! but you remember what Dr. Jowett said, ' Tha must be born again.' " He preached one of the Heckmondwike Lectures again in 1900, and once more in 1920.

A harp string is invisible when it is vibrating to its true note, and when a minister of the Gospel is doing his proper work he makes no " copy " for the newspapers. It is when he does, or says, things outside his proper sphere that he provides headlines for the secular Press. Jowett felt this. He hated what Dr. P. T. Forsyth called a " footlights ministry," and it was an immense relief to him when after some occasion that brought him under the searchlight of the Press, he could shrink back out of the glare of publicity to do his own work quietly and unobtrusively.

CHAPTER VIII

CALLED TO AMERICA

(*Æt.* 46–47)

A HOLIDAY spent in America, in company with Mrs
Jowett, in the summer of 1909 proved a turning point
in Jowett's career. It was his first visit to the United
States, and he went, primarily, on the invitation of Mr.
Will. R. Moody to preach and speak at the Northfield
Conference. His intention was, however, to have a
travel holiday and he had no idea that the visit would
have a supremely important bearing on his whole
future. He spent some time in New York, where he
preached at Plymouth Church, Brooklyn—Henry
Ward Beecher's old pulpit—and at Montclair Church,
New Jersey—a pulpit indissolubly associated with the
name of Dr. Amory Bradford—and at Fifth Avenue
Presbyterian Church. Then he went on to Northfield.
A fortnight in the Yellowstone Park rounded off the
delightful trip. "Yellowstone," he wrote to Mr. S. E.
Short, "baffles all description. I have nothing but
exclamations for it—my ordinary means of expression
pitifully fail."

Northfield surpassed his anticipations. This educational and Evangelical settlement in one of the lovely
New England valleys perpetuates the work of D. L.
Moody, the famous evangelist, who established there
a series of schools designed to meet the needs of young
men and women whose scanty means preclude them
from the regular colleges. Each summer a sequence

of religious Conferences is held at Northfield, with speakers and preachers of the highest standard drawn from England as well as America. Jowett found the Northfield atmosphere quite congenial, and he entered with abandon into the spirit of the Conferences.

> *East Northfield,*
> *Mass., U.S.A.,*
> *August* 16, 1909.

To Rev. Edgar Todd.

The Northfield Conference is now over and we are leaving to-day. We have had a very great time and there have been experiences which have exceeded all my expectations. I was led to expect great things, but the reality is greater still. The attendance has been enormous, including four hundred ministers. I had the privilege of preaching yesterday to three thousand people, and have frequently had the same opportunity during the last two weeks. I am perfectly sure that English ministers just now have a tremendous opportunity in the States. Our messages have been received with positive hunger, and we are all deeply grateful for the results. We have heard from scores of ministers that the Conference has meant a revolution in their life, and I cannot but think that the influence of Northfield will be felt throughout the States.

Early one morning he went out from Northfield to conduct a camp meeting in the woods for men drawn from the Jerry McCauley mission for " down and outers " in New York. Before Jowett spoke one of the men prayed for him. " Oh, Lord, we pray for our brother. Now blot him out ! Reveal Thy glory to us in such blazing splendour that he shall be forgotten." Jowett declared that this supplication was inspired, and expressed a hope that it was answered.

In a letter to Mr. John G. Hurst, Jowett gave his impressions of America and the Americans, and also the first intimation that New York was casting envious eyes on Birmingham.

To Mr. J. G. Hurst.

" Stands Scotland where it did "? America appears to stand us very well, and is most evidently determined not to be disestablished. She—I mean the aforesaid America—has done her level best to disestablish us—I mean by " us " self and spouse adored (*Ego et meus rex*). She—America—has tried overwhelming kindness, overwhelming heat, overwhelming crowds, overwhelming convulsions by rail and sea—and now here we are 8000 feet up and she is trying a new game. . . . We have been shivering to-day in the blue margins of boiling springs and I am about disestablished and inclined to " fully surrender " as friend Sankey has it.

A wonderful people ! I should think they are. In some respects we are infants in arms (I almost spelt that word " alms," and it would have been equally true). They can beat us hollow in imagination, speculation, expectoration ! In regard to money-making we English folk — you and I— are living in the glacial period (I don't know enough geology to be able to announce in definite terms the period at which they have arrived, but it's as plain as a pike-staff that they are there !)

Religiously I can't make Uncle Sam out. He's continuously " on the wink " and I can't get him with a serious eye. The only time when you get him with a fixed eye is when you criticise him ; and then the rigid optic has no religion in it : so that it gives one no stuff for a judgment. But the Convention type is odd and I haven't got his measure, and so I shall have to make a guess at it. I am going to formulate my guess when I am on the Atlantic and Sam's shores are left behind. And Sam wants me to live with him and take up my abode at Fifth Avenue,

K

New York. But this, too, is immeasurable, and I refuse to flirt with him. He is making the wires hot with telegrams : but, as Billy Bray used to say, " Praise the Lord, He keeps me cool."

And now home is calling, and I hear and heed. It sounds very gracious, and the old land lies very sweet in the Northern sea. And my friends are very dear, and you among the first of them. Yes, I'm ready for home and work again.

Though Jowett had refused to enter into any flirtation with Fifth Avenue Church, where he had preached on two Sundays, the New Yorkers were sufficiently in earnest to proceed to a definite proposal, and on Christmas eve a crisis was sprung upon him. A letter, posted from an incoming Atlantic liner at Queenstown, intimated to him that a deputation was on its way to invite him to the pastorate of Fifth Avenue Church, New York.

Since his return from America he had received no communication from Fifth Avenue Church, either by letter or word of mouth. Then came the message from Queenstown, followed swiftly by a deputation of three gentlemen from New York who, with what Jowett described as " abounding grace and spirituality," presented him with a formal call to Fifth Avenue. During five days at Rhos-on-Sea Jowett and his wife carefully deliberated over the situation, and he virtually determined to accept the call. Meanwhile cables from New York announced to English newspaper readers that the invitation was in Jowett's hands. Immediately he was bombarded with communications from his Church and from all parts of England pressing him to stay in England. A counter-bombardment of cables from America begged him to go to New York. For ten days he was absolutely bewildered and confused. During this period of uncertainty a Church meeting was convened at Carr's Lane, but before it met 1400 signatures had been attached to a resolution, petitioning him to remain in Birmingham, in the following terms :—

To our Beloved and Honoured Pastor the Rev. J. H. Jowett, M.A.

We, the undersigned, members of the Church and congregation worshipping under your leadership at Carr's Lane, have heard with deep concern of the invitation recently given to you by the Fifth Avenue Presbyterian Church, New York.

We are all conscious that the choice you are now called upon to make is one of the most vital and momentous character. We want to assure you that your decision is being made the subject of earnest and continued prayer by us all, and of our belief that God will surely guide you to a decision in accordance with His will.

We are not unmindful of the great opportunities that would undoubtedly be yours in America. At the same time we should like you to know that we are all deeply impressed by the opportunities that are yours among your own people in the City in which for the past fourteen years you have so faithfully laboured, and in the country in which, with the growth of years, you have won so wide and so commanding an influence. For the way in which you have led this Church into increasingly wide opportunities of service, and for all you, and your wife, have been to every one of us, we desire to render our most hearty thanks by personally signing this letter. In addition to what you have been to us here it has been given to you to guide the thought and spiritual life of the country in a unique way, and it is our prayer that if it be God's will you and your wife will remain in our midst and that as minister of this united Church you may continue to lead us and all your

own countrymen who regard you with unstinted
loyalty, devotion and love, and to render to England
in the critical time which lies before us even yet
wider and more fruitful service in the Kingdom of
God. (Signed by 1400 signatories.)

The feeling in Birmingham may be judged from the
fact that the Lord Mayor took the unprecedented step
of sending Jowett a memorial signed by the City
magistrates expressing concern at the possibility of his
removal from Birmingham, and adding a hope that
" in the interests of all that is best in our civic life "
he might see his way to continue in the pastorate at
Carr's Lane Chapel. Meanwhile he faced up to the
issue.

In conversation with one of his friends in the previous
spring Jowett had disclosed a doubt in his own mind as
to his own future. He was forty-seven, and if he thought
of changing the scene of his ministry he was at the age
to do it. So he approached the Fifth Avenue call
with a mind at least open to influence. The wealth
and prestige of Fifth Avenue Church rather repelled
him. He dreaded the possibility of a social atmosphere
that might be uncongenial, possibly even hostile. As
to money, he had told the deputation at once that
he would, if he accepted the call, only become their
minister at a stipend equivalent in American purchasing
value to that which he received at Carr's Lane. They
replied that they were actually offering him £600 a
year less than they we ̧ authorised to offer. It was
the unique opportunity that tempted him—the " opportunity of preaching an Evangelical Gospel to a thirsty
people in the heart of cosmopolitan New York." A
further three days' retreat spent in his old home at
Halifax with his Mother left him with his course
undecided. Then he determined to consult three of

his most intimate friends, Rev. Edgar Todd, Mr. J. G. Hurst and Mr. H. F. Keep, and to take his decision from them. " I want to hear ' the voice,' " he wrote to Mr. Todd.

On arriving home at " Clydesdale " he found these three friends awaiting him in one room and the three delegates from New York in another room. For four hours he discussed the matter with his Birmingham friends and finally came to the conclusion that he must decline the offer. His decision was at once communicated to the New York deputation, and next day he announced it to his people at the morning service at Carr's Lane. " I have been led," he said, " to the conclusion that the New York ministry is not for me." For a moment there was silence, and then, spontaneously, the congregation burst into applause. Someone started the Doxology, but Jowett with a peremptory gesture, stopped the demonstration which to his sensitive spirit profaned the decencies of public worship.

Having so emphatically declined the invitation to New York, Jowett threw himself whole-heartedly into the work that was at hand. He never, he said himself, worked so hard as he did in the succeeding twelve months. The New York Church allowed six months to elapse and then returned to the assault. In June 1910 Jowett received a cable telling him that the call was about to be repeated and that a second deputation was being sent. Within two hours he had cabled to stop them. " Finally declined," was his laconic message. So the deputation was not sent. In the ensuing autumn Dr. J. D. Jones of Bournemouth, who was visiting the United States, preached at Fifth Avenue and made so strong an impression upon the Church that a few weeks later, when he was in Boston, a deputation went up from Fifth Avenue Church and

invited him to the pastorate.   Dr. Jones deferred giving
an answer until his return to England.   When he
consulted his friends, Rev. C. Silvester Horne and
Dr. Jowett, Mr. Horne urged that the Congregational
Central Fund was in Dr. Jones's hands and would tie
him in England for four years at least.   Dr. Jones
agreed and straightway declined the overtures from
New York.   Then the Fifth Avenue Church turned
once more towards Jowett.   On December 15th he
received an urgent cable begging him to reconsider his
decision.

Jowett had never been quite free from the sense of
the urgency of the call.   It had been upon his mind and
his conscience.   Although he knew he had done right
in declining it in January, the persistency of the New
York appeal, and his realisation of the unique opportunity Fifth Avenue Church presented, haunted him.
And in a letter to Mr. S. E. Short he said he sometimes very seriously wondered whether his appeals had
not lost their power.   " A congregation," he wrote,
" can get accustomed to a man, and his words lose
weight because of their familiarity.   They grow into
his way of putting things and his message lacks the
element of surprise."

The first invitation to New York had unsettled his
mind by compelling him to contemplate the possibility
of uprooting himself from Carr's Lane : the second
invitation found him in a mood when the contemplation
of that possibility was no longer a novel and unthought-
of contingency.   The officers of Carr's Lane Chapel,
recognising that the situation had changed, refrained
from bringing the full pressure of the Church to bear
on Jowett's decision.   He was certainly not left
without clear indication of their ardent wish that he
might again decide to cleave to Carr's Lane : but no

Church Meeting was convened, nor was any petition organised. He was not unmindful, they all knew, of their confidence and affection and of their desire to retain him. Public opinion found expression through *The Birmingham Daily Post*, which, in a leading article, said that "Birmingham has still great need of Dr. Jowett's ministry," and urged him to "stand to the post which he has held so long and which he has filled with such rich results." But Jowett felt that this was "a deep, fundamental, irresistible, imperative call," and five weeks after he had received the cabled invitation he decided to accept it and communicated his decision to a Church Meeting at Carr's Lane on January 25th. His statement was heard with tense interest, though its tenour was fully anticipated. He felt, he said, that the appeal Fifth Avenue Church made to him was as a mighty opportunity. It was a Church doing a work in the slums far bigger than at Digbeth, and supporting eighteen missionaries in the foreign field. He had been told that he would find no needier place than Birmingham; but when he compared the needs of that great, new, raw city across the water, with the needs of the privileged city of Birmingham he had no hesitation in saying that if the decision were to be made in accordance with the need, then he had no doubt what the decision should be. He was not going among a congregation of millionaires to live under the most luxurious conditions, but to minister to a church which was not merely fortunate in its wealth but in the work it was trying to do at home and abroad. He took the opportunity to repeat that he had intimated that he would not accept the salary the Fifth Avenue Church had offered him. It was larger than his needs. He should only take the equivalent of the salary he had received at Carr's Lane. "My people here know," he said, "that I have never been out after money (applause). You have offered me increases of salary which I have refused . . ." If money came his way in New York, he said he should give it away. He did not want it. There was no boasting about that. He simply wanted to do the work that awaited him there. A resolution brought forward by the deacons was submitted to the meeting by Mr. J. G. Hurst and carried in these terms :—

The members of the Church and congregation worshipping at Carr's Lane profoundly regret Dr. Jowett's severance from the great work which he has so successfully carried on as their pastor during the past 15½ years, but, having heard the statement that he has now made, they desire to assure him that the call which he has once again received from the Fifth Avenue Church, New York, is one in which they also recognise the voice of God. They therefore commend him in all tenderness and Christian sympathy to their brethren across the sea, and assure him that they will follow him and support him in his new ministry with their constant prayers.

With fine magnanimity the Carr's Lane Church sent from the same meeting a message of goodwill to the Fifth Avenue Church, New York. What was happily described as "the resolution of resignation" was welcomed by Jowett. He regarded it as the seal of Carr's Lane upon his work, and a sign, if he had wanted one, that he had done good work there. "I very much question," he said, "whether anything like this has ever been known before in the history of the Congregational Churches of this country. I feel proud that I have been minister of this Church. I feel far more proud of Carr's Lane Church than of any little ministry of my own."

Jowett had to run the gauntlet of a succession of formal and informal farewell meetings, luncheons and dinners during his last two months in England.

King George commanded his presence at a State Dinner at Buckingham Palace. A few days later (addressing a Free Church Council meeting) Jowett made a personal reference to that occasion. " Great honour had been done him," he said, " by the King in inviting him to dine with him last Friday night (March 3rd, 1911). He took it not as a personal honour, but as a recognition of the work done by the Free Churches and further as a gracious act on the part of a gracious monarch towards the (American) people whom he (Jowett) was going to try to serve. He thought he should not be breaking a sacred confidence if he said that the last words spoken to him by the King, when he gave him a quarter of an hour of personal fellowship, were, ' I want to tell you that you go with the goodwill of your King and Queen.' "

The National Council of Evangelical Free Churches took leave of Jowett at Portsmouth, where its annual Conference was in session, on March 7th. He had just completed his Presidential year and had the " gracious privilege " of welcoming his dear friend, Rev. Charles Brown, as his successor. The new President's first duty was to present a farewell address to Jowett and to acknowledge his great services in his Presidential year, " especially in those wonderful conventions which had made an impression which would not easily be effaced." The address presented to Jowett on behalf of the Assembly expressed heartfelt affection and esteem, and deepest sorrow and regret at his departure.

We desire to record (said the address) our deep gratitude to God for your wealthy gifts and for their

complete consecration to the holiest service, for your
high Christian character, the certitude of your
message and your unfaltering loyalty to Evangelical truth.   We give thanks to God for the great and
illustrious ministry which has lifted preaching to
its true dignity and importance, and for the seals
to your ministry which He has granted you.

Jowett, in reply to the address, expressed his belief
that while there was every reason in the world why he
should not go, there was one reason why he should—
that if he had not gone he would never again have
been happy in his work in England.

He had still to receive the valediction of his own
denomination and the adieux and God-speeds of his
own Church at Birmingham. The denominational
farewell took place at a luncheon to the members of
the Congregational Council. The company at the
Holborn Restaurant was representative of Congregationalism from Northumberland to Cornwall and from
Carnarvon to East Anglia. The Chairman of the
Congregational Union, Rev. C. Silvester Horne, M.P.,
presided and in his happiest vein lifted the occasion out
of lugubriousness by his delicious banter. Dr. Jowett,
he suggested, had " merely made a mistake over a
complicated railway guide and had really taken a ticket
for London *via* New York." He was merely travelling
to the metropolis by the " Great Western route."
London would be his eventual destination, though he
might be delayed a little while changing at New York.
" We are," said Mr. Silvester Horne, " merely negotiating
a loan—we could do nothing less when a sister denomination found herself hard up for preachers, but we surrender none of our rights in Dr. Jowett. This is only
a lease to America : the freehold remains in our
possession. Dr. Jowett belongs to us. He is a

Congregationalist and he remains a Congregationalist, and as a Congregationalist he will be an invaluable home missionary in that denomination which has at least one grace left to it—it knows good preaching when it hears it." Dr. J. D. Jones struck another note. He was persuaded that Jowett was entering on the work and opportunity of his life. Fifth Avenue Church was an auditorium from which the preacher's voice would go to the ends of the world. America needed a convinced Evangelicalism united with a modern intellectual outlook, and Fifth Avenue Church presented the greatest opportunity in the whole non-episcopal Protestant world.

Jowett, who confessed that the strain of the last few weeks had robbed him of all elasticity of brain, evidently felt acutely the tension of this farewell to his brethren in the ministry. One assurance he gave them—forget that he was a Congregationalist he never would. He owed everything to Congregationalism. He was born in it, in the home of a father and mother who loved it. He was cradled in it, received his first inspiration from it and found his first hero—Dr. Enoch Mellor—in it. He acknowledged, too, his lasting debt to St. James's Church, Newcastle, which welcomed him when he was " a raw apprentice " and to Carr's Lane Church which had surrounded him with confidence and affection such as no Church could possibly surpass. " So you see I owe everything to Congregationalism and I am not leaving the marrow and virtue of Congregationalism in my new sphere."

The farewell to Carr's Lane and to Birmingham was, inevitably, an even more poignant occasion. Though invitations were restricted to his own people at Carr's Lane, the famous Town Hall was none too large for the meeting. Many sacred memories link Carr's Lane

with the Town Hall. Dr. Dale preached there when
Carr's Lane was undergoing structural alterations, and
it was there that he was welcomed back to Birmingham
after his Australian tour—welcomed with the famous
banner-scroll bearing the words, " We love you and we
tell you so." Year by year Jowett had preached the
Carr's Lane Sunday School Anniversary sermons in
the Town Hall. The presence of the Lord Mayor
(Alderman W. H. Bowater) in the Chair gave a civic
character to the gathering, and speaking for the citi-
zens of Birmingham he declared that Jowett's work in
their city was an imperishable heritage. There were
presentations—which Jowett acknowledged in gracious
words. The choice, by the deacons, of a gold watch
for himself, liberated a flow of banter. The only watch
he had ever found that would keep time was a five
shilling one he was then wearing. In a few phrases
he reviewed his sixteen years' ministry at Carr's Lane
and paid generous tribute to his loyal deacons—" not
a single word has ever fallen in the deacons' vestry that
I would wish recalled." Then he spoke of the two
sovereign aims of his ministry. " I have tried to
preach the good news of Salvation," and " I have tried
to secure that the Evangel should find a translation
into good deeds of social service." Family farewells
and final visits to intimate friends filled Jowett's days
during the ensuing weeks.

Halifax,
March 10th, 1911.

To Rev. Thomas Towers.

  I am here in the old home for a couple of days
with my Mother. The quiet is delightful.
  What a gracious act you have done to me.*
I cannot tell you how deeply I appreciate it.
When I am getting out of terrible bunkers the

---

 * Mr. Towers had sent him a niblick.

implement will remind me of our friendship, and of how often we have taken counsel together about bunkers of a more serious kind.

The last few days were spent quietly in the country.

Church Stretton,
March 18, 1911.

To Rev. Edgar Todd.

What a lovely quiet Sunday we are having! And what restful days and sleepful nights. Your prescribed ten hours is being more than satisfied. It is all glorious after " the garish day." We are imbibing good things in body, mind and soul.

We thank you and Mrs. Todd for your most gracious thoughtfulness in sending the golf balls. It is very kind and means so much. If you should find a good " Challenger " ball in your garden it will be one of my " sliced " balls. Send it on.

The Congregational minister here * is a choice soul. His text this morning was " They that wait upon the Lord shall renew their strength." Hurrah! That sounds hopeful for New York! And for you too! So again I say Hurrah!

* Rev. W. A. Simcox.

CHAPTER IX

DELAYED by a stormy voyage, the " Mauretania,"
in which Jowett crossed the Atlantic to begin his
ministry in New York, did not reach her berth until
midnight. The officers of Fifth Avenue Church—
some of whom awaited him on the quay—had engaged
a suite of rooms for Dr. and Mrs. Jowett at the Gotham
Hotel and the chef had been instructed to stay on duty
to prepare their supper. The order to the chef,
telephoned from the ship to the hotel, was that " Dr.
and Mrs. Jowett would like two bowls of bread and
milk."

The story is almost a parable of the spirit in which
he began his ministry in America. His arrival was an
event of primary interest to New Yorkers. He was
the foremost living British preacher, in whom the King
of England was personally interested and he was
intimately acquainted with Mr. Lloyd George and other
British dignitaries. The American sensational Press
made a " stunt " of his arrival. Flaring block-type
headings, running across the front pages of the newspapers, announced his coming. It was the event of
the week. A cohort of reporters interviewed him as
soon as the ship reached the dock. The reports of the
interviews suggest that Jowett puzzled the New York
journalists. In their own parlance he did not " deliver
the goods." They expected, no doubt, an exuberant

personality who would talk lively " copy "; but they found a shy, reticent man with a singular serenity of manner, and an immovable reluctance to say anything whatever that would justify sensational headlines. Jowett was never the man to be lured into extravagance, and his caution was proof even against the seductive influence of the far-famed New York harbour interviewers.

Hundreds of people struggled unsuccessfully for admission to Fifth Avenue Church when Jowett began his ministry on Sunday, April 2nd. As it was, those admitted were said by *The New York Herald*, the next day, to have formed the largest audience the church had ever held. Placards bearing the words " Church filled to utmost capacity " were displayed at least an hour before the service began. Though Jowett's concern for what he called the decencies of public worship always made him reluctant to introduce anything extraneous into divine service, he read a cable, which he thought was not out of keeping with the spirit of the day, from Carr's Lane Church, Birmingham, " praying that your message to-day may be filled with the Holy Spirit's power, and that the joy and peace of God may rest upon you." His first sermon as minister of Fifth Avenue Church was on the Compassion of Jesus for the multitude—interpreting Christ's compassion as " a cloudless sense of right, a blazing resistance against wrong, a sensitive perception of human infirmity, and a glorious purpose to ransom and redeem. " This," he said, " is the Gospel I have come to preach to you, the Gospel that has saved me, and helped me and blessed me, and holds me—the Gospel that is more than sufficient for the infinite pathos and suffering of human life." It was a strictly expository sermon, but (says one of the reporters), " it held the

congregation in a spell for forty-five minutes." Jowett
spoke in an easy conversational tone. " One could
tell," wrote *The New York Herald* reporter, " that the
pastor is an Englishman from his manner of speech,
but his accent is by no means of the pronounced
English variety." The newspaper comments on
this inaugural sermon all convey a suggestion of
bafflement. Jowett announced no plans about his
future work. As *The Continent* observed, he made
no attempt to capitalise the interest his coming to New
York had created. If the reporters expected rhetoric,
they got none. If they anticipated topical allusions,
they were disappointed. " I have to speak," said
Jowett, " in ignorance of your conditions," and it was
never his habit to rush in " where angels fear to tread."
It was recorded by *The Tribune* that the congregation
" buzzed with eulogistic comment " while filing out of
the church; but *The Herald* observed that many of
those who were most pleased appeared to be more than
a little puzzled as to just how the effect had been
produced, adding, " although they had read that
some of the English papers were inclined to rank
Dr. Jowett as perhaps the greatest living preacher, they
would have had difficulty in picking out a single passage
which critics would rank as eloquence." Jowett's
own impressions of his new sphere of work were
recorded in letters to English friends :—

New York,
April 10th, 1911.

To Mr. H. F. Keep.

  . . . Of course we have had enormous crowds
 to the services, but that counts for nothing.
 Curiosity is very keen, and some of it will die
 down. My ministry will not provide permanent
 excitement for the American Press. The real test
 will come when the preliminary sensations are

over and I get into the ordinary stride of my
ministry. . . . The conditions of work are very
novel, and we are face to face with surprises every
day.

New York,
April 13, 1911.

To Rev. Edgar Todd.

. . . . The opportunity in New York is all I
dreamed about. The people are hungry for the
Bread of Life and I believe the ministry is waking
to supply it. I had a long visit yesterday from the
Bishop of New York, and he told me that the people
are starving on merely social topics and essays on
remote themes. He believes there is a tremendous
opening for evangelical preaching, and he graciously
assured me that he thought I should find a place in
the ministry of this great city.

The greatest surprise I have had has been in
reference to the character of Fifth Avenue itself.
I sometimes said in the old country that I should
be altogether grateful if some day Fifth Avenue
could become another Carr's Lane. It is another
Carr's Lane ! There is the same wonderful body
of praying women and a fine devoted set of men.
The services are reverent and orderly and I do not
know that there is an item I care to change. . . .
This has greatly surprised me, as I was expecting
that there might be elements that would not be
congenial to me. You may imagine, therefore,
my delight when I found myself surrounded by
internal conditions so happy and favourable.

I am learning to resist almost every hour of the
day the tremendous forces that would push me here
and there. I do not know what time ministers
here spend in their studies. They are evidently
engaged in a hundred outside works which must
leave them very little time to prepare their
message. I am going to stand steadily against
this pressure, even at the cost of being misunder-
stood. When I get into my own home I shall

L

allow nothing to interfere with my morning in the study. If the pulpit is to be occupied by men with a message worth hearing we must have the time to prepare it. I feel the preaching of the Word of God is incomparably my first work in New York.

New York,
May 1, 1911.

To Mr. H. F. Keep.

I am glad that all the preliminaries are over and that I am getting out of the public Press into a quieter life. One thing is perfectly clear. The opportunity is stupendous. Whether I have the gift to seize it can only be revealed by time. At any rate there is very much to cheer me. I am not thinking of the vast crowds that attend the services. Those may mean something or nothing. I am thinking of the praying people in this church and of the delightful mid-week service. The latter is giving me unbounded satisfaction. Everybody is wonderfully good, and the leaders of the church are doing everything to make my ministry fruitful. Of course what I shall want to see is the evidence that the Holy Spirit is at work in the Church, and that we have a witness in conversions and in the enriched lives of the people.

New York,
May 16, 1911.

To Mr. H. F. Keep.

. . . You will be glad to know that I am settling down to my work and am enjoying more peaceful conditions. I felt more at home last Sunday than I have done since I arrived, and you will be glad to know that real good was accomplished and that men and women found the Light of Life. I have got to a time of life and to a mood in life when mere crowds would offer no satisfaction. I am more thankful than I can say that the deeper things are being given me in this city.

New York,
June 1, 1911.

To Rev. Thomas Towers.

By the time you receive this letter we shall probably be on the water. We leave on Monday by the " Adriatic " and hope to be in London on Tuesday of Coronation week.

There is one thing about this city which is very delightful, the glorious blue skies that we have day after day. I think we must have had forty successive days of these lovely blue skies without a cloud. There are very few days when there is not plenty of sunshine. We shall, of course, always be away from here in the time of extreme heat. The work practically finishes at the end of April and I shall always finish at the end of May. My congregation is one that goes away into the country by that time, and I am left with the people who are visiting the city.

You will be glad to hear that I am greatly encouraged in the beginnings of the work. Of course I do not misinterpret these early signs. I know that a new ministry is watched with much curiosity, and I shall not see the true state of things until next winter, but certainly just now I am having a very great opportunity of preaching the Word. The Sunday congregations are enormous and the services are marked by great reverence. I confess I have been a little surprised by the way in which I have found things fit into my own tastes and desires. . . . One thing is perfectly clear—there is a great hungering for the Word of God and a great desire to have its contents made known.

One of the things I have had to do since I came is steadily to resist the enormous number of invitations to do all kinds of things in all parts of the United States and Canada. It seems to me that ministers can be employed anywhere and everywhere rather than at their own immediate

work. I simply will not do it, and I should think
my typewriter would almost acquire the habit of
declining these things of its own accord. I am
perfectly sure that what is needed here is concentration upon one's own particular work.

The people have been wonderfully kind and in
every way have tried to make the change as little
troublesome as possible. They could not possibly
have done more for us in helping us to a happy
settlement. . . .

New York is a strident city, flurried and feverish
in the eyes of a Londoner, and bewildering even to New
Yorkers. Dr. Fort Newton, himself a Middle-Westerner,
has described the American metropolis as " a human
hotch potch. . . a vast far-spreading encampment of
many races, a gigantic medley of wealth and want, of
palaces of pleasure and hovels of poverty, an apocalypse
of America at its brilliant best and worst; at once a
problem, a challenge and a prophecy." Into this
maelstrom Jowett plunged believing that he had a
Gospel which was adequate to meet its utmost needs.
Some feeling of trepidation was in his heart, as he
confessed. His experience, up to now, had been in
provincial cities. Neither Birmingham nor Newcastle
had prepared him for the clash and clamour of New
York. On one of his visits to England during his
sojourn in New York he spoke of his amazement on
entering a New York street-car one morning and notic-
ing that only one of his fellow passengers was reading
a paper printed in English. The rest were intent over
newspapers in German, Yiddish, Italian or other
languages. At a newspaper stand in East Forty-
Second Street he counted papers published in eleven
different languages. The cosmopolitanism of New
York glared at him, and profoundly affected all his
subsequent thinking.

In his first three months in New York Jowett was content to explore the situation patiently, and to acclimatise his ways to the New World. Fifth Avenue Church realised and even surpassed his rosiest expectations. The beauty of the building itself with its " storied windows richly dight " and its quiet reverential atmosphere met every requirement of his æsthetic instincts. Its central situation just where the palatial end of Fifth Avenue begins to merge with the busy business life of the city, linked leisured ease with ceaseless toil, and gave the church, he felt, a commanding place in New York. Its immense prestige throughout the United States made its pulpit a sounding board spreading its minister's message over the Western world.

When, at the beginning of June, Jowett returned, for the summer, to England, any doubts that might have lingered as to his wisdom in settling in New York had been dissipated. He arrived in England in high spirits just in time to be present at the Coronation of King George V in Westminster Abbey.

London,
June 20, 1911.

To Miss Alice Slater.

I have just been to see about my dress for the Coronation. Fancy me engaged in such a quest ! Cassock, scarlet gown, white bands, knee breeches, silk stockings, buckled shoes, cocked hat ! Shades of my infancy, what have I come to ! And how am I going to get to the Abbey in such attire ? Well, well !

Fresh from America, where even a short experience of absolute religious equality had made its impression on his mind, Jowett felt—and expressed the feeling in an article he wrote—the anomaly of the exclusion of the Free Church ministry, representing perhaps half of the British nation and the whole of the overseas

Dominions, from any active part in the Coronation ceremony.

On the eve of his return to America Jowett was summoned to Halifax to the death-bed of his mother. She had survived his father for five years. Jowett felt her loss very severely. From childhood she had been an inspirational force in his life, and his filial sense of obligation to her, as well as his affectionate pride in her, had deepened with the passing of the years. His greatest comfort was that he was in England, and by her side, when she passed away. " We have never," he wrote to a friend who about the same time was similarly bereaved, " advanced so far in life as not to feel the sense of a great blank when a good mother goes home." After the funeral he wrote to Rev. Edgar Todd saying, " The Light of the Grave was over everything." Death itself had no terrors for Jowett —and the tomb no victory. " Death," he said, " is but a change of clothes, not a change of character. It is just a brief transition. It is a mere changing of the sites, a plucking up of the tent pegs on the plains of earth and a shifting of one's quarters to the heavenly fields."

One of Jowett's sources of happiness in New York was the renewal of an old friendship. When he was a boy at Halifax, and a scholar at Square Sunday School, he came into contact with Mr. John Pells, who served the school as its secretary for ten years (1876–1886) and, as Jowett said, " was everybody's friend." Mr. Pells married a daughter of Mr. John Whitley (whose encouragement and help in his early years Jowett always remembered) and had removed to America. Soon after Jowett settled at Fifth Avenue, Mr. Pells became a deacon of the church, and the old association was revived and strengthened. " There is one compensation," Jowett wrote to Mr. Pells, " in growing older—friends grow dearer."

Winter in America suited Jowett physically and temperamentally, though he confessed that occasionally he felt homesick for a day of drenching rain.   He found a tonic quality in the wintry air.   " Even the cold," he said, " is a cheery cold, dry and sunny, and zero in New York is more comfortably borne than a cold rainy day in England when the thermometer is 50 degrees higher in the scale.   An American zero still gives you freedom when an English 40° puts you in bonds."   A month after resuming his ministry at Fifth Avenue for the second winter, Jowett wrote home in an enthusiastic vein :

New York,
Oct. 31, 1911.

To Rev. Edgar Todd,

I am getting over the feeling of strangeness. Of course the change has been tremendous, and for a time I walked with somewhat uncertain feet.   But now I am seeing fruits to my ministry, and I have got the old confidence of the Carr's Lane pulpit.   The morning service presents me with an overwhelming opportunity.   The place is crowded with over two thousand people.   We have all sorts and conditions of men from State Judges to stewards from the " Mauretania."   I feel sure that the new way of putting things, the English mind and the English phraseology, are gripping the people and holding them with a strange surprise. The second service is at four o'clock, and this presents a more difficult problem.   In most churches the attendance at this service is almost nil, and the ministers have lost all expectation, and have settled down into contentment with it. I could never do that, and I shall judge the real fruitfulness of my ministry in New York by that service.   At present we have a congregation of from twelve to fifteen hundred people. It seems strange to think of Birmingham without you and ――. But things have been ordered very wonderfully, and I think we are all in our right places.

New York,
Nov. 29, 1911.

To Mr. J. G. Hurst.

I am getting into the stride of things. The pulpit is becoming more familiar to me and I can look out on the general field with more knowledge and competency. . . . The thing that strikes me every week is the immense area of possible influence which this pulpit commands. We have people present from every part of the world. I am amazed after every service, when I speak to scores of people, at the immense areas they represent. Last Sunday week Mr. James Bryce and his wife were in the congregation. He came up to me at the close of the service and I had an interesting conversation with him. He is deeply in love with the American people and they are deeply in love with him. He seems to know them through and through, and all they have done, and sympathises with all their aspirations.

New York,
Dec. 4, 1911.

To Miss Alice Slater.

I think probably the most novel thing in my ministry over here is the exposition of the Scriptures. Generally speaking the sermons in this country are topical and are not devoted to the immediate exposition of the Word of God. Such expositions have therefore the suggestion of novelty. I am glad to have so many students and ministers attending the services, as I have the opportunity of turning their minds to real delving work in the Bible. I am perfectly sure that what the churches of this country need is the nutriment of spiritual truth distributed at every service. I have met with many ministers who have confirmed my judgment.

News about his old Church at Carr's Lane was fragrant to Jowett during his New York ministry, and he hailed as " glorious " the tidings that the Church was seeking his successor in Rev. Sidney M. Berry, M.A. " There will be few happier men than I," he wrote, " when I know that Carr's Lane is happily settled." Three months later he is writing again rejoicing in Rev. Sidney M. Berry's acceptance of the Birmingham pastorate :—

New York,
May 17th, 1912.

To Mr. H. F. Keep.

The news from Birmingham is altogether delightful. I am bound to say I have steadily and firmly expected it. I cannot imagine such action as the Carr's Lane Church took when I gave up its ministry not being honoured by the Lord. There was something so sacred in the attitude of the Church at that time that I felt perfectly certain that God would look to the succession, and here we are receiving the answer in most abundant measure. I cannot tell you how I feel at the prospect. To know that my work is going to be carried forward to richer fruitfulness is inspiring in the highest degree. The great Church is justifying herself to the fullest and her gracious story promises the continuance of even greater service.

The signal honour of being the Lyman Beecher Lecturer on preaching came to Jowett in the spring of 1912. He delivered his course at Yale in the Spring and the lectures were published in the Autumn, in England and America, under the title " The Preacher, His Life and Work." He spoke " as a prophet to a leave me? The morning congregation which had dropped to six or seven hundred, invariably crowds the building and numbers have to be turned away. The afternoon service (which is the far more difficult of the two, and which had dropped to three or four hundred at the most) gives me a congregation of fifteen hundred. The mid-week service, which I found practically extinct, has now a steady congregation of between four and five hundred. All this is vastly encouraging, but, as you will know, this will not give final satisfaction. The great point is this—can I open the immediate door to the American soul? I may interest him, but can I lead him to conviction? That I do not know; it is still to be proved. I am almost ashamed to put it in that way, in the face of all the resources which are ours in Christ. But you will know what I mean. One thing is clear. I can see that it is becoming increasingly significant for the pulpit of Fifth Avenue to be filled with an expository evangelical ministry. We get crowds of ministers, and their thoughts have been turned in altogether new directions.

To sum up. I am perfectly clear that at present I am where I have to be. When Free St. George's, Edinburgh, invited me last February, I had not a moment's hesitation; and I declined by return of post. How it will be two years hence I cannot say. I cannot say "yes" or "no." It may be that I shall find myself more firmly rooted here. It may be I shall feel I can return to my own country. Of course I hope I may some day return to England. I should wonder what had happened if that desire were dead.

The winter's work in New York confirmed his decision that Fifth Avenue, for the time being, was his right and proper sphere. He thrust aside everything that might divert him from his one business of preaching the Gospel, and was rewarded by the results.

New York,
Decr. 16, 1912.

To Mr. J. G. Hurst.

Altogether apart from the numbers, which are very great, I feel, as I have never felt before, as if there is a Springtime coming over the Church. Last Sunday, at the Communion service, we received 40 new members, some of them with testimonies like romances. Three of them came to us from Roman Catholicism; others came right out of the world. I think the final impulse with many of them was a sermon on " The Friend of Publicans and Sinners." I felt the place was swept with holy power.

Then I feel an altogether deeper spirit in the services. Sometimes I am overwhelmed at the most evident movement of the Spirit of God. I cannot but think that we are being led into some wide and blessed evangelical ministry. I feel altogether firmer and more certain about everything. I am quieter in mind and heart and I feel more settled in the saddle. . . . I am sending by this post a Christmas sermon. We are giving 6,000 of them away on Christmas Sunday. That, too, is another way by which the " Word " is spread. So, altogether I am in excellent spirits.

New York,
Feby. 24, 1913.

To Rev. Edgar Todd.

. . . It is absolutely clear that for the time being I am in my right place. I could not have said this with such confidence a year ago, but I have growing evidence that that which I came to do is being done. . . . From the point of numbers I have every encouragement. But then it is the deeper thing which one wants, and which alone will bring satisfaction. I want to know that the wills of men are being changed and that the sorrows of people are being transfigured, and this I am seeing on every side. I have begun a series year, the year when any slave can gain his freedom in the Lord. I deliberately sought to bring things to an issue, and so I had decision forms printed on our Calendars. I am quietly and confidently expecting that a large number have to-day "crossed the line." There is nothing for it in New York, of all places in the world, but to bring the soul close against the eternal realities : and this winter, God helping me, I mean to do it with all my strength. . . . I have greatly enjoyed my work since my return.

This is a marvellous place. I sat in the vestry on Wednesday to see people who wished to join the Church. Among those who came were two Swiss, a German, a Scotchman, and several Americans. This morning I saw four Japanese come into the church, one of whom is the vice-mayor of Tokyo, a very pronounced Christian who is at present studying municipal administration in this country. This afternoon after the service the last four men I spoke to were an American, a Spaniard, a Greek and an Italian. "All nations and kindreds and peoples and tongues."

Though he was a Congregationalist by upbringing and conviction Jowett had made the transition into Presbyterianism without feeling that he had sacrificed any principle. He made light of denominational barriers. One Good Friday he conducted the three hours' service at St. James's Episcopal Church, Madison Avenue, where his friend Bishop Courtney was Rector. Occasionally, too, he visited the Jerry McCauley mission for drunkards and outcasts—a mission which is now closed owing to the operation of Prohibition. Though the novelty which had excited the curiosity of the crowd had by this time worn off, and though, to his infinite relief, his ministry no longer engaged the attention of the sensational Press, his church was always full. It was so difficult to seat the people that Jowett insisted that unless the seatholders were in their places when the services began, the vacant seats should be filled. This was tantamount to a revolution in Fifth Avenue custom, and Jowett had to fight a mild battle. He persisted and got his way.

New York,
Jany. 9, 1914.

To Rev. Thomas Towers.

We are now in the thick of the winter's work and opportunity opens out on every side. The difficulty is only found in the lack of strength to cope with it. I am more and more emphasising the spiritual side of things and bringing the naked evangelical truth to bear upon the lives of men. Nothing else is worth anything simply because it accomplishes nothing. I sometimes wonder if the times are growing ripe for another John Wesley who shall shake the nations out of their materialism and bring them to view the Unseen and the Abiding. I know some who are praying that this may come about, and that some mighty servant of God may arrive whose power shall awaken the world.

Beyond interesting himself very actively in foreign missionary work in the Near East and serving on the Presbyterian Mission Board, Jowett confined his energies to his own church and its home missionary activities. This was from deliberate choice, even from a stern sense of duty. As a sojourner with an English point of view he shrank from interfering in American domestic problems. He was fully aware that this apparent aloofness was misinterpreted by some New York ministers who thought he was exclusive see Smyrna, and Ephesus and Sardis. I stood in the ruins of the very theatre where the uproar occurred about Demetrius. . . . I stood on the very stage of the theatre and looked on the ascending tiers of seats, and I read aloud the story of " Great is Diana of the Ephesians ! " The excavations are just proceeding at Sardis. They opened a tomb while we were there, and we looked into a dead world. Jewellery, coins, pottery are in the tombs in abundance.

But the Holy Land ! We saw it at its best, and the charm and interest are indescribable. My New Testament has got an inconceivable vividness by this tour. Standing on the Mount of Olives ! Bethany yonder ! And Bethlehem ! And away yonder the Dead Sea, and Pisgah beyond and Nebo ! Nazareth was bewitching. The view from the hill behind the village ! And then Carmel and Cana and Nain, etc. ! My wife and I walked down to the Lake of Galilee on a supremely lovely day. We walked on the Mount of Beatitudes and she gathered flowers. We sat on the hillside above the lake all the afternoon. Just below us was Magdala, where the Magdalene lived : away to the right Tiberias : yonder to the North Capernaum, Chorazin, Bethsaida, and beyond — Hermon covered with snow ! Then Damascus ! We saw it before we arrived. There it gleamed, and all Saul's story was before me. We walked through the " Street called Straight." Damascus is in many ways just what it was in Paul's day ; so I have got new setting and colour.

We leave here on Thursday for Greece. Next Sunday we spend at Athens. I hope to spend a quiet hour on Mars Hill. We are going to call at about six places on the Dalmatian coast. We purpose reaching Venice on June 1st. We shall stay there a few days and then begin the motor tour through the Austrian Alps. It is all a very great privilege, the like of which I never hoped to enjoy.

I am shocked with the news of Horne's death.*
I cannot realise it. It seems so strange. But he
went too fast. But, again, what a fine day's
work !

To the Clerk of the Session at Fifth Avenue Jowett
reported that " every yard of it (the Holy Land)
teemed with significance, and added new light to the
Sacred Word." " There has been nothing to disturb
our peace of mind for a single day . . ." he added.

Jowett and Mrs. Jowett made a leisurely journey
across Europe after this yachting tour and were joined
by their daughter in Switzerland, where they spent a
few weeks. The European war-clouds burst just as
they got back to England.

Seascale,
31 *August,* 1914.

To Rev. David Young.

But what a time this is for the preacher ! Congregations tense, strained, burdened, wanting
some glimpse of spiritual things amid this riot of
material things, and yearning for a glimpse of the
things which abide in all the fierce rush of things
which are transient. I have an idea that this is
going to be a great harvest-time for the Kingdom. At any rate many folk who have only
hugged creeds are going to get faith, and many
folk who have lived on opinions are going to
obtain convictions.

I am glad to have been here (in England) these
last few weeks. It has been worth living through.
We have crossed a watershed in national history
and we shall only become really aware of it when
the war is over and we begin to look round on
our new environments.

What a mercy it is that Asquith fills the front
place ! And how he is filling it ! I had a letter

* Rev. C. Silvester Horne, M.P., who died on May 2nd, 1914,
while crossing from Niagara to Toronto.

from New York yesterday from one of the best known men in that city, and he regards Asquith's position as superb. He writes of these pressing days as being " one of the brightest epochs in England's history."

I shall leave here for New York with very mixed feelings. My duty lies across the waters, and every man best helps the Kingdom by sticking faithfully to his own post. But I shall want to be here among my own people helping to bear the heavy load. But I can help yonder.

Jowett's " confused thoughts and moods," born in the welter and chaos of those bewildering days, found expression in another letter :—

Seascale,
26 *Aug.,* 1914.

To Miss Alice Slater.

. . . For there isn't much song in the world just now. I haven't quite got my bearings. There are times when one knows he is on rock but he knows that his feet are not in a large place. Well, I have standing ground but no liberty. I feel like Ezra : " When I heard these things I was astonied " ! Where are all the Christian influences? And what has the Church of Christ been doing in England and Germany these last twenty years that peoples have arrived in conditions like these? That is what holds me just now. Has the Church been faithless? Or has she been asleep? Has her really vital witness been comparatively silent so long as to be drowned beneath the clamour of the world and the devil? Perhaps what is happening will awake the Church, give her back her power of witnessing and restore to her something of the moral vim and aggressiveness of the Old Testament prophets. What is Christ thinking about it all? And those angels who sang over the plains of Bethlehem, what do they think about it? And what are the so-called

DR. AND MRS. JOWETT WITH MRS. KENNEDY (IN VENICE).

[*To face p.* 168.

heathen nations thinking about it, the onlookers in China and India? These are questions which make me think furiously, and they should be like goads to prayerless souls. I am not afraid of the issue. God reigns! And He shall reign! But I want to know the signs of the times and I want to hear the voices of the Highest.

I wonder if we are getting a stage nearer to the time when the Orient will take the leadership and when once again wise men will come from the East!

On his last Sunday in England he fulfilled an engagement to preach at the Metropolitan Tabernacle. A war-sermon preached that day was issued as a booklet entitled " They that Wait " and proved a heartening message to thousands of distressed and anxious English people.

A new atmosphere awaited him in New York. Englishmen who had to spend the first two years of the war in the United States had a very unenviable experience : and few of them escaped mental agony during their exile in a country so studiously neutral as America was at that stage in the world conflict. He had been warmly welcomed after his prolonged absence and he found relief in the work at Fifth Avenue.

New York,
Nov. 19, 1914.

To Mr. J. G. Hurst.

I am greatly enjoying preaching. The long absence enabled me to think out my subjects and to have a better grasp of them.

Last Sunday we had the President, Woodrow Wilson, at the service. He came very quietly and we made no fuss about it. He is a very fine man and I am inclined to think he will play a notable part in any peace settlement.

Of course there is no subject here but the war. The papers give enormous space to it, sometimes three pages a day. There is a very deep and strong feeling that the British censorship is acting very unwisely, and I am sure it is having a prejudicial effect on American opinion. The suppression of news like the destruction of the "Audacious" is also regarded with great suspicion. People ask what other disasters Britain is hiding. I am sure it would be a good thing to relax the censorship, and also to give out more news. . . Opinion here is practically solid for the allies. Of course the folk of German extraction have German affinities and sympathies, but speaking generally America is with us. Extraordinary efforts are made from time to time to create a pro-German feeling, but it's no good. I shouldn't be at all surprised if America is eventually drawn into the war.

As the European situation grew more and more anxious for the Allies Jowett felt the depression and he ached to be in the homeland.

New York,
Decr. 28, 1914.

To Miss Alice Slater.

We never feel as though the clouds are away. Europe, and particularly England, presses upon us continually, but I am not going to say it is all cloud. It is like the cloud on the Mount of Transfiguration, it is a bright one. All the nobility of our country is revealing itself in wonderful splendour and I marvel at the stories of sacrifice which come our way. I often wish I were in the thick of it.

New York,
Jany. 5, 1915.

To Rev. Thomas Towers.

. . . I often wish I were in England just now. I covet the privilege of sharing the common burden and I often long for the opportunity of bringing cheer and inspiration to my own countrymen. But no one helps the cause of the Kingdom by disloyalty to his own post, and it must be from this part of the earth that I am to help my native land. I sometimes wish I could just be transferred for twelve months that I might give what strength I have to sharing the yoke, but I am not going to force any doors. They must be opened by a higher Power.

Notwithstanding the tension arising out of the war Jowett's work at Fifth Avenue that Winter was "crammed with encouragement." He saw signs of a general quickening of the Church life—one of the surest being a men's Bible class for the study of the Word and for that only, and attended by one hundred and fifty men. The New Year Communion service was the largest in which Jowett had ever taken part anywhere. "The Spirit is at work," he cried, with something like holy joy.

In the cosmopolitan congregation at Fifth Avenue there were Germans by birth and pro-Germans by sympathy, but without, in the pulpit, violating the hospitality of a neutral State Jowett lost no valid opportunity for presenting the case for the Allies against the Central Powers. A son of Dr. John Hall —one of Jowett's predecessors at Fifth Avenue Church —espoused the German cause, and Jowett forgot his own shrinking from controversy in challenging Professor Thomas Hall's statements. The correspondence between them—part of it was published in the New York Press—was sharp and vigorous. It came to an end with an irate conversation over the telephone when Jowett for once in his life was curt and explosive.

New York,
Jany. 29, 1914.

To Mr. J. G. Hurst.

. . . This is certainly the best Winter I have had since we came. There's a new life making itself felt. We have just elected seven new elders, and seven of the finest men in the church have been chosen and have consented to serve. One of them is a German. . . .

. . . These last two Sundays I have been appealing for foreign missions asking that we should make a sacrificial offering as a witness that we mean to send the Gospel to the ends of the earth in spite of all the chilling influence of the war. We took the collection last Sunday morning and took £8,000. It is magnificent, and represents fine giving throughout the entire church.* But better than all this I have continued evidence of changed lives every week. . . . So that altogether we are having a good winter.

And yet I wish I were in England. I feel awfully out of it. It is a great mystery that I am here. And yet, perhaps, something is accomplished in the mere fact of an Englishman having the principal New York pulpit, and preaching there three times a week. I cannot but think it may have some influence on American opinion. That opinion is steadily with the Allies. The New York papers are solidly one in the matter. But I do hope we shall not have many articles like the one in this week's *Spectator*. That was cabled over, and irritated folk exceedingly. I wish Strachey could be muzzled, and Bernard Shaw too !

Jowett and Mrs. Jowett celebrated their silver wedding on May 20th, 1915, and were almost swamped

* One lady sent Jowett her ring set with lovely large diamonds for the collection. "It is the most precious thing I possess," she said.

by the beautiful gifts poured upon them by their
New York friends. In quiet ways Jowett tried to
serve the homeland from which he was separated, and
Mrs. Jowett organised the ladies at Fifth Avenue
Church into a working party to make bandages, etc.,
for the wounded soldiers. " It's a bit of splendid
work," wrote Jowett to his daughter, " and it helps
mother to feel that she is doing something for the
old country."

June 1915 found Jowett again in England, but this
time in indifferent health. Neuritis was causing
insomnia, and he bore obvious traces of nervous
strain. The war-made gaps in the homes of his friends
grieved his spirit sorely.

Amberley Ridge,
Stroud, Glos.,
June 22, 1915.

To Rev. Edgar Todd.

It is grand to be in England again. We decided
to dare the dangers of the submarines to be here,
and I am devoutly grateful to be allowed to get
my shoulder underneath the common burden.

From New York in the winter of 1915–16 Jowett
wrote in a happier strain, owing no doubt to the
growing appreciation in America of the vital world
issues at stake in the war.

New York,
Jany. 13, 1916.

To Rev. Thomas Towers.

. . . . I notice that the English papers are
very much disturbed about the attitude of America
to the situation in Europe. The action of the
American Government has certainly not been as
strong and as positive and as cosmopolitan as I
should like it to have been. All the people
whom I meet feel that the great opportunity
was missed when no protest was made about

Belgium. But there is no uncertainty where
the sympathy lies. It is altogether with the
Allies. . . . I do not know what Germany's
game is just now. I hope that she is not hastening to a settlement of all her disputes with America
in order to induce America to be unwisely aggressive about our interference with her commerce.
I hope that America will not be more intensely
concerned about the dollars than she was about
the liberties of Europe. I have confidence in
Woodrow Wilson, and I think affairs will be
wisely piloted.

Early in the New Year two lady members of Fifth
Avenue Church offered to contribute $100,000 each for
an endowment fund if the congregation would raise
another $100,000 during the year. In one week in
April the remaining $100,000 was contributed, and a
provision of £60,000 was thus made for sustaining
the church and its mission work whatever the future
may have in store.

Jowett's interest in the life and work of his friends
was never diminished by time or distance, and when
Rev. Thomas Towers was invited to become a deputation secretary of the London Missionary Society
Jowett wrote :—

You need not have the smallest fear for the
future if you take the post. . . . Your own passion
for missions would be bound to kindle others
and you would have fires burning all over the
Midlands. . . . But what about withdrawing from
the pulpit? There's the rub. Of course I know
you will be preaching, but it's not the same.
Preaching is at its highest and best when the
message is new each week, and you could not
possibly do this. If I thought it would mean a
permanent withdrawal from the pulpit-pastorate

I would immediately say—don't take it! The permanent ministry cannot spare you. . . . If it means only three years I should incline towards it. As for getting another church, of course you would. There is much about Congregationalism that is wooden, but it is not so wooden that it can't tell the difference between a bone button and a pearl.

Another letter shows how he sought to serve the Allied cause while in America :—

New York,
Dec. 5th, 1916.

To Rev. John Loosmore.

Your letter came at an opportune moment. On the evening of the day when I received it I was appointed to address what is called the Presbyterian Union. The subject on which they asked me to speak was English Religious Life as affected by the war! Of course I do not think any of us can speak very definitely about matters which are still dim. But I was glad to have your own testimony, and your own judgment. I think I can see signs in the political life of England, and in her church life, and in the broad realm of literature, of movements which will be favourable to the Kingdom of God.

I told the Presbyterian Union last night that I thought there was an even more important thing than the effect of the war upon English religious life, and that was the effect of the war upon church life in America. Our nation will be saved by its sacrifices : this nation has no such saving salt, and therefore its peril is all the greater. The best thing about this nation just now is its uneasiness about itself. The best men and women are disquieted and dissatisfied and would like to be differently related to what is going on in Europe.

We are now in the thick of our Winter's work. I could not wish for a greater opportunity of service.

When at last the United States entered the war, Jowett's spirits revived, for though he never doubted right would triumph, the wearisome waiting for the tide of victory to turn in favour of the Allies tried him severely. He was now free to unburden his soul, and to take effective part in propaganda. Meanwhile his position in New York as a preacher—and he sought no other position—had no parallel in the city. It was difficult to find a seat in Fifth Avenue Church. " Church Full " boards had always to be displayed.

But events were shaping themselves across the Atlantic to bring Jowett's New York ministry to an end; and they moved swiftly.

CHAPTER X

RECALLED TO ENGLAND

(*Æt.* 54–55)

INDIRECTLY Jowett's recall to England came through the City Temple. When Rev. R. J. Campbell resigned his ministry in 1915 to enter the Church of England, the City Temple deacons wrote to Jowett, then in New York, saying that they were unanimous in desiring to submit his name to the Church. The City Temple had always had a subtle attraction for him. Its pulpit and that of Free St. George's, Edinburgh, had seemed to him to present the greatest opportunities in Britain for an Evangelical preacher. Just before the war he had closed one of these two doors by declining an invitation to Free St. George's. And now the other door seemed opening before him. If he was ever to return to England—and his letters show that he never seriously contemplated a permanent settlement in America—the City Temple would offer him a perfect sphere for his future ministry. Doubtless the memory of an earlier episode in his career quickened his interest in the overture from the City Temple. Dr. Parker had more than once told Jowett, in his Birmingham days, that he hoped he would be his successor. He also wrote Jowett to this effect, and through this suggestion from Dr. Parker, Jowett probably began to look to the City Temple as the ultimate scene of his ministry. But Dr. Parker, whose vagaries were curious, had nominated more than one

man to succeed him; and upon his death his mantle
fell upon the shoulders of Rev. R. J. Campbell. If
Jowett was disappointed at that time, he concealed
his feelings, and he preached Mr. Campbell's induction
sermon. So when this closed door seemed once more
reopening—at a moment, too, when the war situation
made him yearn to be in his own land—he unhesitat-
ingly told the City Temple deacons that at such a
time any Englishman away from England would feel
the strength of a call home. He could hardly have
replied less ambiguously. For reasons which it is not
pertinent to detail here—since they have no personal
relation to Jowett—the City Temple deacons were
overruled and their scheme for inviting Jowett to the
pastorate went agley. Jowett heard no more from the
City Temple until he saw from an English cable in a
New York paper that an invitation had been sent to
another British minister, then in New York. Jowett
went on quietly with his work at Fifth Avenue.

British without insularity, his love of England burnt
brightly all through the years spent in America—and
especially in the war years. Through his letters home
a strain of home-sickness runs insistently.

New York,
Jany. 24, 1913.

. . . Don't think I feel just as " settled " here
as if we were in England. I don't. I miss
everything, and this week I have felt a bit flat.
But if I missed nothing when I have left country
and friends—— !

Llandrindod,
June 24, 1913.

. . . The homeland is very very dear, and the
friends in it grow dearer. I see Aked has been
disowning his country and has become American-
ised. I can tell you that before I take that step

I'll eat my—— Well, put it in this way, you'll have some nice grey curls hanging pendant-like, and your century will be well in sight.

New York,
Jany. 11, 1914.

Oh, these blue skies. They do offer some compensation for exile.

Amberley Ridge,
24 *June,* 1915.

It was good to get one's feet upon one's native land. I have longed to be at home all the winter, but desire and duty were at conflict. Perhaps I have been holding an outpost of the holy cause. I think I have.

Banff, Canada,
3 *Sept.,* 1917.

Give me that gray, misty, cloudy island (England) first and last.

The fact that Jowett had so frankly told the Deacons of the City Temple that a home call would be acceptable was not kept a secret. So when Dr. Campbell Morgan withdrew from the ministry of Westminster Chapel eighteen months later the deacons there, led by Sir Albert Spicer, took prompt steps to secure Jowett as their minister. Dr. Campbell Morgan closed his pastorate in February 1917. Within a month (*i.e.* on February 26th) a special church meeting, by " a very enthusiastic and entirely unanimous vote " had invited Jowett to the ministry. The unusual course was taken of re-enforcing the formal " call " of the Church by letters signed by the Chairman and ex-Chairmen of the Congregational Union, and by leading men closely associated with the London Congregational Union and the London Missionary Society, urging Jowett's acceptance of the invitation. " Come over and help us " was the spirit of their cry.

The Prime Minister wrote a personal letter to Jowett pressing him to return home.

> Westminster (wrote Mr. Lloyd George) is a centre of influence, and a preacher of your power and distinction would, from that pulpit, exercise a great and beneficent sway on the national life at a highly critical period in its development. England needs your inspiration at this moment.
>
> It seems to me that you would render to your country, by your return, a great religious and patriotic service by voice and influence in the work of reconstruction after the war. England, and London itself, will need prophetic voices as never before.

As President of the Free Church Council, Dr. J. H. Shakespeare wrote " expressing the thought of every Free Church leader " that " your return to your native land would be a patriotic and inestimable contribution to our national and religious life." All these letters were dispatched from England so as to be in Jowett's hands immediately after the cabled invitation to Westminster had reached him. It was stated in the American Press that King George V " commanded " Jowett's return : but this statement was utterly erroneous.

On April 9th Jowett cabled his readiness to accept the call, but—with America just entering the war on the side of the Allies—he expressed his conviction that he could best serve the common cause by not leaving his post until the next Spring. In reply the deacons at Westminster cabled that they were quite prepared to leave the date of coming to him. " Whatever date " (ran the cable) " let us announce acceptance as soon as possible." On April 14th Jowett sent a cablegram accepting the call.

Across the Atlantic in New York, Jowett had been

subjected to almost irresistible pressure to stay at Fifth Avenue. The Church even offered to grant him six months every year to spend in England, while still paying him his full salary. President Woodrow Wilson and other eminent Americans joined in urgent appeals to him not to leave America altogether. Jowett withstood the pressure firmly. The English call for his service was *Vox Dei* and he could not disobey it.

In announcing his decision to return home, at Fifth Avenue Church on Sunday, April 15th, he said he recognised the wonderful opportunity presented by his American pastorate, but Westminster Church had interests equally grave and its opportunities appeared unlimited.

> And its call (he continued) comes to me at a time when the men of my country are fighting in the cause of freedom and for an enduring peace and fraternity. I love my country. You would never wish me to do anything else. If I held my own country cheaply, I should disparage yours. I love my country, and if she thinks I can serve her I must obey her call and do the remainder of my work on her soil.

Two days later Jowett sent a letter to " the members of the Church and Congregation at Westminster " confirming his cabled acceptance of its pastorate :—

> I understand (he wrote) that you are calling me to the ministry of the Word, and that it is your will that I should give my life to the proclamation of the Gospel from the pulpit of Westminster Church. To this great end I shall consecrate my whole mind and strength, and I shall depend upon fellow labourers for the accomplishment of other work which the church may determine to do. A church which is placed in the heart of a great

city gathers a very cosmopolitan congregation, and it will be my constant prayer and aspiration that from Westminster Church there may go forth a spiritual power which will not only help to leaven our own country, but, through the visiting friends from other nations, may reach even to the ends of the earth.

Letters written to intimate friends in England reveal Jowett's feelings when the crisis was over :—

New York,
14 April, 1917.

To Mr. J. G. Hurst.

I have just decided to accept Westminster. I haven't bothered you about it; but I have wished a hundred times that you were here. I have never been faced with a more difficult problem, except perhaps when I decided to come out here. The pressure on both sides has been tremendous. Of course I required no urgent pull from England. That has been there all the time. But I have been fairly perplexed what I ought to do with the Church in New York. I have a very long personally written letter . . . from the British Ambassador in Washington, Spring Rice, strongly urging me to remain in New York, and to do so in the interests of England. I have also had a very impressive letter from Lansing, the American Secretary of State, urging the desirability of an Englishman who has won the ear of the American people, remaining here, especially at a time when America is moving in strangely new ways in closer co-operation with Europe. Then I could not overlook the fact that the crowds which this winter have sought admission to the Church have been greater than ever. We always turn hundreds away.

Still I could not put the call away. I felt that if I declined it my relationship to England would be entirely changed. I could not face the future with that prospect. I had no peace along that line. From the very first I have had a sort of sense that I must accept the call, although I wanted it to be an enlightened judgment. . . .

So, next Spring, London! And I am already anticipating those nights when you are up in London. No more hotels! The new " Clydesdale "! And may your London engagements multiply until, as Billy Sunday might say, your bed is never cold.

New York,
April 30, 1917.

To Rev. John Loosmore.

. . . I was never in any doubt as to what my heart told me, but I was in considerable uncertainty about my judgment. Fifth Avenue Church offered me the plan of spending six months in New York and six months in England. At first that appealed to me, but I soon saw that the English side of it would not work out. I could not do without a holiday, and that would mean that the English ministry would have to be reduced to an exceedingly short season. But I shall try to maintain some sort of vital relationship with America, and shall come over as frequently as possible.

I think Westminster will offer a great opportunity in coming days. I intend to give my whole strength to it, and not scatter my energies over a hundred things in every part of the country. As far as I can see, any ministry in the City of London which has been effective has been one to which the man has given all he had.

New York,
May 8, 1917.

To Rev. Edgar Todd.

I am overwhelmed with messages from the old country, and they are all laden with grace. I know I have done right in accepting the call and I have perfect peace of mind and heart.

East Northfield,
Mass., Aug. 3, 1917.

To Rev. Thomas Towers.

   I am looking forward with great expectation
to my work at Westminster.   It was by no means
an easy matter to decide to leave Fifth Avenue
Church. . . . The congregation is gathered from
the ends of the earth, and is composed of all the
races of the world.   But I think that Westminster can also be a great cosmopolitan centre
and I am sure I shall have the atmosphere which
I so absolutely require.

The Summer vacation of 1917 was spent by Jowett
in Canada, travelling from the Atlantic to the Pacific—
from New Brunswick in the East to British Columbia
in the West.   The new cities of the Dominion impressed
him deeply, while the boundless expanse of the great
prairies enthralled him.   The heat and the constant
travelling, however, subjected him to physical strain,
and he returned to New York for his last Winter's
work there without the sense of renewed invigoration
derived, in previous years, from the Atlantic voyages
and short sojourns in Scotland.

New York,
Oct. 17, 1917.

To Rev. Edgar Todd.

   I am back now in New York to begin what
appears to be my last Winter in this city. . . . I
have not been very well this Summer, and I have
not my full resources at present, but I am gradually
recovering. . . . Of course no one knows what
the future may bring, and even now I sometimes
feel uncertain as to where my future ministry
will be.   The world is full of upheaval and one
cannot plan months ahead about anything.

   I believe we are going to have tremendous
opportunities in the cause of the Kingdom.
There are many adversaries but the door is opening.   Everything depends upon the loyalty of

the Church to its Lord. I am just burningly eager
for Christian unity. I have many dreams, I hope
they are visions, of the Churches of England
coming together in spiritual fellowship and social
service. I feel that the first great step must
be pulpit interchange between the Nonconformist
and the Episcopal Churches. I shall not have
been in London long before I seek an interchange
of that kind. Once that is done the barriers will
begin to fall like icebergs in tropical seas. We
want a few men who will dare to run amuck against
all denominational traditions in the interests of a
holy freedom. I care less and less for denominationalism, but I care more and more for the
Church of Christ.

The fourth Christmas of the war found the European
nations still interlocked in deadly strife and the future
obscure and menacing. Even Jowett seems to have
had some misgivings :—

New York,
Dec. 26, 1917.

To Mr. John Pells.

What will the New Year bring to the world?
And to you and me? What a mercy " our eyes
are holden " so that we have the privilege of
walking by faith and not by sight! For if we
saw something very attractive ahead, we should
spoil our present work in our impatience to reach
it. And if we saw something unpleasant ahead,
we should spoil to-day in our fear of to-morrow.
So the New Year is in God's scroll, and we are in
God's hands. And that is the best every way!

In some respects this Winter of 1917–18 was, at once,
the most successful, and the most trying of Jowett's
ministry in New York. The crowds were greater,
and the queues longer than ever, but Jowett rejoiced
most in the response which was given to his preaching.
His letters to England, however, struck a wistful note.

New York,
Jany. 3, 1918.

To Rev. Edgar Todd.

Now that the New Year has begun I am face to face with the great change in my own life. I am somewhat disturbed just now by the urgency of appeals that are being made to me on this side, but on the whole my guidance seems clear and constant. I am trying to be very quiet in the face of the coming weeks, and I know I shall be guided to do the right thing because I want to do it.

New York,
Feby. 18, 1918.

To Rev. Thomas Towers.

I am beginning to feel as though my time was short in New York. I have the most divided feelings and sometimes I am greatly bewildered. There is not a single reason why I should leave New York except that I feel the call of the Homeland. The work here has never been so signally blessed, and I have never had so large an opportunity of preaching the Word of Life. I am a little concerned about this great church at Fifth Avenue. The Committee has no one in sight to succeed me. But I can cherish the faith, as I did when I left Carr's Lane, that if it is the will of God for a man to leave a certain post, God will attend to the succession.

New York,
March 18, 1918.

To Rev. John Loosmore.

I received your letter on Saturday, March 16th, two days ago.

When I saw the Hampstead address I said " they have gone there so as to be near Horton." . . . I have the greatest admiration for Horton and I have asked him to offer the prayer at the Recognition Service which will be held at Westminster. I am going to have no Recognition meeting with all sorts of eulogies flying about. We shall have a service, with Kelman as preacher, and Horton and Shakespeare taking the devotional service.

In bidding farewell to Fifth Avenue Church (on April 14th) Jowett explained once more that his return to his homeland was prompted by the call of duty "No soldier," he said, "has heard the bugle more imperatively than the summons comes to me. . . The spiritual mood of a people, its moral resources, the deep wells of virtue and Godly passion in which alone unshrinkable springs of endurance can be found—these are the vital things which are going to count in the next few months or years." Jowett spoke with tender affection of America and its people. "There will," he said, "be no public man in all Britain who will be able to speak with such intimacy as I shall command, of the heart of the American people. I return as an ambassador of your affections."

Leaving New York proved a wrench to Jowett. A love of America and the Americans had grown with the years, and the buoyant life of the United States, where no one is afraid of to-morrow, found a responsive chord in his optimistic spirit. His friends at Fifth Avenue were magnanimous to the last. He had never expected, he said, that another church would behave so chivalrously as Carr's Lane Church did when he left Birmingham; but Fifth Avenue proved equally gracious in the hour of parting. He reached England in mid-May, and on arriving in London found mountains of messages rejoicing in his return. Among them was a letter from the Bishop of London, warmly welcoming him to London, and a cordial greeting from the Vicar of the parish in which Westminster Chapel stands. Both messages were a source of deep satisfaction to him.

CHAPTER XI

WESTMINSTER

(*Æt.* 55–59)

JOWETT came back to England sharing the common
illusion that the war, or at least the Peace, would
quicken the spiritual sensitivity of the English people,
and that the Christian Churches would have an opportunity hitherto unequalled for influencing the national
life. He thought then—though later he revised his
opinion—that London is the dynamic point in the
conquest of the world. " Fail in London," he had said,
" and we fail everywhere." An uneasy sense that
Westminster was a peculiarly difficult place caused him
some misgivings, but he was satisfied that its pulpit
could serve as a fulcrum for righteousness through the
faithful and fearless preaching of the Word. " During
the last seven years," he said, " I have found no new
Gospel. I have found that the old Gospel is all-sufficient
for the needs of the world."

But Jowett soon made it clear that he had come back
to England ready to throw an emphasis on certain
implications of the old Gospel which he had not con-
spicuously stressed either in Birmingham or New York.
The social and international aspects of Christianity
and the obligation to work towards Christian unity
took, henceforward, a much more definite place in his
pulpit messages, and gave a fresh impulse to his work
and thought.

His ministry at Westminster, which opened on

Whit Sunday (May 19th, 1918), was destined to be short, chequered by ill health, and closed by a complete breakdown : but Jowett regarded the four years he spent there as the capstone and culminating achievement of his life work. Conditions in London were distinctly unfavourable for a preacher when Jowett assumed his new work. Londoners were utterly war-jaded. Air raids had set up a general "nerviness." The food shortage was acute. Almost every able-bodied man, and indeed woman, had been drawn into some form of national service. The military situation on the Western front was acutely critical. Just seven weeks earlier the severest defeat ever inflicted on a British army had planted the German host on the Marne, and Ludendorff was massing his forces to capture Paris. Conscription was being applied in England to men of fifty : boys of eighteen were being hurried over to France to be flung, half trained, into the battle lines. The general atmosphere in London was sodden with damped hopes and grim forebodings. Church attendance was hampered by curtailed railway facilities and by the abnormal conditions of life. Congregations all over the Metropolitan area were at their nadir. A hard materialism was dominant. Things were in the saddle riding mankind. Truth, as always in war time, was on the casualty list, and the rigid Press censorship made people suspicious of all they read and credulous of any gossip they heard. It was a period of moral sag and spiritual defection. Any man less confident than Jowett in the final victory of good over evil and of truth over falsity might have quailed before the prospect of opening a new chapter in his career at such an unpropitious hour.

But Jowett's serenity of soul was undisturbed, though in one of his first letters he wrote after reaching England he conceded that " everything contributes to keep one's nerves strung up a little more than is healthy." He felt, however, and said, that it was a happy circumstance that obeying the call of duty had called him home among his own countrymen when every form of service was a privilege and when satisfaction could only be found in perfect consecration to the common good.

Notwithstanding all the adverse conditions Jowett found an abounding welcome awaiting him at Westminster. On the Sunday morning when he assumed the pastorate the congregation filled every nook and corner of Westminster Chapel. Mr. and Mrs. Lloyd George were present, and the Prime Minister went into the vestry to give Jowett a cordial greeting. President Woodrow Wilson sent a personal message in which he said : " While I am deeply sorry you are leaving America I am glad you are taking away an intimate knowledge of our people which will enable you to interpret them to those on the other side of the water who have not always understood them." From the City Temple came a message right heartily welcoming him " at a time when every sweet voice is needed to comfort and command." If there were gloom and uneasiness outside, glow and inspiration reigned inside Westminster Chapel that morning. Jowett struck a note of glad assurance in his invocatory prayer, and he read the 27th Psalm,—" Though an host should encamp against me, my heart shall not fear "—with exultant emphasis and a contagious confidence in his voice. The subject of his first sermon was the springs of endurance. Righteousness, justice, truth, freedom were the " Alpine " words upon which he dwelt. Seek inspiration by all means, he cried, at these historical founts. But all these, he declared, were minor springs of endurance. The great central spring came from intimate communion with the Living God. " Yes, we can endure," he said, " but we must endure as though at any moment we might see the visible presence of our Lord on the road. We must act as though we saw Him at our side." With an almost infallible intuition he gave his hearers just the inspiriting spiritual message demanded by the circumstances of the hour. He led them to the mountain tops and left them radiant on the spiritual heights.

Some marked differences were noted in Jowett and in his preaching on his return from America. He had described his period in New York as " a time of continual enlargement," and the seven years in America had, he said, given him " ten thousand new points of view." Even his voice had a fuller note and a wider range; his manner was more confident and his style of speech was more vigorous and direct. " It is a robuster, profounder Dr. Jowett," said *The Christian World*, " that Fifth Avenue has sent back to Westminster Chapel."

The multitude of greetings from all over England overwhelmed Jowett during his first month at home. A very simple service of dedication was held at Westminster Chapel on the Thursday after Whit Sunday. Dr. John Kelman (who later became Jowett's successor at Fifth Avenue Church) preached. Dr. Stuart Holden, Vicar of St. Paul's, Portman Square, offered prayer, Dr. J. H. Shakespeare read the Scripture lesson and Dr. Campbell Morgan gave a message of greeting. " I bid you welcome," Dr. Morgan said, " with my whole soul, on behalf of the Church, on behalf of the nation and of the saints of God in the land we love." Abundant evidence was given Jowett that his return home was welcomed among all classes of the community.

The most noteworthy gathering held in his honour

was a dinner at the House of Commons given by Sir Joseph Compton Rickett and Sir Albert Spicer, and attended by over sixty members of Parliament. The Prime Minister found time, even at so crucial a stage in national affairs, to be there, and several members of the Coalition Government were present. Mr. H. H. Asquith, who could not attend, wrote saying that " he was glad that Dr. Jowett's voluntary exile has come to an end, and that he is with us to exercise his great and beneficent influence on our national life." The occasion was, in the strictest connotation of a much-abused word, unique. No preacher had ever been shown such honour in the Houses of Parliament. Mr. Lloyd George, in a brilliant impromptu speech, paid tribute to Jowett in felicitous phrase and with warm-hearted feeling. He had had a share, he confessed, and was proud of it, in bringing Jowett back to his native land. Indeed he regarded the kidnapping expedition as an important piece of national service, because England needed all her great preachers and moral and religious teachers in view of coming events. The loss of a great preacher was an irreparable loss, and he felt they had achieved something worth while in recovering Dr. Jowett, one of the greatest of them. He had been almost overwhelmed by protests from America when it became known that he was taking a hand in inducing Dr. Jowett to return—protests from official sources even, made on the ground that Dr. Jowett's presence in America was of infinite value to the United States in its hour of crisis. But it was a national service to England to get Dr. Jowett here. A new England was emerging. After the war, which had upset everything, there would be great social and economic disturbance. But what especially concerned them was the moral and spiritual disturbance caused by the war, for all the

Photo. Reginald Haines.]

MRS. JOWETT.

[To face p. 192.

future of England depended on that. That is why he wanted Dr. Jowett home. No country in the world owed so much to great preachers as Great Britain, and there had never been a time in our history when our future depended so much on the strength, the penetrating power, the influence, and the spiritual appeal that would be made to the multitude. Jowett, who was obviously moved by the Prime Minister's speech and by the equally generous personal tributes which followed it, replied with his natural modesty and bright humour. He recalled his boyhood visions of a Parliamentary career, adding that the mystic mysterious hand which interposes so strangely in human life touched his life, and instead of becoming a politician he became destined for what he felt was something higher—a place in the Christian Church. So he would never, he imagined, get nearer to addressing the House of Commons than he was at that moment. In coming home he had done only what countless thousands of Englishmen had done, obeyed the call of his country. He had heard the call, and asking no questions, he had come, for a man must be of strange and faulty metal if when such a call came he did not respond. Mr. J. H. Whitley, now Speaker of the House of Commons, expressed his joy at Dr. Jowett's return because, important as was " man power " for the purposes of the war, the power of the spirit was greater still. Sir Joseph Compton Rickett expressed his pride that though Jowett belonged to the nation he had been produced by Congregationalism, and Sir Albert Spicer indicated his belief that under Jowett, Westminster Chapel would be a great force for national righteousness.

Of necessity Jowett had left his furniture and the bulk of his library behind him in New York. For a while

o

he made his home at an hotel in Kensington, but finding that hotel life becomes a bore after a time, he took a furnished house at Ealing. It was many months before he finally settled in a home of his own at Croydon. Though the inconvenience of being homeless hampered him in many ways he took up his work in a spirit of hopefulness and high endeavour. His fixed intention was to concentrate on preaching at Westminster, and he had to sweep aside the invitations showered upon him to speak and preach elsewhere.

After the exhilarating climate of New York in Winter and early Spring the twice-breathed air of London began to sap his energy and nervous force. London has a strange way of exacting a heavy toll upon men who enter her gates after the age of fifty; and Jowett made this discovery almost at once. He was glad to get away to Scotland for a holiday. Braemar, which he visited for the first time, sent him into ecstasies— it easily eclipsed anything he had seen in Britain. " I felt glad," he wrote, " that all this natural beauty was in Britain and that we can get to it without crossing the seas." It almost goes without saying that his Scottish holiday included a sojourn in his beloved Arran.

A Thursday week-day service at Westminster was one of Jowett's projects. One service was held on October 20th, but he had to abandon the idea with no hope of its resumption. " It is purely," he announced on the following Sunday, "a matter of health and strength, but since Thursday I have had medical counsel which leaves me no option but to give up the idea of a week-day service. For the past twelve months I have had very indifferent health, and have often gone lamely along the road. However, I am left in no uncertainty, and my work will have henceforth to be confined in somewhat narrower lines. I do not want you to think there is anything organically wrong; there are some functional difficulties which I have to watch. I can go on as I have been doing, but without this additional strain of a Thursday service."

Such a set-back at the very beginning of his London work and just after his return from a refreshing holiday naturally gave him much concern. In public he made light of the physical weakness, but in a letter to one of his closest ministerial friends his distress at having to economise his energy is evident :—

> *Buckingham Gate, S.W.,*
> *Nov. 5, 1918.*

To Rev. Thomas Towers.

. . . You ask about myself. I vary a good deal. The fact is I was knocked over last year in America. The extreme heat of August did for me. I had a bad time all through the winter and I have not got over it. I am troubled with some weakness that the doctor says I shall get over if I go guardedly for a time. But it is more than a little disappointing at the beginning of one's work. However, it is something to be able to take Sunday services.

As he had anticipated, Jowett found at Westminster Chapel a glorious opportunity for preaching the Gospel. Crowds flocked to his ministry from its beginning; and he felt, too, that his work was fruitful and, in the highest sense, rewarding. Wide avenues of usefulness opened before him and, given the necessary strength, he was bent on exploring and seizing them. But Westminster Chapel, from its situation in the back streets in the area between Victoria Street and St. James's Park and also from its inherent defects as a building, subjected him to an immediate strain and constraint. " The very building," he said " seems to be possessed

relating it to a Providence which has enlightened our counsels and blessed our arms."

He recalled the " bugle " period at the beginning of the war, when the nation was called to a rough and stormy road, "black with the menace of tragedy and death." Swiftly he glanced over the heavy gloomy years and thanked God for the " sustenance of hidden manna given by an unseen hand " which preserved the national unity unbroken. To the brave men who had borne the terrible burdens of the day he paid tribute and he tenderly remembered " our gallant sons " who had fallen in the fight—" lives that had passed through sacrifice into the exalted ministry of still larger service." But though they had reached the end of the fight, they had not reached the goal of the entire campaign.

The moral strength which has overturned a universal menace must now be consecrated to even greater tasks. . . . The fraternity of destructive warfare must be transformed into a fraternity of constructive peace. The sword must be beaten into a ploughshare and the spear into a pruning hook, and the moral spirit of the nations must provide a moral climate in which every people will be able to mature its own genius and make its own contribution to the common treasure of the race.

And so we are here to dedicate the coming years in our own land. We are here in order to make great history possible, to create an atmosphere in which great things can be done. My fellow countrymen, the moral strength which has destroyed one thing can construct a better. It has crumbled a fortress; it can build a house. It has cleared a jungle; it can make a garden. It can go through the highways and byways of our national life and make the crooked places straight and the rough places plain. So, while we thank God for a great victory, we are here to enlist for a new crusade.

After the service both the King and Queen thanked Jowett for his solemn and inspiring words. The King had, by a personal message sent through a friend at Christmas 1911 given Jowett a mark of his appreciation while he was in New York. On this occasion, the Queen, in her conversation with Jowett, asked him if Rev. F. W. Newland, M.A., of Claremont Central Mission (which she had visited years before, and in which she had shown a constant personal interest) was in the Albert Hall congregation. Jowett, who shared Her Majesty's admiration for Mr. Newland's long and self-sacrificial work in one of the grimiest slum districts in London, had great satisfaction in conveying to Mr. Newland the Queen's solicitous inquiry.

A slight recovery of strength, though not of weight—a significant symptom—encouraged Jowett to expand his range of operations in the year following the Armistice. He joined the Board of Directors of the London Missionary Society and attended its Eastern Committee meetings assiduously. He preached at the Spring meetings of the London Congregational Union, delivering a sermon in which he presented Jesus as the democratic leader. Though not in any sense a political sermon it had pronounced political implications of a progressive character. In various other ways Jowett showed that as far as his strength permitted he was anxious to take his rightful place in the general religious life of London and of his age. In the Summer of 1919 he went to America, to revive friendships and to preach and speak in fulfilment of engagements he had made, but he was somewhat disturbed to find a decided change in American feeling towards England and Europe. He attributed this unfriendly mood to the "politics," preceding the Presidential election.

" When that gets out of the way," he wrote, " we shall see our American friends in their best mood again."

Soon after his return to England, Jowett confided to a friend that he intended to accept at once any invitation he received to preach in a Church of England pulpit.   In the Autumn of 1919 Bishop Welldon asked him to preach in Durham Cathedral.   Jowett had been taking part in conferences on Unity held at Mansfield College, Oxford, between members of the Church of England and of the Free Churches.   He was one of the signatories to a resolution declaring that recognition of equality within the Church of Christ was a fundamental to any approach to the realisation of a reunited Church and that the approach should be along the lines of (1) interchange of pulpits (2) mutual admission to the Lord's Table, and (3) acceptance by ministers of such authorisation as should enable them to minister freely and fully in the churches of other denominations—such authorisation not to be taken as reordination or as a repudiation of their previous status as ministers of Jesus Christ.   He had, moreover, declared his belief, in a sermon at Westminster, that " if ever reunion is to be brought about it will be through spiritual communion."

Within a month of the issue of the Mansfield College Conference resolutions, the Dean's invitation to preach in Durham Cathedral reached Jowett and without hesitation he accepted it. Sunday, February 15th, 1920, was fixed for his visit.   The acceptance of the invitation made history. Since the time of the Commonwealth no Nonconformist had preached in an English Cathedral. The opportunity to break this age-long tradition of separatism in religious life seemed to Jowett to be a signal occasion for demonstrating the new spirit of unity, war-bred, actuating the British Churches.

He was scarcely prepared for the furore to which the Durham invitation gave rise. As soon as the announcement was made through the Press, a storm burst over Bishop Welldon's head. He was attacked by High Anglicans for violating the proprieties, and pressure was put upon him to withdraw the invitation, which one Rector denounced as " ecclesiastical Bolshevism." Jowett, too, was bombarded with protests from irate Anglicans, some of whom seemed to think that the appearance of a Free Church minister in a Cathedral pulpit amounted to an act of sacrilege. " They evidently imagine," he wrote to Mr. W. R. Moody, " that my presence will corrupt the venerable pile." Many of the communications addressed to Jowett were scurrilous : some of them were studiously offensive. A few were merely amusing. The storm left Jowett quite unperturbed. If the Dean held to the invitation Jowett intended to adhere to his acceptance of it. " I shall pay no heed to their screamings," he wrote, " and I shall make no fuss about it."

Croydon,
Jany. 30, 1920.

To Rev. David Young.

. . . Yes, I see that the Church papers, both daily and weekly, are lifting hands of horror that I am to be in the Cathedral. *The Morning Post* is particularly vicious. I feel absolutely unmoved by it, and whatever they say I shall go. I see that Rev. Arnold Pinchard, a very notorious High Churchman, says that my very acceptance of the invitation proves my insincerity. What can you do with a man like that? And what has the war taught him? I had hoped that that awful convulsion would shake the dead wood out of the ecclesiastical tree, and indeed I do think that much has been done. We must not allow the fierceness of a few to hide the goodwill of the

many. The laity of the Episcopal Church are
magnanimous, and they have welcomed the
invitation with goodwill.

When the time came to fulfil the engagement to
preach in Durham Cathedral, Jowett bore himself with
his characteristic serenity and dignity, though it proved
a trying ordeal. Few events in the ecclesiastical
world have, in recent years, excited so much interest.
The North of England, where, from his Newcastle days,
Jowett was a personality of great popular interest,
was especially stirred. Long before the service the
Cathedral was crowded. The congregation, numbering
seven thousand, had been drawn from all over the North-
eastern counties. Durham City Corporation, headed
by the Mayor, attended in state. The Free Church
Council and the Salvation Army marched in procession
to the Cathedral. The officials of the Durham Miners'
Association went as a body; so did the University
students and the Grammar School boys. All the
Canons were in their stalls. Though he decided not to
be present, the Bishop of Durham (Dr. Handley Moule)
had written expressing his sympathy with the ideals
which prompted the invitation and reiterating his
" reverent esteem for Dr. Jowett as a Christian minister
and teacher." The Archdeacon, alone of the Chapter,
was noticeably absent. Jowett, who wore a Geneva
gown and his Edinburgh D.D. hood over a cassock,
walked with Bishop Welldon in the procession of
clergy, and during the service occupied the Lord
Lieutenant's stall. The Bishop of Jarrow (Dr. Quirk)
and the Dean read the Lessons prescribed for the even-
song of the day.

A jarring incident disturbed the harmony of the
memorable service. Jowett had entered the pulpit
and, after offering the invocatory prayer, was just

announcing his text when a clergyman seated in the nave stood up and in a loud voice shouted : " I am the Vicar of Wheatley Hill, and I call upon all loyal Churchmen to protest. . . ." Angry voices drowned the rest of the sentence. In the momentary confusion a group of Durham miners started to sing " When I survey the wondrous Cross " and during the singing the protesting clergyman was hustled out of the Cathedral. Apparently unperturbed, Jowett stood watching the scene, and then quietly he announced his text and began the sermon. His subject was " Supplementing the Sufferings of Christ." He made not the slightest reference to the peculiar nature of the service, and his sermon was quite free from any controversial suggestion. Into every part of the Cathedral his resonant voice penetrated clearly. He spoke in a tone of quiet but intense impressiveness and was heard with rapt attention by the congregation.

The Vicar of Wheatley Hill, who, casting aside dignity and reverence, made his unseemly protest against one who was not episcopally ordained preaching in the Cathedral, had, by letter, warned Jowett beforehand that there would be a " scene " at the Cathedral service and had called on him " to save us from this, and from such traitors as the Dean of Durham." An icily polite reply was sent from Jowett to the Vicar.

I have (he wrote) received your letter. I have received multitudes of letters during the past week, but none like yours. I could not understand it until I reached the end of the letter, when I found the explanation in the information that you attach to your name.* I will only permit myself to say that I assume from your explanation that you are no longer in the Nonconformist

* The Vicar explained that he was formerly a Baptist minister.

ministry. As your letter is signed you can appreciate why I am assuming that there is no objection to my forwarding it to the Bishop of Durham.

Having crossed the rubicon, Jowett on several subsequent occasions preached in Anglican churches. He exchanged pulpits with his friend Dr. Stuart Holden of St. Paul's, Portman Square (the Bishop of London, who was consulted, offering no formal objection), and he preached in St. Matthew's, Croydon, at the request of his neighbour and friend, Rev. W. E. Daniels. The only protest ever made was that by the Vicar of Wheatley Hill.

After the Durham Cathedral service Dr. and Mrs. Jowett proceeded to Newcastle-on-Tyne to be the guests, with the Bishop of Newcastle (Dr. Wild), at a public luncheon and later in the day to attend a reception arranged in his honour at his old church—St. James's—a very happy reunion, reviving sweet memories of his first pastorate.

Jowett seldom preached a polemical sermon : but on the Sunday after his appearance in the pulpit of Durham Cathedral he departed from his rule and, before an exceptionally large congregation at Westminster, he vigorously asserted the claims of Free Churchmen against the exclusive claims of the High Anglicans. On the sacerdotal issue he was adamant and unyielding, and he firmly repudiated any High Church claim to monopoly of churchmanship, ministry or sacramental grace. . . . With Priestism, he declared, he would have no traffic. "I am no priest. No Bishop's hands have been laid on me. My orders are like St. Paul's—he was ' called ' to be an apostle, not of men but through Christ." In claiming for Free Churchmen the right of personal touch with Christ without the intervention of any human priest, the right to commune with Him and to membership of His Church he spoke with unaccustomed vehemence, and for once he did not try to suppress the audible approval of some of his hearers.

Another sermon in which Jowett struck the new " social " note in his Gospel attracted some attention about this time. He dealt with strongholds that ought to be pulled down and mentioned four fortresses which he declared Christians of to-day ought to assail. (1) The British Factory System, (2) Money worship, (3) Carnality, and (4) International jealousy and ill-will. Jowett had always stood four-square against what Miss Evelyn Underhill calls " devotional basking in the sun while allowing the maiming influence of environment to press myriads of other souls back to the animal levels," but he had never placed such resolute emphasis upon the collective responsibility of Christian people for social and economic wrongs as in his preaching at Westminster. Unfortunately, by his own express direction, none of his manuscripts are to be published posthumously. Consequently many of the sermons which struck a quite new note, and lent a fresh distinction to his last years of ministry by the revelation of a white-hot passion for social justice, will not now see the light. With this sterner note in his preaching he retained all the winsome persuasiveness of his spiritual appeal. His essential Gospel remained unchanged. In merely speculative theology he displayed less interest than ever. The core of his message was the call to Christ.

Christ Jesus asks us for the full surrender of our life to the governance of His will and to the power of His saving Grace : He calls us first of all to bring our life and offer it to Him as our Saviour and, then, secondly to use that offered life in obedience to our Lord.

That was the dynamic energising all his preaching at Westminster. Donald Hankey's phrase that " true religion is betting one's life that there is a God " was, he pointed out, a ready measure for testing the reality and value of religious professions.

We need not begin (said Jowett) with prolonged investigation into the length and details of our theological creed. I have known men and women with a creed as long as your arm, but they had no more spirit of venture than a limpet. Their theology is like a mountain, but they have not the courage of a mouse. Our jealousy for orthodoxy is no proof at all of the value of our faith. What do we hazard for it ? The measure of the hazard reveals the vitality of our faith, and nothing else reveals it. It is not revealed by our controversial ardour. It is not revealed by our stern guardianship of orthodox spoils. It is not revealed by the scrupulous regularity of our attendance at Church and worship. No, all these may mean nothing at all. What do we hazard for Christ ? What have we staked on the venture ? How much have we bet that He is alive and King ? . . . Twopence a week, or our life ? . . . That's the test.

The Autumn of 1920 brought him reasons for grave misgiving about his health. He was losing weight progressively. Fatigue followed the slightest physical effort and sometimes fainting fits followed. Almost for the first time in his life he found preparation for the pulpit burdensome. In October he was ordered a prolonged rest. A winter in the Riviera offered few attractions for him, but he accepted the fiat of his doctors.

Croydon,
Oct. 28, 1920.

To Rev. Edgar Todd.

I have been struggling on for the last two years, but I have been losing ground lately and it is well that I should be face to face with the realities of things. The specialist leaves me no option, and therefore I obey, but very reluctantly. He assures me, however, that if I take his counsel I shall recover my strength. I may find many other things as well along this road which I have never seen before.

The first few weeks of enforced rest at Cannes effected a distinct improvement in his health, but he sought a more bracing spot and found at Sospel, in the Maritime Alps behind Mentone, just what his condition required. He moved there at the end of February. Though all his life Jowett had worked with slender physical resources he had never had a serious breakdown, and when he remembered that his ministry covered a period of thirty exacting years he felt that he had no reason to complain.

Cannes,
24 *Feby.*, 1921.

To Rev. John Loosmore,

Just a word or two to report on myself. We are leaving Cannes to-morrow. I feel I have got all it can give me. I have rested, rested, rested—and now I want energy. So we are going inland a few miles to a little village on the hills. . . . I am hoping that a more bracing air may finish the job. I have been lying fallow—no sermon-making, not much reading, merely dreaming, dreaming. I wonder if I shall know how to preach when I turn to it again.

What about the Sunday services? (at Westminster). Are they keeping up? Are the men preaching the Gospel? I mean Christ's good

news? When I sit in the pew Sunday after
Sunday I feel I want to hear about nothing else.
And our men too often discuss smaller matters,
interesting but not vital. They don't pierce to the
heart of things.

The snappy bracing air at Sospel gave him an access
of strength, and his letters to home friends all enthusi-
astically proclaimed his confidence that his vigour was
being renewed. That his interest in public affairs in
England never flagged while he was abroad is shown
by an ejaculatory postscript to a letter to Mr. John
Pells—" Harry Whitley, Speaker ! How fine." On
the homeward journey from Sospel he spent a few days
in Switzerland to " cool down," and reached England
looking a rejuvenated man with the tan of outdoor life
on his cheek and a new spring in his footstep. Immense
congregations welcomed him back to his pulpit.

It was lovely (he wrote to Mr. A. Mackillop) to be
back at Westminster on Sunday, and although I
felt somewhat nervous and excited after six months'
silence and in face of such congregations, I got
through it in comparative comfort.

Unhappily the strength regained at such cost was soon
exhausted. The old symptoms of mysterious weakness
reappeared within a few weeks. He struggled through
the summer and got away for his usual holiday. But
at the beginning of the Winter's work he saw that he
was losing ground quickly. A friend who visited him
at Croydon in December found him looking very tired
and old, and very nervous about himself. He was
emphatic that he could not continue under the same
strain as for the last three years. It was not fair to the
Church or to Mrs. Jowett. He still loved preaching
above everything, he said, but preparation was becoming a burden. And unfortunately, he said, he was so

slow in preparing sermons and speeches. The future seemed to him very uncertain, but he was sure he would not be at Westminster more than three years—perhaps less. A crisis came within a few days of the friend's visit, and before the end of the year he had had to tender his resignation of his Westminster pastorate.

Croydon,
Jan. 31, 1922.

To Mr. H. F. Keep.

. . . I have sent in my resignation to Westminster Church and the whole subject is being discussed this week. It is simply futile to think I could go on as I have been doing, and a breakdown which I had a fortnight ago made some decision imperative. I can go on preaching once a Sunday, and do it with comfort and perfect safety, and I shall not go beyond the reduced capital upon which I can draw. The whole question before me is as to how that can be arranged. . . . .

I have had a splendid innings and I am not going to complain if I have to go more quietly. I shall be very glad to get out of the glare and have a chance of exercising a quieter ministry.

I think " Painted Windows " is a very indiscreet book, with very unbalanced judgments and a frightfully unfair attack upon Orchard. Orchard is no idol of mine and I bemoan the fantastic ways in which he clothes his ministry. But he cannot be set aside in the way Begbie tries to dispose of him. . . . He is too big a man for that.

Two other letters written to old ministerial confidants throw a little further light on Jowett's hopes and fears at this juncture.

Croydon,
4th Feby., 1922.

To Rev. Edgar Todd.

I have taken a step which has been long foreseen, as it was perfectly evident that I could not

P

go on as I have been doing. But I do not want my friends to think my working days are over. I am amused at some of the letters which are coming to me from friends who write as though I was nearing the end. I have plenty of strength in me and some days I feel as though there is nothing the matter : but then I know there is, and I have quite sufficient experience to make the days burdensome when they arrive. I have had thirty-five years of pretty hard public life and all I need is a somewhat quieter road. I have some half-formed plans in my mind for continuing to preach in London, but not before next Autumn. How these plans may mature I do not know : but I think they will give me the opportunity I want.

I am surprised at the intimation of your own early retirement. I have always looked upon you as like Johnny Walker, " going strong " till 90.

Croydon,
6th Feby., 1922.

To Rev. Thomas Towers.

Many thanks for your very kind letter. It is lovely to have all my old friends gathering round me at one of the critical moments in my life. I have had two or three decisive periods in my ministry. It was very difficult when I had to decide to leave Newcastle-on-Tyne and take up the work of Dr. Dale. It was a momentous thing when I had to face the possibility of leaving Birmingham to go to New York, and I found it equally trying when the call came to leave New York and come to London. And now the obligation is very clear that I have to lay down my work at Westminster. I feel it quite imperative, as I could not go on as I have done for the last two years. I shall seek quieter ways of work, still continuing to preach, but in ways and methods that will not be so exacting. I have had a splendid run for 35 years and I do not feel inclined to murmur if the pace has to be slackened.

The letter to the Westminster Church tendering his resignation left his people no other course but reluctant acceptance.

> When you called me from New York to be your minister (he wrote) it was in the gloomiest depths of war time, and I answered your call without the slightest hesitation, as any other man would have done who wished to share in the labour and travail of his country. I came hoping and praying that I might be an additional spring of comfort and inspiration, and that I might bring courage and cheer to the hearts of all to whom I ministered. I trust that hope has been in some degree fulfilled.
>
> From the very first days of my coming home I have been like a bird with a broken wing. I have had frequent breakdowns in health : indeed it is true to say that there have been very few days when a sense of weakness has not robbed me of an efficient discharge of my work.

A sub-committee of the deacons was appointed to confer with Jowett, who, at their request, agreed to continue to preach at the morning service at Westminster until May. This, his medical advisers thought was within the limits of his diminished strength.

> *Croydon,*
> 20 *March,* 1922.

To Rev. John Loosmore.

> . . . I have just returned from Birmingham, where I went to be under the dentist's care for a week. I shall be very glad when I can be poorly in private, and not have public intimations of one's sickness. I feel perfectly certain that these paragraphs make one feel twice as bad. However, you will be glad to know that the lessening of the burden and the limiting of myself to one service on Sunday is acting very beneficially, and I feel a difference already. Of course it means just half the output, and that keeps me within my limit. I fully expect that by next Autumn I shall be

competent to do anything I want to do. I am still planning for the mid-week service, and I have decided to have it at Whitefields. . . . I am inundated with invitations to take this church and that church from all parts of Great Britain, and, indeed, from all parts of the world. I have fully decided not to take another church, but just to choose here and there, and preach up and down the country.

As the days of his Sunday morning ministry at Westminster neared their end, Jowett preached with undiminished power and zest—burning the last drops of oil in his lamp. It was during this half-time period that he made his first great pronouncement on the Churches and World Peace. In May he went North. In August he was at Copenhagen, and after an invigorating stay on the Yorkshire moors he felt well enough in October to enter into an arrangement to preach at Westminster on Sunday mornings until the end of the year. At no period of his London ministry was popular interest in Jowett so manifest, nor the eagerness to hear him more evident. The queues before the Church doors extended along Buckingham Gate, and not all who sought admission secured it. In November the King conferred upon him the order of the Companion of Honour, to the great joy of Jowett's friends. " I only hope," he said in reply to a congratulatory letter, " that its influence on my life may be to enlarge the scope of my ministry." He was planning his Peace Campaign and summoning up what reserves of strength he could gather for what was really a Quixotic enterprise in his then depleted condition of health. The effort drained all his resources. On Sunday, December 17th, he preached his last sermon at Westminster—the last sermon, in fact, that he ever preached.

CHAPTER XII

HIS GOSPEL

"THE glory of a popular preacher," Lord Haldane once said, "is very great." For thirty years this glory shone upon Jowett. He came dangerously near being apotheosized in his lifetime. His presence in any pulpit invariably crowded the building. His words went forth to the outposts of the British Empire and indeed to the ends of the earth. The explanation of such world-wide popularity is not to be found merely in his being possessed of a beautiful voice, of perfect elocution, of all the arts of oratory. Such endowments might give a man an ephemeral popularity, but they could not account for a preacher continuing through a quarter of a century to be both a magnetic influence in the pulpit and a power in the thoughts and hearts of men scattered all over the world.

What then was Jowett's message? What was the Gospel, preached as he preached it, that perpetuated this grip upon the public mind? " I have had but one passion," he said himself, " and I have lived for it—the absorbingly arduous, yet glorious work of proclaiming the grace and love of our Lord and Saviour, Jesus Christ." The supreme note of his preaching was the proclamation of the all-sufficiency of Redeeming Grace in its relationship to the worst. His interpretation of the Christian ministry was that of a Greatheart facing the highways of life carrying with him all that is needed by fainting, bruised and broken pilgrims, and at the very centre of his message were Comfort and Grace. Like Ian Maclaren, he believed that one of the great functions of a preacher is to comfort and hearten his people. Men and women, he was convinced, are almost all weary and heavy laden, and experience taught him that they seek not primarily intellectual enlightenment, but the word which will " put heart into them for the coming week." Jowett quoted approvingly Dr. Parker's advice to preachers —" Preach to broken hearts." He recalled Professor Elmslie's words to his wife, " What people need most is comfort," and he remembered that even Dr. Dale had declared that " People want to be comforted." A heart of compassion, he felt, was essential in a preacher, and he was certain beyond all peradventure that only in the unsearchable riches of Christ would the sad, tear-stricken, heavy-laden children of men find their satisfaction. To this ministry of consolation he dedicated himself, and he sought to express his message in terms of tenderness " born of the refining and chastening ministry of a Great Companionship." " We cannot preach without tenderness," he said— quoting the story of Robert McCheyne hearing from Andrew Bonar that he had been preaching on " The wicked shall be turned into Hell " and asking whether he was able to preach it with tenderness. To be a teller of good news, Jowett believed was the first mission of the preacher. His function was to be a herald of salvation. And what, he asked, is to be the theme of the " good news "?

It is to be good news about God. It is to be good news about the Son of God. It is to be good news about the vanquishing of guilt and the forgiveness of sins. It is to be good news about the subjection of the world and the flesh and the devil. It is to be good news about the transfiguration of sorrow and the withering of a thousand bitter roots of anxiety and care. It is to be good news about the stingless death and the spoiled and beaten grave. . . . We preachers are to go about our ways finding men and women shattered and broken, with care upon them and sorrow upon them and death upon them, wrinkled in body and mind and with the light flickering out of their soul. And we are to bring them the news which will be as vitalising air to those who faint, which will be like the power of new wing to birds that have been broken in flight.

This *sursum corda* note rang through Jowett's preaching. The Eternal love of God was his basal doctrine of Christianity, and he proclaimed the illimitable love of God with unwearied insistence. This "apprehending love grip" he believed to be equally true of those existing in dreary rooms and tenements and of the weary souls in stately castles confronting wide domains. "I have proclaimed," he said, "that everybody is in the love grip of the Eternal. Is there a bigger thing than that to say to anybody? Can I get anybody to tell me of a bigger thing than this infinitude—'God knows them and loves them with an everlasting love'"? "They that bring sunshine into the heart of others," says Sir James Barrie, "cannot keep it from themselves," and Jowett's message of comfort, deriving from his certitude of the everlasting love of God, sustained his own soul and actuated his life.

Jowett's second basal doctrine of Christianity was the reality of sin. The guilt of sin and the fear of death are, he believed, the most real of all the terrors that afflict men and women. He never wavered in his sense of the sinfulness of sin. So Reconciliation in Christ was the keynote of his gospel. The nearest approach to a *credo* which Jowett has left behind him is to be found in a sermon he preached at the Centenary of the Congregational Church Aid and Home Missionary Society in May 1919. Whatever changes and adjustments and readjustments are needed—he was arguing—the cardinal necessity is for the Church of Christ to recover the fullness of the Holy Gospel which will equip her with all sufficient power for the new-shaped needs of our own time. "What," he asked, " was that Gospel? " and, in answer, he defined it in terms embodying his own message :—

The Holy God who had veiled His mysterious and awful presence between the Cherubim had shown His face. He had been seen ! Where ? He had been seen in Jesus. Jesus of Nazareth had lit up the vast abyss of the Eternal Mind, and men beheld His glory full of Grace and Love. At Bethlehem God became incarnate, entering into our estate through very lowly doors. At Calvary the incarnation of the Godhead became superlatively wonderful, unfolding itself in nameless sacrifice, unveiling a lamb which had been slain before the foundation of the world. In the life and death of this Jesus were revealed a power of redeeming love and grace which could lay hold of all life that had lost the divine image and superscription—men and women who had been perverted, deformed, defaced, and brutalised by sin,—and restore them to the spiritual likeness of the Lord. That is the outline of the marvellous story. That is the strange alphabet from which is woven the unanswerable literature of redeeming grace.

In conversation with Dr. Dale at Llanbedr in 1892, about the time when Jowett was just getting into his stride as a preacher, Dr. P. T. Forsyth said " the time has come to get back the word Grace into our preaching : word and thing have too much disappeared." Jowett emerged with his tireless emphasis on Grace as a fulfilment, almost, of Dr. Forsyth's prophetic perception of this need. To the literature of Redeeming Grace Jowett made a rich contribution by his sermons and books. It was the " big theme " to which, above all others, he returned again and again, as if, of all truth, it was the one facet that entranced him.

Mr. A. Clutton-Brock, writing on " What is the Kingdom of Heaven ? " has noted that Jesus found it hard to explain what He meant by the Kingdom of Heaven, and yet laboured incessantly to do so. " He tried," Mr. Clutton-Brock said, " to express it in one image or parable after another, always insisting that it is the greatest thing in life, and that what is needed above all things is to find it, to be aware of it." To Jowett, Redeeming Grace was the fulcrum of the evangelical message. " With all my heart," he said, " do I believe that this Gospel of Redeeming Grace is the cardinal necessity of our time." In a hundred sermons he proclaimed it. All his wealth of imagery and illustration was lavished upon this theme. " I cannot do anything better than magnify the Grace of God," he said. " One could preach twenty sermons on it." Grace was Jowett's sovereign word. He was always probing into the depths of its meaning and discovering some new aspect of its unsearchable riches. Each discovery he heralded with satisfaction. " You cannot define it," he said on one occasion, " but then you cannot define anything that is really lovely, still less can you define love itself. As soon as you begin to describe a garden you feel you have only just got the alpha of the great alphabet and all the rest is left untouched. I feel just like that when I begin to try to say anything about Grace."

Even Jowett, with all his spacious vocabulary of definition and description, confessed that the multitudinous connotations of Grace baffled him.

There is no word (he said) I have wrestled so much with as Grace. It is just like expressing a great American forest by a word. No phrase can express the meaning of Grace. If anyone is in love you do not take down a dictionary to find out its meaning. But how much further can you get in dealing with these primary exercises—these primary elements in the life of the soul? You cannot diagnose. But there is nothing negative about it, nothing merely passive. When we speak about the Grace of God there are so many who think of Grace as favour, conciliatoriness and kindly sentiment. I want to say that there is nothing in God that is aloof, nothing of mere composure, nothing of passive regard, nothing apathetic. Every attribute of God is a fountain of vitality and the throne from which flows the river of the Water of Life. Grace is favour, but it means more than this. It is holy love radiating from the soul of the Eternal into the soul of His children and radiating holy love into His children, transforming them to His likeness and equipping them for His service.

On another occasion, attempting a definition of his theme, he said :—

Grace is more than mercy. It is more than tender mercy. It is more than a multitude of tender mercies. Grace is more than love. It is more than innocent love. Grace is holy love, but it is holy love in spontaneous movement going out in eager quest toward the unholy and the unlovely, that by the ministry of its own sacrifice it might redeem the unholy and the unlovely into its own strength

and beauty. The Grace of God is holy love on the
move to thee and me, and the like of thee and me.
It is God unmerited, undeserved, going out towards
the children of men, that He might win them into
the glory and brightness of His own likeness.

In one of his last articles for *The British Weekly*,
written in a period of physical weakness, he made
still another attempt to answer the question he was
always posing in his own mind—what is Grace?

It is God (he replied) in the infinite ministries of
His own love, moving to the destruction of the
tyrannies of sin and death. It is the full strength
of the Godhead set against man's supreme foe in
uttermost self-sacrifice. There is nothing of rights
on the side of man; it is entirely undeserved. It is
never a bit earned; it is all given. It is not even
asked for; it anticipates even the cry of our need.
Grace moved to the Cross to set the bondsman free
and to proclaim an amnesty to all mankind. At the
Cross the grim monarchies of sin and death die in
the unutterable death of the Son of God. And it
is all of Grace. "The gift of God is eternal life
through Jesus Christ our Lord." Grace reigns in
the reign of the Saviour.

The practical theology underlying all Jowett's
preaching was that men and women must establish
right relationships with God by establishing right
relationships with Christ. "Make a full surrender of
your life to the governance of the will of Christ and to
the power of His saving Grace." That was the verdict
he preached for. "He calls us first of all to bring our
life and offer it to Him as our Saviour, and then to use
that offered life in obedience to our Lord." Make the
surrender to Christ, Jowett iterated and reiterated,
and then streams of Redeeming Grace will flow through
your life, redeeming you from your sins, radiating

qualities undreamed of from your character and
ensuring you a peace the world cannot give. " Salvation and peace," he declared, " are to be found only
in the surrender of the personal life to the Saviourhood
and comradeship of Christ."

> No one (he wrote) can gaze in silent lowliness
> upon the Christ and lift to Him the incense of
> prayerful desire and aspiration, without having
> from the Lord, in some way or other, some clear
> expression of His will. I shall come to know what
> He wants me to be like, in my home and in my
> ministry, and you will know what He wants you to
> be like in your daily life and calling, both in private
> and in public relationships. And when we know
> His will, the reverence which bowed in lowliness, and
> aspired in prayerfulness, will now obey in faithful-
> ness. That is to say, true reverence will offer the
> Lord the gold of obedience.

This Evangelical insistence on the Lordship of Christ
and His redemptive power was central in all Jowett's
preaching. Ruskin, he reminded the theological
students at Yale, had said that if you were to cut a
square inch out of any of Turner's skies you would find
the infinite in it, and Jowett urged that if a square
inch were taken out of a sermon men should find a
suggestion which would lead them to " the throne of
God and of the Lamb." For this reason he had no
patience with preaching on trivialities. He took the
great texts—the fat texts as he called them—and
treated them spaciously. A member of his Church
at Carr's Lane took notes regularly Sunday by Sunday
of Jowett's texts and to them he added a short epitome
of the sermon. A study of these notes reveals that
Jowett throughout the Birmingham years, with rare
exceptions, dealt with the great themes of the pulpit
as he himself enumerated them—" The Holiness of

God, the Love of God, the Grace of the Lord Jesus, the solemn wonders of the Cross, the ministry of the Divine Forgiveness, the Fellowship of His Sufferings, the Power of the Resurrection, the Blessedness of Divine Communion, the Heavenly Places in Christ Jesus, the Mystical Indwelling of the Holy Spirit, the Abolition of the Deadliness of Death, the Ageless Life, Our Father's House, the Liberty of the Glory of the Children of God." Though he saw very clearly the peril of divorcing ethics from theology, Jowett, until his return from America and under the pressure of the post-war social unrest, was rarely tempted into preaching sermons bearing directly on social or economic or political subjects. He was content to suggest the implications of Christianity on such questions, without any immediate emphasis on current issues. The danger he saw was that " the broadening conception of the preacher's mission " might lead to the emphasis being laid " on the Old Testament message of reform rather than upon the New Testament message of redemption." The life of society as a whole, he was satisfied, must be uplifted by the individual regeneration of the men and women composing it and not by Acts of Parliament, however well devised and however strongly they commanded his own adhesion as a politician. " Ye must be born again " was an injunction of Christ's, from which Jowett preached more than once and with pressing urgency. Removal of social evils and economic injustices was, to him, a matter of sweeping away obstacles to the individual " rebirths " which would redeem society.

The perennial freshness and appealing power with which Jowett proclaimed the grace and beauty of the Christian life explain the eagerness with which his message was welcomed. He concentrated his strength on edifying the saints, comforting the sad, and illuminating the pathway to the peace of mind that is the Christian's inalienable reward. His own mental and spiritual experience had not fashioned him for laying the spectres in questing minds, or dealing with the intellectual problems of men and women perplexed by doubt, hesitation and pain. The problems that baffle the modern mind left him serene and unperturbed in the uplands of assured faith into which he seems to have soared without any tragic crisis in his religious experience. It has been written of him that " he invested the Christian life with an aura of Grace and beauty and made one feel that it was the completion and crown of the natural life rather than a violent reaction from it."

Theological questions *per se* did not greatly interest him. His practical Yorkshire mind had no trend in that direction. Mere speculation was not his bent. He appealed to faith which is intuitional, rather than to belief which is intellectual. Quarrying in the regions of experience, he found there rich veins of precious ore. And from it he minted the sterling coin of his Evangelical message. Even upon the Higher Criticism of the Bible he never, from the pulpit, indicated his own view, though in the last year of his ministry he publicly expressed his profound agreement with Dr. W. B. Selbie, who had been pleading that there should be no juggling with the truth, but that the accepted findings of Biblical Scholarship should be wisely and fearlessly taught in all our churches and schools.* " There is now," Jowett said, " widespread unrest and confusion. Our young people do not know where they are. They are in the bonds of antiquated

* *The Daily Telegraph* (Oct. 17, 1922), to which he contributed a periodical series of " Free Church Notes."

methods and conceptions. Much of their bondage
would be released by a more candid and fearless dealing
with their difficulties and more particularly by teaching
methods of approach to the Bible in which many of
the difficulties would solve themselves."

The problem of the miraculous did not disturb
Jowett. In the miracles of modern science he saw
possible substantiations of the miracles of Jesus.

> We are rapidly approaching a time (he said from
> his pulpit at Carr's Lane in October, 1907) when
> the miracles of our Lord will be lifted clear out of
> the circle of the unnatural and the incredible and
> will be interpretable in certain clearly recognised
> conditions, and explained according to the operations
> of established but as yet unknown law. He believed
> that Jesus of Nazareth, by the very uniqueness and
> grandeur of His Being, controlled and exercised
> mystic forces which were only to be discovered in
> the evolution of the years. He moved in realms
> into which the ordinary man had no entry, and in
> which he moved perfectly oblivious of the mar-
> vellous energies by which he was surrounded. It
> was not that Jesus was unnatural, but that His
> range of the natural was more extensive. In His
> very Being He had the key to larger worlds. . . . It
> may be (he added) that we are now (through scientific
> discovery and development) gaining glimpses of
> forces with which Jesus was familiar, and there may
> be finer energies still which men may discover in
> the process of the years, but which Christ consciously
> exercised in the common relationships of His day.

He found a suggestion for stimulating sermons in what
he called the ministry of sacrificial suffering, and he
pressed the principle of sacrificial suffering upon the
individual as well as upon the Church. " The sacrificial life," he said, " is life pooled for the public good."
" It is life with the emphasis placed upon our brother."

In this connection he used one of his most famous and memorable illustrations.

> I was crossing (he said) the shoulder of one of the lower Alps, the Fürren Alp, whose bold, rocky head looks down into the lovely valley of Engelberg. My guide-book told me that I should reach a place where the visible track would cease, but it vouchsafed no further information. I reached the place, and with the place the end of the beaten road. For a time I wandered about uncertainly, guided only by the somewhat vague and capricious counsels of a compass. And then I caught sight of what seemed like a splash of blood upon a rock, and then at some little distance another similarly splashed, each one I came to bringing into view another further away. And then I inferred that these were to be my dumb guides across the trackless waste. I was to follow the blood marks. By the red road I should reach my destination.

The red road is the path of noblest influence, Jowett urged. The self-crucified man becomes identified—nay incorporated—with the Lord Jesus Christ. " If the Church of the Living God were sacrificial she would thrill the world."

Though faithful to the Evangelical message, Jowett refused to be a bond-slave to the old Evangelical phraseology. Each generation, he recognised, has its own thought-forms, and the thought-forms of a previous generation are obsolete and without significance. Jowett spoke oftener of Readjustment than of Atonement. What he never did was to use an old word after emptying it of its historic content. In " the newness of carefully chosen expression " he discovered a fresh power for his own generation, and at Carr's Lane he led his people out of the nineteenth-century language of Dr. Dale into the currency of twentieth-century idiom. Just as sickly people are often stimulated into eating by a change of the pottery ware on which their food is served, Jowett felt that the new phrasing of religious truth gives a fresh and appetising taste to familiar spiritual food.

No theological school of thought could claim Jowett as exclusively its own. He described himself, or acquiesced in his description, as a Broad Evangelical; but he told an intimate friend that he agreed with, and preached, eleven-twelfths of what Rev. R. J. Campbell called the "New Theology." The other twelfth, which was Dr. Campbell's view of Christ and of sin—his own two centralities—he utterly disbelieved. He visited the Keswick Convention and found himself in warm sympathy with its emphasis on "the wonderful and glorious privilege of the Christian believer to have holy and intimate companionship with the Holy Ghost." While he criticised the Old Testament exegesis at Keswick as "often fanciful," and could not identify himself with its mental methods and instruments, he appreciated its recovery of a lost emphasis. When he attended a meeting to welcome Rev. H. Tydeman Chilvers to the pastorate of the Metropolitan Tabernacle, Jowett, quite consciously perhaps, exposed himself to misunderstanding. His presence was regarded as a side-step to the extreme theological Right : but to Jowett it was just a generous gesture of sympathy with, and goodwill towards, an historic church—associated with the name of a great preacher whose memory he honoured—which was making a new start at a time of extreme difficulty. Jowett bridged the theological chasms that separate the Christian hosts not merely by varying theologies but by conflicting ecclesiastical systems. With all his responsiveness to the upheavals of popular thought,

Q

his early and provident fear of hasty decisions saved him from being stampeded into premature departures from old positions. But new modes of looking at things, new ways of expression and the absence of familiar catchwords had no terrors for him.

I believe (he said in one of his last sermons) that we are entering upon a day when we shall encounter many new terminologies. Men will be saying old things in new words. They will be giving new expressions to old truths. I plead that we never let a new phraseology frighten us into a sense of spiritual bereavement. Let us look very reverently and expectantly at the new presence, and we may find that in the very moment when we are tempted to think that we are pathetically bereaved we are face to face with the risen Lord and in open communion with His grace. The Son of God, who is the sun of righteousness, reveals His presence in rushing change and transition just as truly as He reveals it in the quiet features of restful peace and settled government. And here, I think, is the part which you and I, and all who share our faith, are to fill in these revolutionary days. It is comparatively easy to discern the Lord's presence amid the green pastures and by the still waters; ours must be the braver vision that can see the Lord in general disquietude, when He leads out into unfamiliar ways of righteousness. It is one thing to see the Lord's banner waving over the triumphant achievements of the past; it is a grander thing to behold Him revealing Himself in a growing moral sensitiveness which is feeling out for larger exploits in the more perfect expression of His will. Yes, it is a good thing to be sure of the Lord in the old tent which has been our dwelling place for many generations; it is an even better thing to be able to say, " It is the Lord " when we are pulling up the old pegs, and striking tent, and setting out for we know not

where, except it be on to " the bound of the waste,
on to the city of God."

Through his writings Jowett ministered to a community scattered over the whole world. His first
regular contributions were made to the columns of
The Christian World, for which he began writing a
monthly devotional article in the New Year of 1907
and continued until his last illness. These articles,
which were drawn from his sermons, appeared simul-
taneously in *The Continent* (Chicago) and were frequently pirated in other religious papers in America
and Australia. For some years he wrote a prayer
and a short unsigned religious article for *The Sunday
Companion*. Later he contributed week by week a
" Meditation " to *The British Weekly*. Some of his
best original work went into these articles. They
were not sermons, but totally independent productions
prepared during his early morning studies, and written
currente calamo and at a sitting. For a time he
published through *The British Congregationalist* his
week-night address at Carr's Lane Chapel. From
time to time his sermons were printed in *The Christian
World Pulpit* and a sermon was published monthly in
The Westminster Pulpit during his London ministry.
With three exceptions his books were collections of his
sermons, carefully revised and arranged to secure a
sequence of thought. The other three volumes were
his Yale Lectures on preaching and two volumes of
prayers.

CHAPTER XIII

HIS METHODS

JOWETT lived to preach. All his energies, spiritual, mental, nervous and physical, were concentrated on preaching and preparation for preaching. He read, observed, thought, meditated and brooded with a single eye to the pulpit; and he scorned delights and lived laborious days to perfect himself for his high calling. " This one thing I do," he cried, echoing the words of a greater. Without vanity he knew that to preach was his *métier :* without egotism he was firmly conscious of his own power in the pulpit, and he accepted it as a bounden duty to dedicate himself to the single end of being a preacher.

Certain initial qualifications for preaching were part of his natural equipment for the pulpit, and he developed and perfected them by painstaking industry. If he had any intuitive genius it was spiritual genius—a sensitiveness that opened the windows of his soul to the softest zephyrs of the winds of God, and this spiritual genius he kept receptive by a disciplined prayer life that kept his soul attune with the Infinite. The genius that Thomas Carlyle defined as the capacity for taking pains Jowett possessed to a superlative degree. It has been truly said of him that given one talent he made it into ten talents by ceaseless effort. A rich musical voice, ranging from a soft, sweet, wooing murmur to a thunderous bass was a precious asset, and he commanded it with a consummate artistry that never suggested the mere elocutionist. Possibly he never wanted to lose—and he did not lose—a slight suggestion of the Yorkshire intonation acquired in his boyhood.

To the spiritual qualities from which his message derived its radiance, and to the beautiful voice with which he proclaimed it, Jowett by his own patient and untiring labour added a rich and flexible literary form of speech. He was *par excellence* the stylist of the English pulpit—an expert in the perfect use of words. No preacher of his time had an equal command of expressive colour in word and phrase. His mastery of the chiaroscuro of language was one of his outstanding marks of distinction. Jowett always acknowledged that it was Professor David Masson who fired him with a passion for exact verbal expression. But his *flair* for literary style came out of self-schooling and out of reading and re-reading the great masters of English prose and poetry. Bunyan, perhaps, influenced him more than any other author. Before he left Newcastle he had made himself possessed of a distinctive style of his own, delicate, full of colour and glow and warmth. Like John Bright he chose simple Saxon words, avoiding the use of Latinity if by any device it could be obviated.

If he can be said to have had any hobby, it was the study of words. It was at once a duty and a pleasure to him. He loved to take a word, as an entomologist takes a moth, and having, figuratively speaking, stuck a pin through it, subject it to a long microscopic examination. One day his friend, Rev. Edgar Todd, walking with him in Sutton Park, wanted to show Jowett how the " Holly Blue " butterfly differs from the " Common Blue." " With the utmost caution," says Mr. Todd, " I approached the resting insect, so that I could lift it off the leaf without injury to show him the markings on the underside of the wings. Jowett watched me in silence and then said, ' That is just how I pick up a word.' "

The derivatives, varying historical connotations and exact values of a word presented a world of fascination to him. He pursued this hobby with scientific thoroughness and knew the pedigrees of words as if he had learned them from an etymological Debrett. This was all a part of his mental discipline for the pulpit, and not merely an æsthetic taste for choice phrases and expressive words. Words were the implements of his craft as a preacher, and no artist studied his pigments with purer delight. All the fine gradations of nouns and verbs, adverbs and adjectives yielded their secrets to his scrutiny and enabled him to wed the inevitable adjective to the inescapable noun with infallible felicity. A fine phrase thrilled him : a delicate *nuance* set him tingling. Once when talking to me of his passionate delight in word study, he likened his hobby to Henry Ward Beecher's habit of carrying precious stones in his pocket so that in odd moments he might hold them in the sunshine and watch the multi-coloured rays flash from their facets. " I do something like that," said Jowett, " only with words."

In Copenhagen in 1922 Jowett met for the first time Professor Adolf Deissmann, whose profound studies of the New Testament Greek text have enriched Biblical scholarship and revealed new significances in the phraseology of the Gospels and the Epistles. Almost the first question Jowett asked Prof. Deissmann concerned the New Testament Greek Lexicon on which the Berlin scholar had been engaged for several years when the war interrupted its progress.

When Jowett heard from Dr. Deissmann that the probability of its completion was quite remote, his face bore an expression of mingled regret and dismay. The thwarted hope of, some day, owning and exploring the Lexicon gave him a pang such as a schoolboy might experience if he were told that *The Boy's Own Paper* had suspended publication.

Even upon the minutiæ of punctuation Jowett was a purist. The careless use of " stops," he felt, debased the currency of words.

> When I was at school (writes his daughter Monica) one thing in which Father took the keenest interest was punctuation. " Not one woman in fifty can punctuate," he always said. We generally went over that part of my composition together, and many and hot were the arguments—for I was very bad at seeing the natural home of the comma. He said I scattered them impartially as from a pepper box.

Carefulness in small things was a very great thing in Jowett's estimation, and his scrupulous care over details constituted a large element in his acquired genius.

Methods of study formed early in his ministerial life served him to the end of his career. Bible study occupied his best hours—the early morning hours. Dr. Griffith-Jones, who crossed the Atlantic with Dr. and Mrs. Jowett in 1916, says he soon realised that Jowett's great gift of discovering the deep wells of saving power in the Christian faith was no secondary thing, but the expression of his own profound spiritual experience.

> It was impossible (writes Dr. Griffith-Jones) to get very near to him without being made to feel that one was in the presence of a soul saturated with

prayers into sections and announced the subject for which he was about to pray. At the close of each petition the congregation responded with the Amen. One of his last literary efforts in the year of his failing strength was to write an introduction to a volume of liturgical Intercession services, commending their use in Congregational worship in the belief that they would " greatly enrich the worship of the sanctuary."

The mornings spent in his study were seasons of strenuous toil, of unremitting labour. He read hard, " read everything," though he gave less time to formal theological works than to the literature of life—poetry, biography, fiction, science and history. If the study is a lounge, he used to say, the pulpit will be an impertinence. He was at his desk before breakfast, and he remained there until mid-day. Family prayers divided his working morning into two parts. Sometimes in the Summer he used the garden as his study and he would walk up and down the lawn penning his sermon on a writing pad.

Preparation for Sunday's sermons began on Tuesday morning, and two days were spent on thinking out and writing each sermon. The best sermons, he said, are not made; they grow. His habit was to carry about with him a tiny note-book in which he jotted down subjects for sermons or suggestive texts, and skeletonised the main line of thought. Occasionally he drew a rough diagram of a Biblical background. There the sermon notes matured under reflection until they were ripe for preaching. Not until the time came when the central idea could be crystallised into one short luminous sentence was a theme ripe enough for Jowett to begin sermon work upon it in the study. He confessed that getting that germinal sentence was the most exacting and one of the most essential elements in sermon

preparation. Two further mental exercises followed.
He made it a habit to ask himself how other preachers
would deal with the subject he had chosen, or which had
chosen him. " I ask, How would Newman regard this
subject? How would Spurgeon approach it? How
would Dale deal with it? By what road would
Bushnell come up with it? Where would Maclaren
take his stand to look at it? Where would Alexander
Whyte lay hold of it? " This practice of looking at his
subject through many windows broadened and enriched
his own conception of the theme, clarified his own mind
and expanded his vision. The second mental exercise
preparatory to writing the sermon was to keep in view
an invisible circle of typical men and women in his
congregation varying in education, temperament, social
standing and spiritual experience—for every one of
whom each sermon ought, he felt, to provide some soul
nutriment according to their several needs. He wanted
to " adapt his light to their form of night " and grant
them " their needed day." This practice kept him
in touch with real life, with actual men and women.
" It keeps me," he said, " on the common earth and
saves me from losing myself in the clouds."

Once the sermon had been completely thought out
Jowett began to commit it to paper. Even in writing
he cultivated what he called the strength of leisureliness.
It was slow work with him, as he often lamented—
done without haste, and at the cost of infinite labour.
" Pay sacred heed to the ministry of style," he counselled the young preachers at Yale : and Jowett did
not advise what he did not practise. The graces of
speech that made his sermons suggest the very artistry
of words cost him ceaseless travail of mind and spirit.
With prayer and fasting he paid the price for those
finished discourses which seemed so artlessly perfect :

but a high purpose moved him in this embellishment of his message by all the graces he could command. "A well-ordered, well-shaped sentence, carrying a body and weight of truth will," he recognised, "strangely influence even the uncultured hearer." Jowett's illustrations and imageries, prodigal, arresting and sometimes unforgettable, also came out of unremitting hard labour. They were born out of the travail of incessant reading and vigilant observation. Nature unfolded her secrets to Jowett's watchful eyes. His garden was a mine of illustrations for his sermons. The sky, the clouds, the Spring resplendence in the woods, the Autumnal decay, yielded him their bounteous harvest of imagery. He saw nature in her benevolent moods, and found parables where Tennyson met problems in the flower " in the crannied wall."

To Miss Jessie Spicer.

Do you remember soon after we got over the brow of the hills behind the British Camp (at Malvern) going towards the monument that we came to a very rutty bit of road, and we found some exquisite tiny white flowers growing on the very lips of the ruts? Do you remember them? And shall I tell you what I thought when we stooped and looked at them? I just silently prayed that when I came in life to a rutty stretch of road people might find exquisite little flowers of grace and courtesy growing in the very ruts. Do you see my parable? You are feeling perhaps that you are back in the ruts again. Well, make it a beautiful country lane. Fill it with God's wild flowers. Spiritual violets are forget-me-nots, and many a beautiful, nameless little grace grows right out of the bare clay. Wouldn't it be a beautiful thing if we could thus transfigure all drudgery into a bit of God's garden, and surprise those who look upon us by our likeness to the Lord? For we can be perfectly sure that our Lord had many a long stretch of ordinary road, with the most ordinary duties, but He just set to work to turn it all into the highway of a King.

Nature " red in tooth and claw " with its incesssant and pitiless struggle, did not escape his vigilant eye, but it did not upset his philosophy of things. He was Wordsworthian in his view of nature.

To Miss Jessie Spicer.

I believe that everything in nature is a sort of language which God uses to speak to us. He is saying something to us in every sunset, and in every wild flower, in every calm or stormy sea. But we are so dense that we cannot interpret it, and it is so often as though our Lord were making no communication at all.

He would probably have chosen Richard Jefferies rather than W. H. Hudson as his interpreter of nature.

In his earlier years Jowett was lavish to prodigality in his use of illustration and imagery. Some of his Newcastle sermons moved from image to image, symbol to symbol and illustration to illustration. He found John Woolman irresistible. " The Pilgrim's Progress " crept into almost every sermon. In print this profuse wealth of illustration suggested a decorativeness in sheer defiance of Ruskin's great principle that no ornament should be without its utility. He was quick to detect this defect in his own work, and the phase passed. He economised in his illustrations, and finally declared that a sermon illustration should be like an honest street lamp throwing floods of light upon the road and not an item of decoration like a fairy lantern. Above all he felt that an illustration that needed explanation was a worthless encumbrance.

The Old Testament yielded pure gold for sermonic service to Jowett. He delved in its wealthy spaces,

especially in the Psalms and in Isaiah. Sir George
Adam Smith's work on the Old Testament revolu-
tionised its interpretation, he said, and in conversation
with a friend he quoted approvingly Dr. Dale's reply to
someone who suggested that he should preach a course
of sermons on Isaiah—" I cannot; I am not ready
for it." In the Epistles of Paul, too, he found an
inexhaustible treasury.

> Every month (he said at Carr's Lane in 1912) I am
> more and more driven to Paul. I think you heard
> " Paul " and " Paul " and " Paul " countless times
> in my ministry here. I think he has got the key.
> I feel that if ever mortal man had the key of the house
> I want opened he has got it.

Though it may seem like leaping from the sublime
into the ridiculous, it should be mentioned that Jowett
read the daily newspapers and religious weeklies with
scrupulous care as part of his preparation for the pulpit.
His function as a preacher was to relate Christian truth
to the life of his own day, and the newspapers served
him as a mirror reflecting the thoughts, emotions
and activities of the age he was addressing from the
pulpit. He always read *The Friend* from cover to cover
and declared it excellent. But he studied all the religious papers, and when he was in New York he had
them posted out to him regularly. Often he spent an
hour in the Free Library at Birmingham glancing over
the files of the Scottish, London and Provincial papers.
They constantly furnished grist for his mill. Nothing
that engaged public attention escaped him. He
attended Christian Science meetings to find the secret
of their cheerfulness, and his interest in Couéism is
described by his friend, Rev. John Loosmore, as
intense and pathetic. Parliamentary debates were read
almost slavishly by him, and an hour in the gallery
of the House of Commons was one of his delights.

He was the Autolycus of the pulpit, picking up unconsidered trifles and beating them into exquisite illustrations.

The value of preparing his own mind and heart for the conduct of public worship was fully appreciated by Jowett.

> He would (says Rev. John Loosmore, who entered into Jowett's innermost life with deep intimacy) retire early on Saturday night, after a restful evening with his wife and daughter, in order to be up early on Sunday morning. Before breakfast he would play on the American organ and sing some favourite hymns. Then family prayers would come. It was a great privilege to join in his wonderfully beautiful, quiet and helpful prayers before breakfast. After the meal he would retire to look over his sermon once more. On the way down to Carr's Lane by train from Moseley he would seek a solitary compartment and read, perhaps, one of Spurgeon's sermons for the sake of its atmosphere. Then he would arrive at Carr's Lane bearing in his mind the ordered and familiar results of a week's honest toil, and in his heart the glorious purpose of the Christian redemption.

The common supposition that Jowett preached without manuscript was utterly unfounded. He invariably took his full notes into the pulpit, and he read every word. Dr. Griffith-Jones—on their transatlantic voyage together—remarked to Jowett that he seemed independent of his manuscript.

> " I may seem to be so," replied Jowett (writes Dr. Griffith-Jones), " but I am not. My method is to think out a sermon beforehand, then write it fully and read it carefully over three or four times. I am then word perfect. But I must always have my MS. before me, or I am lost. I turn the pages over, and once I see the first word of a page, I know all that comes to the end of the page. If I had not the MS. there I should get into a panic, and possibly

forget what was coming. My method of delivery is to ' think ' each sentence over as it comes, so that however often I may repeat a sermon I go through the whole process of thought each time I give it, as though it were the first. A mere mechanical repetition of a sentence would be impossible and repellent to me as an honest man. As soon as a ' traveller ' becomes too familiar I drop it for some other subject. In this way I am able to keep myself fresh in delivery and, I suppose, to put the right expression into each word."

Continuing the conversation, Dr. Griffith-Jones told Jowett he had always envied him his elocution and management of his voice, and asked him how he had mastered the art of public speech to such perfection.

He at once turned upon me in surprise (writes Dr. Griffith-Jones) and said he had never studied elocution under anyone—had never taken a lesson in the art in his life; he simply spoke and used gestures without any conscious art at all, but only as the thought or emotion he was expressing prompted him at the time. Then, very impressively and lovingly, he said, " If I owe anything to anyone for such gifts of speech as I may possess, I think I owe it all to my dear Mother. She was one of the most beautiful speakers I ever met. She had a great command of words and could tell a story with inimitable effect. She was full of a natural eloquence and humour."

On Saturday nights, the week's work in the study finished, Jowett would join his wife and daughter round the fire with their books—for he was essentially a home-lover—and he would often say to Mrs. Jowett with a glad note in his voice, " I have a great message for my people to-morrow." Work was his consuming passion, and the sense that he was doing it well was a benison to his soul. It was all the reward he sought.

CHAPTER XIV

IN LIGHTER MOODS

A LONDON journalist who described Jowett as a "flame in ice" gave Jowett's intimate friends occasion to smile. They knew better. Behind a veil of apparent austerity, which was an amalgam of shyness and modesty, there was an inexhaustible vein of Yorkshire warm-heartedness in his nature—expansive, affectionate, unconcealed. Among his intimate friends he bubbled over with sheer gaiety of spirit. A shrewd sense of humour—which, like all his qualities, he attributed to his Mother—was an endowment that he both prized and cultivated. For a happy story or a bright witticism he was always ready, and his ringing laugh was infectious. His home, in his interludes from work, resounded with his hearty laughter. A sense of humour, he often said, was essential to a Christian minister if he is to keep his spirit fresh and buoyant. "If our equipment for the knowledge of man is to be even passably complete," he told the theological students at Yale, "we must exercise a genial sense of humour by whose kindly light we shall be saved from pious stupidities and from that grotesqueness of judgment which sees tragedy in comedy and griffins in asses and mountains in molehills." "I have always preached," he said at Carr's Lane, "that laughter is a part of piety," and in a letter written to his daughter at school he told her that "a bit of humour is a good

R

safeguard against a too narrow and bitter theology."
He defined humour as " a certain juicy moistness
which—like the humour of the eye—helps vision, and
a certain geniality of spirit which preserves life from
hardness—not," he was careful to explain," the petty
triflings of the punster or the unconsidered flippancies
of the comic spirit." What Henry Ward Beecher
called " the countenances of constitutionally dismal
Christians " repelled him, and David Brainerd's
saying that " there is nothing that the devil seems to
make so great a handle of as a melancholy humour "
was one of his guiding maxims. Jowett hated forced
seriousness as much as he hated levity. He dis-
criminated between sobriety and melancholy, but in
his sobriety he left a large place for healthy laughter.
He loved children and was perfectly at home with them.

My earliest memory of father (writes his daughter
Monica) was when I was about three years old. Every
morning, never later than six o'clock, I sat up in
my cot asking for Blackie and Grey, and then father
would begin, or rather continue, his tireless story
of the erring young cats, Blackie and Grey. Their
adventures continued for nearly two years, varying
with our own movements. If we were at Malvern,
then Blackie and Grey climbed the Beacon with
uncanny mishaps. Local colour was always supplied,
and the interest never flagged. Finally we left
them, having fallen off the pier at Cromer and going
home in wet clothing for a deserved scolding.

Then there was Christmas with the children's
party. Father was the centre and soul of these
parties and he became for the time just one of us.
It was he who started all the games, told the story
of General Post and wherever the crowd of laughing,
shouting children was the thickest father was in the
centre, more often than not entirely lost beneath a
scrambling party of would-be elephant riders.

I remember one Christmas when he and mother had arranged one of the early phonographs in the chimney in my nursery. It was the kind that plays the home-made cylindrical records. First they prepared the record—father speaking as Santa Claus to each member of the party by name. After supper, the nursery door was unlocked and we all trooped in to hear Father Christmas. It was as much a surprise to me as to the others. When Father Christmas finally said good-bye and we heard him scrambling up the chimney, father pulled a string and a load of parcels, all snowy with cotton wool, came tumbling down into the grate, and scrambling among them all, we each found one bearing our own name.

Children, even strange children, never showed the slightest fear or shyness with father, and he was always perfectly at home with them. His never failing imagination developed the most extraordinary things from an old key ring, and I shall never forget " Markey," a three-fold pocket magnifying glass which in father's hands became—well anything and everything a child could wish.

He loved making things for me and they were always original things. I remember one late Summer when we were staying at Wyche near Malvern. It had been very hot that year, and the bracken lay parched on the hillside. So father made me a sledge on thick wooden runners and on this I spent my time tobogganing every hill. And then when winter came he always flooded our top lawn, and there gave me and my staggering friends our first lessons in skating.

Whenever Jowett was inveigled into the after-dinner speech, he almost invariably started a continuous ripple of laughter.

Sometimes on public occasions his humour " would out " and an unfamiliar Jowett revealed himself. When Mr. Silvester Horne completed twenty-five years in the ministry and celebrated the occasion at

Whitefields, many of his friends in the ministry gathered to pay him tribute. Rev. Thomas Yates, who succeeded Mr. Horne at Kensington, commented playfully upon the array of eminent preachers on the platform and with happy audacity offered a few parodies of the sermons the distinguished preachers might preach with Silvester Horne as their text. Jowett did not conceal his glee when Mr. Yates imitated his easily recognised methods of sermon-making, and he joined heartily in the laughter. When his turn came to speak, Jowett declared that whenever he tried to make a speech he invariably preached a sermon. And he had, he said, thought of a sermon about Silvester Horne. He recalled the audacities of Silvester Horne's early ministry and said he thought that " Let no man despise thy youth " would be the inevitable text. The divisions would be simple and obvious—first " The Youth," second " The Despising " and third " Let anybody try it on."

Humour had its place and he gave it its place, but he had a positive dread of witticisms in the pulpit. " I have always," he wrote to a friend, " sought to avoid them, and I have thought that a danger signal was ringing when I unconsciously aroused the suppressed laughter of my congregation." He felt that there is so much that is frivolous and flippant in common life that the exercises of the sanctuary cannot be too serious and devout and dignified. But while studiously keeping humour out of the pulpit, he just as studiously cultivated it in his intimate relationships and his letters, or at least those he wrote to two or three friends from whom no secrets were hid, coruscated with happy conceits and jollities.

I really think (he wrote to Mr. J. G. Hurst, in reply to a congratulatory telegram, on being made a D.D. of Edinburgh) that a Doctor ought to write in red ink ! But perhaps mentioning the colour will do all that's wanted. Eh ! it's grand to be a doctor ! The " elevation " it gives you is fine.

Since I got it the Malverns have shrunk into molehills, and as for the Welsh Hills I " havena' seen 'em." Everybody seems to be looking at me, I walk wi' such dignity ! And all so natural like ! The D.D. gets at once into your legs : they say it mounts at last into your " nut," and I'm living in hourly expectancy that the doctorial sap will reach that lofty eminence. I'll be sure and write when it does.

Meanwhile I have been thinking of my deacons. Words fail me ! They look like ants ! I'm just amazed at the revelation. For fifteen years I've deluded myself into thinking that they were men : Man, they're just midges. Doctors of Divinity call them " ephemera," and that's just what they look like.

No wonder you sent a telegram ! A letter would have been paltry. It was sixpence well spent. If D.D.'s did such things I should thank you for it. But I've " nae doot " ye're just glowing.

Yours majestically,
THE DOCTOR.

The grim figure of John Knox even suggested comicalities to Jowett.

I have just been reading (he wrote from New York to Mr. Hurst in 1913) the life of John Knox over again. Eh, man, but John was a Tartar. I wonder how his somewhat volcanic temperament would have stood our experiences in that hotel at Dundee. I think another article would have been added to his creed, if he had seen those scones. And I wonder what would have been the length of his reforming face if he had seen that cake unearthed from antiquarian lore ! Eh, Joss, Johnny Knox would have had a bug !

Satirical banter crept occasionally into his letters.

> I see (he wrote to Mr. Hurst from New York
> in 1915) that you have been holding forth on the
> 20th anniversary of the death of Dale. Did you
> wear mourning, or were you satisfied with a ring
> of crepe on your arm? Rather a lively topic for
> war time! By the way, John Angell James died
> 50 years ago. Why not have another, wearing
> the crepe on the other arm? And by the way
> again, wasn't there a William Bullivant who died
> 75 years ago? Wouldn't it be exhilarating to
> unearth that brother, and hold a wake? In fact
> you might have a cheerful winter of it! Still
> you are engaged in a worthy pilgrimage in seeking
> out these footprints on the sands of time. Mean-
> while I'm thankful that I'm alive. However, if
> you take my hint, and have a series of them, one
> every week, you might let me have a programme
> so that I can reserve the hours for silent meditation!

A whimsical description of a Billy Sunday Revival
meeting enlivens a letter written from New York in
April 1917, just after his decision to return to England.
It was addressed to Mr. Hurst :—

> As I have just been to hear Billy Sunday, the
> cultured evangelist : and as he addressed me as a
> " white-livered, black-hearted mug," I think I'll
> pass the compliment on to you. His tabernacle
> holds 20,000, and the ministers are penned in an
> enclosure immediately on Billy's right, and as
> he knows just where we are, he fires his torpedoes
> at us before we even show a periscope. He lets
> go a fiery shot at us and then retires across his
> huge platform making sile-t n~-'s at us. At one
> moment, observing that one or two of us looked
> slightly resentful, he raced a&̲   ds us
> shouting, " I don't care whether your collars are
> buttoned at the front or the back." That was
> too much for me, and if I hadn't had a collar round
> me, in the shape of a Jaeger belt, one of Billy's

audience would have gone all to pieces, and would have been seen no more.

Another pleasant remark he made in the course of a sermon on Pentecostal power, a remark which he addressed to the 10,000 women who were present, was this, " Never mind your spring cleaning ! Come out to the services ! The bugs have been there so long, they'll do no harm by staying a few weeks longer." What about that for Carr's Lane ? Wouldn't there be a squealing from those vaults under the " long-drawn aisles " ? Another classic remark which will bear quotation was as follows : " What we want is stewards that will stew, and deacons that will deac ! "

Then the evangelist deplored the way in which the church runs to machinery and organisation while the vital personal element is lost. Regarding which he ventured this remark : " I expect to read before long that somebody has invented an electro-huggographo-squeezeophone so that a fellow can stand in New York and hug and kiss his girl in Chicago ! " What about that 4000 miles of briny Atlantic when Billy's invention comes along ? But Billy's a rum 'un. I have never heard his like. As to his significance, that's another matter. But he has given me many a good laugh in a very serious week, and perhaps his humour is the best part of his endowment.

We both need those old walks to Barnt Green and a few times of laughing till we ache. I want some of those old laughing times back again. My ! how I've missed them.

A letter congratulating his friend Rev. John Loosmore on his appointment as a Pelman School examiner has its glint of humour :—

You must have got hold of an extraordinarily interesting piece of work. . . . I have sometimes thought of taking the Pelman course ; it would be a prime lark if my papers went to you for examination.

From the South of France, when he was recruiting his strength in the winter of 1921 he wrote :—

Sospel,
Mentone,
March 25, 1921.

To Mr. J. G. Hurst, K.C.

I have been watching thy planet in its wide orbit—King's levees, complimentary dinners to Viceroys, etc., etc. But much as levees, etc. make me envious, thy weight makes my " thin hair " straighten out with emulation. Dost thou say twelve stone five? Whence came it, dear brother? I abide at 10s. 4 lb. stedfast and immovable. Is it law or grace that is adding the avoirdupois? I wouldn't mind climbing into the pulpit at West (Good old West : Mrs. H. loves that name : so do I) *à la* Sir John Falstaff, but I cannot find the particular brew of sack to do it. Fancy the looks of the Westminsterians if they saw me with Sir John's environment. I fairly missed it when I turned from the bar. There's something in the mineestry that ill fits good digestion. Muz flourishes, and so does your beloved; but their secret is hid. I am a lean pantaloon.

. . . By the way, have you any spare francs? Is the bar running over? Deflect the gracious stream to Sospel! I find that sixpence doesn't go very far. Man, it's just astonishing how the bawbees fly. Well, I'll put my blinkers on and trudge on.

The hotel is very quiet—perhaps thirty or thirty-five all told. The Bishop of —— is here, but we haven't touched yet. John Ediwardy * can't play up to his Lordship. But I can beat him

---

* When Jowett was a very small boy, a still smaller boy with an impediment in his speech, used to come to Jowett's mother and say, " Please Mimi Dado, can your John Ediwardy come out to play? " The name stuck, and by one or two of his most familiar friends Jowett was sometimes called John Ediwardy. In fun he occasionally used it himself.

at " legs." To think of being reordained by anybody with legs of this order is incredible. If the Lord took pleasure in the legs of a man, the whole Episcopal bench would be disqualified. No ! in legs we have it. And with our laity at twelve stone 5 we have them there too.

A month later he returns to Mr. Hurst's 12 stone 5 in a mood of merry raillery :—

> Well, that extra avoirdupois of yours ! I can't forget it. Perhaps it is the erratic record of a " penny in the slot " and the species flatters you for all you are worth. There's one at Croydon Station—a perfect dream of a machine for sending the figure up. I never give a penny away with more delight—every time up to 13 stone. I walk away like an Alderman. But there's one down at Cannes—a mean little beggar in a chemist's shop that gets the staggers, and trembles, and stops a little above 9 ! " Croydon for me," say I.

Occasionally Jowett courted the poetic muse— confessing that his Pegasus was an unwilling pony— but what verses have survived the waste-paper basket reveal a blithe spirit rather than a natural gift for versification. If he ever attempted serious poetry he seems to have abandoned it early and, like Disraeli, to have " hurled his lyre to limbo." A few lines written to Sir Evan Spicer on his seventieth birthday strike a facetious note with an undercurrent of affectionate regard.

At Seventy.

I used to think that seventy was far on in the years,
Autumn time of falling leaf and catching breath and fears.
that's the baldest nonsense, as now I've learned to sing,
It isn't even summer time : it's only late spring.

How can a man be growing old who's fond of birds and flowers ?
And loves to play upon the turf, and saunter through the bowers ?
If you would see a real young man, then kindly please take note,
A bird sings in his laughter, and a flower is in his coat.

If capacity to appreciate a joke against one's self is the criterion of a true sense of humour, Jowett stands the test. He was travelling in the North on one occasion when a woman got into the railway carriage and straightway announced that she had just come out of " quod "—for being drunk. Jowett asked her about her parents. " My mother is dead," she said, "and there isn't an honester angel in heaven." He tried to put in a timely word against drinking; but she shut him up at once. " You look as if you had had a drop yourself " she said—to the infinite amusement of Jowett, who told the story afterwards with great glee.

He loved to tell one story that recoiled, boomerang-like, upon himself, about a holiday visit he paid with Mrs. Jowett to a quiet village on the North-east coast. On the Sunday morning he went to the village chapel and took his seat almost unnoticed among the little congregation. The time approached for beginning the service, but the preacher for the day had not arrived. The deacons consulted together anxiously, and agreed to ask the stranger if he would take the service in the emergency. Jowett said he " would try." He preached a sermon with which he was familiar—one that had served well at Carr's Lane, and as a " traveller," but he found the congregation strangely unresponsive. The deacons expressed their thanks to him for getting them out of their difficulty. Later in the week one of the religious newspapers announced that Mr. Jowett of Birmingham was holiday-making at ——. On the Friday a deputation from the village church waited on Jowett at his lodgings and asked he would preach on the following Sunday. Astonished at the request, Jowett answered, " But I preached for you last Sunday!" " Oh, yes, we know that," replied the spokesman of the deputation, " but we did not know then that you were Mr. Jowett of Carr's Lane Chapel."

A very characteristic touch of Jowett's humour leaps from a note addressed to one of his Carr's Lane deacons.

> I am delighted with your most gracious and generous " arrangements." You see, I am " groping " for a word.

Evidently there must have come to his ears a story, probably quite apocryphal, which circulated in varying guises for many years, of a commercial traveller who dropped casually into Carr's Lane Chapel one Sunday night and heard Jowett preach. In the course of the sermon Jowett paused and said " I am groping for a word." He waited for a moment, then seemed to snatch the very word he required out of the air and proceeded with his discourse. On the Thursday following, the same commercial traveller was at Halifax and saw a poster announcing that Jowett was to preach that evening at Square Church. He stayed to hear him. Jowett, quite naturally, preached the sermon he had given at Carr's Lane on the preceding Sunday evening, and once again he paused and, feeling the air with outstretched hand, said " I am groping for a word." The note to his deacon indicates that the story, whether true or not, amused Jowett himself and carried no barbed point.

> It will astonish some people (writes Rev. Edgar Todd) to know that no one could be more ir̄ ̄sibly ridiculous. The first time I saw this co ̄   ̄n, it startled me. I had a horrible dread that it was some terrible consequence of overstrain. It was nothing of the sort. It was first class comedy, but almost unbelievable. His whole aspect changed.

One eyelid drooped dolefully, the other eye took on a
stare of stupid vacuity. His mouth became loose
and he spoke with the broadest West Riding accent.
I always called this person " Billy " when he emerged
and he would sometimes emerge on the most unlikely
occasions. I never quite got over my first astonish-
ment at it, and Jowett knew it and sometimes put it
on for that very reason.

Like all ministers Jowett occasionally received
anonymous letters commenting with varying degrees of
disparagement upon his sermons. One correspondent,
who always wrote on a post-card and in the second
personal singular, peppered him with messages, thus :—

Friend, thy supply was above the average. The
matter was good but the style was poor.
Thy head is like Shakespeare's. They are both
bucket-shaped.
Thou art a marvel. What a lot thou makest out
of a rubbish heap.

These candid comments gave Jowett no concern. His
sense of humour was proof against little darts of that
type. He showed them to his friends.

When a man, obviously irresponsible, strode one
Sunday up the pulpit steps of Carr's Lane when Jowett
was preaching and announced in a loud voice that he was
Judas Iscariot, Jowett's ready humour obviated an
awkward situation. " Oh," he said, in a tone of kindly
surprise, " then take a seat, please." The man sat
down looking perplexed at the unexpected welcome
and remained seated until a deacon entered the pulpit
and quietly led him out.

Once in a way Jowett's equable temper gave way
under extreme provocation. After a service at Carr's
Lane one Sunday a young man made his way to the
vestry and told Jowett in a rude tone that his sermon

was all wrong. "There is no shadow with God," he said. Jowett asked him to what church he belonged. "To the Church of Christ," was the answer. "Yes, but what building does it worship in?" "None, it is the Church of Christ." "Then," said Jowett, "you are one of those men who pester ministers who are foolish enough to let you into their vestries." "That's a lie," the young man truculently replied. "There's only one reply to that," said Jowett, who promptly took the man by the coat-collar and bundled him out of the room.

On their bicycles Jowett and Mrs. Jowett made many long holiday tours, and for health's sake Jowett exercised for a time on horseback, but the only sport in which he delighted was golf. He enjoyed the game far better than he played it. When I once asked Sir William Robertson Nicoll to be one of a team of journalists to play a team of ministers, he replied that he thought he had better not as "my golf is a thing best played 'at dead of night with the lanterns dimly burning.'" Jowett's golf was of about equal calibre with Sir William's. His score usually pendulumed between a hundred and a hundred and fifty—which in serious golfing circles is regarded as evidence of assiduity rather than an aptitude for the "Royal and Antient" game. As befitted a good Yorkshireman, he followed cricket in the newspapers, and took a patriotic pride in the Yorkshire team. Though he did not play tennis he liked to watch it, and he spent a long happy day at Wimbledon during the summer Championship Tournament of 1922. He knew the literature of fishing, especially Izaak Walton's "Compleat Angler," and while he admitted that he was a poor hand with a rod himself, he got the suggestion for one of his very best sermons on preaching from that classic.

Gardening was a perennial joy to Jowett. At Clydesdale, his home at Moseley, on the outskirts of Birmingham, he had a garden that was a never-failing source of interest and pleasure to him. He watched all its changing moods and colours and phases with eager eyes. Without claiming to be an expert horticulturist, he loved to " potter " about the flower-beds and occasionally to earn a little honest backache by a spell of real spade work upon mother earth. A neighbour at Croydon who saw Jowett in his shirt sleeves building a chicken run, saw nothing exceptional. He had no indoor recreations and played no games : but he could always spend a pleasurable hour over an " odd job " about the house. One room in his home was always set apart as a " carpenter's shop."

In his lighter moods, especially when on holiday, Jowett was as care-free as a child. He loved the Yorkshire moors, but the island of Arran claimed his fondest allegiance, and when in America his thoughts flew often to the heather-clad hills around Corrie. In one of his merriest letters written from New York to Mr. Hurst—who with Mrs. Hurst and their family frequently made holiday with the Jowetts at Arran—he played upon the figure he was going to cut in " plus four " tweed knickerbockers and " looking like a squire out collecting the rents." Three letters to Miss Alice Slater reek of holiday abandonment :—

Arran, N.B.,
29 *August*, 12.

A thousand thanks for your kind Birthday remembrance and for all the varied tokens which expressed it. They " went off " admirably. You should have seen me sporting the tie, waving the flag and holding aloft the umbrella. Fardy Hurst was yellow with envy ! He hasn't a tie in his well-stocked drawer that is within miles of it. His colours are all dull compared with my aurora. Let me congratulate you on your choice as I indeed congratulate myself on its possession. All your gifts will cross the Atlantic.

New York,
May 27, 1913.

This is just to say that when you get this letter we shall be on the water. Hurrah! How can we sing the Songs of Zion in a strange land? Yes, but in Arran we not merely sing them : we shout them. We " cry aloud and spare not." I am going to practise deep breathing on the Atlantic so that I can make the barrister hide his thin wheeze in shame and confusion of face.

Llandrindod,
24 June, 1913.

This is the laziest man in broad England. I wish I could give you his type in the Old Testament, but my knowledge cannot drag out the necessary Patriarch. Isn't there something somewhere about somebody " waxing fat," and doesn't it go on to say that he " kicked "? That is something like it, only in my case I'm afraid I'm too fat to kick. And isn't there something somewhere about " settling on the lees "? . . . You might just look up all the references to the fat people and the easy-going pilgrims, and you will have glimpses of the returned missionary from New York. They say the climate of New York is like champagne. I do not quite know what cordial I should use to describe the climate here. It wouldn't have to be one of the gingery ones. . . . Still I'm lazy and I'm not ashamed. My mind is lying fallow. I run over it occasionally with a novel, but that does not leave a seed, nor does it awaken one. I suppose you never feel like this : I am very sorry for you !

CHAPTER XV

CAMPAIGNING FOR PEACE

(*Æt.* 58–59)

THE Peace Campaign to which Jowett dedicated the last six months of his active life—for which, in fact, in sober truth, he sacrificed his life—in the early Winter of 1922 was not born of any sudden impulse. His New York ministry, bringing him into close acquaintance with the conditions of life in the United States—where the peoples of the nations who exist in enmity in Europe dwell in amity side by side under the Stars and Stripes—had developed in Jowett an " international mind." He returned to England from America cherishing hopes, as most high-minded people did, that the end of the war would be followed by a stable peace in Europe. In that hope he was grievously disappointed. But what concerned him most profoundly was the reluctance of the Free Churches in England to slough the war mind and to cast out the spirit of hate that had sprung up, choking all charity, during the fierce struggle. I heard him express, very strongly, in conversation with an eminent Free Church minister his conviction (though he had not actually reached the pacifist position, he said he could never give his support to another war) that if the Christian Churches, should another war occur, followed the precedent they had set themselves, in all the nations, when the war broke out in 1914, the very future of the Church itself would be in grave danger. He argued

DR. JOWETT (AT THE AGE OF FIFTY).

[*To face p.* 256.

this view with a touch of asperity, such as he rarely displayed, and it was clear then that his mind was uneasy. Indications of growing concern were given in several sermons at Westminster, and on May 7th, 1922 (while the futile Conference at Genoa was in progress), he spoke out with a passionate vehemence that had been awaiting expression for months. The broad suggestion he made was that a world Conference of Christians should be summoned to endeavour to solve, face to face, the problems which the politicians were showing themselves incapable of solving. Give Christianity a chance to settle Europe, he cried. Let the Archbishop of Canterbury, the Cardinal Archbishop of Westminster and the leaders of the Free Churches of Britain summon a world Conference to open out the channels of Christian understanding, sympathy and goodwill.

Suppose (he said) that during the coming week, instead of a meeting of the Congregational Union of England and Wales we had a Conference of enthusiastic Christians, drawn from every nation in Europe, nay, from every nation in the world! Suppose we had enthusiastic Christians coming here, sent as the ambassadors of their Churches—some from France, some from Germany! . . . " Ah, now you are dreaming! There you touch the impossible. Talk practical politics, and we will listen to you! " Yes, but the impossible is just the way of Christ, as indeed it was just the way of the Cross. In all merely business reckoning the biggest impossibility that has ever darkened this planet displayed itself at Calvary. And yet, in that impossibility all human possibility was born, and from that bleak terminus roads open out to the very heart of God's bright heaven. So that the impossible need not daunt us.

s

Behind the politicians and the diplomatists and the militarists and the destructionists there were, Jowett believed, in every nation vast, silent perplexed multitudes of people yearning to see peace on earth, goodwill among men.

> Let this Conference then (he said) be held and let its members meet in the name of the Lord Jesus, face to face—Briton and German, and American and French, and Austrian and Russian and representatives from every Christian nation in the world—let them meet and survey the world in the spirit and purpose of Him who died for the world. And who knows but that in such an assembly we have the embryo of a fellowship which will shape the destinies of mankind?

This appeal from the Westminster pulpit received wide publicity in the English Press and was cabled all over the world. The response showed that the Christian world had been waiting for some such tocsin.

Jowett was overwhelmed with letters of appreciation and promises of support. On appearing on the Congregational Union platform two or three days later he received an ovation which indicated that his co-denominationalists were ready to march under his standard. It happened that on the same morning the Dean of Worcester was speaking from the platform of the Congregational Union on behalf of the World Alliance for Promoting International Friendship through the Churches. The World Alliance was actually preparing for an International Conference of all the non-Roman Churches of Europe, America and Japan to be held in Copenhagen in the following August, and the Dean was seeking the co-operation of British Congregationalists in that enterprise. Jowett's pronouncement had created an atmosphere of enthusiastic sympathy, and Dr. Moore Ede found he was engaged in forcing an open door. Thirty years previously the Dean and Jowett had been neighbours in the North— Dr. Moore Ede being Vicar of Gateshead when Jowett was ministering in Newcastle, just across the Tyne. After some playful reminiscences of their earlier associations the Dean explained that the Copenhagen Conference would be just such a Conference as Jowett had suggested, and he asked that the Congregational Union should send him to Copenhagen as its representative.

Jowett spent the weeks between May and August in the North of England recuperating his strength. Up to the last moment it was doubtful whether his health would allow him to go to Copenhagen, but he finally decided to take the risk. The crossing to Denmark tried him severely, and he arrived with Mrs. Jowett at Copenhagen inexpressibly wearied by the exhausting railway journey through Holland and Germany and up the Baltic coast. He looked pathetically feeble when he arrived at the Palast Hotel; but a night's rest revived his spirits and energies, and day by day his sojourn in Copenhagen seemed to renew his strength. He enjoyed to the full the fellowship with friends from America like Dr. Nehemiah Boynton, Dr. Merrill, Dr. Jefferson, Dr. Faunce, and with Continental leaders of thought and life like Professor Deissmann, Dr. Julius Richter, Dr. Wilfred Monod and the Archbishop of Uppsala, as well as happy fraternity with Britishers like the Bishop of Oxford, Sir Willoughby Dickinson and Dr. Alexander Ramsay. This Copenhagen Conference was his first experience of an international convention, and the babel of tongues and the quaint costumes worn by some of the South-eastern Europeans delighted him. He scarcely missed a

session in the Studenterforeningen, and he attended all
the public gatherings and services connected with the
Conference.   Jowett had promised to write an article
about the Conference for *The British Weekly*, and with
his inveterate conscientiousness he allowed this responsibility to become a burden.   During the sessions he
deserted the block of seats reserved for the British
delegates, and in order to be nearer the tribune and
the interpreter's desk he sat among the Roumanian
delegates close to the platform, taking voluminous
notes for his article—ten times as many as he could
possibly use.   " I'll never undertake to report a Conference again," he said to me with a sigh.   " It isn't
my job.   You seem to take it in your stride, but it's
hard work for me."

The swiftly changing moods and tenses of the
Conference cast a spell over Jowett.   An international
Conference is like the surface of an inland lake—
placid for hours together and then, caught by a sudden
breeze, lashed into a furious squall.   Jowett watched
these alternating moods with curiosity and amusement.
Quite candidly he had confessed that though he had
advocated holding such a conference he had been
sceptical as to whether anything of any value could
be achieved by it.   The Copenhagen Conference
dispelled his doubts.

Jowett spoke only once at Copenhagen and then for
scarcely ten minutes.   His intervention came during a
session devoted to disarmament.   The purpose of the
discussion, obviously fraught with difficulties, was to
ascertain what degree of common agreement could be
reached by Christians from all over the world upon the
general question of national armaments.   The issue
brought the German and French delegates into sharp,
clashing antagonism.   Professor Deissmann, speaking

for the German delegates, argued that Germany had been disarmed, but that her disarmament had been achieved by chicanery and by a violation of one of President Wilson's " Fourteen Points " (expressly confirmed by Mr. Lansing, the American Secretary of State, in a letter written on Nov. 5th, 1918, the eve of the Armistice), that disarmament would be general. That promise, Dr. Deissmann insisted, had been broken. " Germany," he declared, " was disarmed and the experts of the Allies recognised it." " We see more soldiers in Copenhagen than in Berlin." Meanwhile France retained her armaments and her armies stood threatening Germany. To Dr. Deissmann's vigorous indictment Dr. Wilfred Monod replied politely, but incisively, that France had not sufficient information to have confidence in the *bona fides* of the German Government and the German people. They had frustrated all the Hague proposals for reducing armaments, but now, in defeat, they sought general disarmament. The clash between Dr. Deissmann and Dr. Monod was conducted in terms of courtesy, but the buttons were off the foils. All that is implicit in national suspicion and fear and hate was manifest, even though it was concealed beneath the surface. Other European delegates took up the gage, and a touch of ferocity crept into the discussion.

It seemed as if a deadlock was inevitable and that the Copenhagen World Conference of the Christian Churches would have to disperse without being able to express any sort of unified opinion on so vital an issue as disarmament. Up to this point not a word had been spoken in the Anglo-Saxon language. No Englishman or American had taken the tribune. Under extreme pressure Jowett agreed to speak. He shrank from " butting in " (as he put it), but it was forcibly represented to him that silence on the part of all the American and English delegates would be gravely misconstrued, and that it might make a very undesirable impression outside the Conference. To this persuasion Jowett succumbed. His sense of duty impelled him again. He agreed to speak conditionally upon being allowed ten minutes in which to write his speech. It was no occasion, he said, for a hasty extemporisation. The Moderator, Dr. Nehemiah Boynton, was made acquainted with the circumstances, and allowed the discussion to rage furiously for another ten minutes before calling upon Jowett. The effect of Jowett's speech was magical. His gift of creating an " atmosphere " was never more dramatically displayed. His first sentences seemed like oil poured on the troubled waters, and the Conference which had been seething with bitter nationalistic feelings was calmed and sobered by his quiet tones and pacific spirit. It was a conquest of sheer personality. The only detailed report of Jowett's actual words appeared in *Goodwill*, the official organ of the World Alliance.

Dr. J. H. Jowett (says *Goodwill*) made an exalted appeal to the Christian spirit of the German and French delegates. Behind material disarmament, he said, was the deeper, more serious and more difficult matter of the disarmament of the mind. To uproot the prejudices out of which misunderstandings arose would do more to make armaments unnecessary than the activities of the Governments. The greatest enemies of peace were lurking fears and suspicions. Their biggest antagonists were illusions. Where did this envy, jealousy and suspicion come from? In the first place it was bred and nourished and cherished in the daily Press by its suppression of facts and perversion of facts, and by statements fashioned by the financial interests and not by moral ideals. He had recently spent six months in the South of France and saw his fellow-countrymen through the French Press and did not know them. When in the United States he saw England through the medium of the American Press and did not recognise his fellow-countrymen. If his French friends were in England they would not know their own land as reflected in the English Press. The first thing they had to do was to look beyond the Press and right over the Press and look at the people themselves. The peril to peace was the morbid patriotism bred by the Press. Patriotism was not something to be denied, condemned or discouraged, but they should cultivate that wider internationalism for which Christ stood and died. Dr. Jowett appealed to the Churches to be forces of reconciliation in the world.

No direct allusion was made in Jowett's speech to the question of disarmament which had created the perilous *impasse*. Evidently this omission was of set purpose. His aim was to lift the Conference " above the battle " into the rarefied spiritual airs where animosities and misunderstandings fade away. Before he sat down a wholly new mood had come over the Conference. He had distilled the dews of quietness. It was interesting to watch the tense faces of some of the European delegates as they listened to the interpreter's translation of Jowett's speech. Knowing no English, they had no doubt very hazy notions as to what he had been saying; but something in the man, his voice, his presence, the atmosphere he created had held them enchained. As at Pentecost " every man heard in his own language "—in the *lingua franca* of the soul. " An atmosphere of goodwill and of brotherly confidence proceeded from him," wrote Dr. Deissmann afterwards, adding, " I shall never forget the wonderful glance of his eye." After the interpreters had repeated Jowett's speech in French and German, Dr. Boynton, from the chair, ruled that the discussion should stand adjourned until the following day, on the understanding that Dr. Adolf Deissmann, Dr. Wilfred Monod and Dr. Hull (an American Friend who had introduced the disarmament resolution which had occasioned the furore) should spend the evening together in an endeavour to agree upon a new resolution. Jowett's cup must have overflowed next morning when a resolution upon which the German scholar and the distinguished French preacher had come to an agreement was proposed by Dr. Deissmann, seconded by Dr. Monod and carried with almost sacramental fervour by an upstanding vote. As the delegates sat down Dr. Deissmann and Dr. Monod were seen standing with hands clasped across the table. The episode was a triumph of Christian Grace, and had Jowett lived to preach on Grace after that memorable event, that scene would have furnished an incomparable illustration for the sermon. It is characteristic of Jowett's modesty that in *The British Weekly* article he made not the slightest mention of his own lion's share in this historic episode in International Christian relationships.

After the visit to Denmark Jowett went to the Yorkshire moors, and a short holiday there did him, he said, " no end of good." In a letter to Mr. John Pells he says : " I felt as I had not felt for years, and you can bet your boots that if I have any return of these things I go North again as fast as a train can take me." In the same letter Jowett makes it plain that Copenhagen was still exercising his mind.

We had a very great time at Copenhagen, and I am very glad I went. When I was invited to go I felt some reluctance. I was a little afraid of my journey : but it was worth any expenditure of strength and time. It was a very great experience to have a little share in drawing the Germans and French together, and in finding a common basis for the settlement of peace.

Croydon,
25 Aug., 1922.

To Miss Alice Slater.

It was a very wonderful experience (at Copenhagen) to have the Germans and French with us at breakfast and to find them moving to closer and more friendly fellowship. I wish that the Church of Christ in every land could put on courage like a robe ! . . . It is like moving mountains, but then we are told there is a way by which even mountains can be moved.

The Copenhagen Conference confirmed Jowett's faith in the League of Nations as the instrument for averting the renewal of war :

Croydon,
Sept. 2, 1922.

To Sir Ernest Hodder-Williams, C.V.O.

. . . I feel that the League of Nations has in custody all our hopes of international fraternity and peace. But what is to give the League its needful dynamic ? That is the crucial issue. On this everything depends. My suggestions are purposed to enable the Church of Christ to feed and invigorate the League by its solemnly expressed determination to stand for international righteousness, international goodwill and peace. I want to get the Church at the back of the League. How is it to be done ?

Out of his experiences at Copenhagen came Jowett's challenge to the Christian Church to array its ranks in solid phalanx for peace. His manifesto issued through *The British Weekly* (on September 7th, 1922)

under the title " What has the Church of Christ to
say ? " was addressed to the whole world and reached
it. He appealed to the Churches of Christ everywhere,
Greek, Roman and Protestant, to join in a three days'
Council of Peace, to be held in London, composed of
distinguished Christian men, not merely ecclesiastics
but drawn also from the wider realms of commerce,
art, literature and labour, broad-minded, deep-hearted
men with personal loyalty to Christ and a passion for
the Kingdom of God, to visualise and demonstrate the
existence of a corporate body which has in its custody
the moral ideals of Jesus Christ, and which intends to
give them their purposed sovereignty in the reconstruction of the world. The spirit of war, he said,
was still present; men were beginning to talk about
the next war. Explosive stuff was lying about all
over Europe. Some day a seemingly trifling match
might fire it. A great spiritual effort was needed to
put against the war spirit the assembled forces of the
great religions of mankind.

For this appeal Jowett had an extraordinary
" press." Almost every British and American paper
published some more or less detailed outline of its
proposals. Many leading articles were inspired by it.
Through Reuter's it was cabled over Europe, and
Press cuttings show that in the course of a few weeks
it penetrated to the remote corners of the globe. No
voice, unless it was the voice of President Wilson in
the later stages of the war, had been heard above the
clamour of the nations as Jowett's words of warning
and challenge were heard in that desperate hour when
it seemed as if all that had been sacrificed in the
war had been squandered in vain. The response was
instant. In a moment Jowett became an international
force. Christian leaders, of all communions, at home

and abroad, answered his call with promises to put forth their strength to make the spirit and will of peace prevail. The Archbishop of Canterbury was abroad, but the Archbishop of York, without committing himself to the idea of the suggested Council of Peace, expressed his readiness to co-operate. One of Jowett's letters to a personal friend shows how the encouragement he had received moved him to further endeavours—even though his health made them unwise.

Croydon,
Sept. 27, 1922.

Talk about correspondence : I am overwhelmed. I simply can't keep up with it. And as for the office of *The British Weekly*, it is snowed under. . . . If nothing more were done I feel that something has been accomplished. But we are moving to something more. We are getting our representative committee formed. I do not think we shall get the Catholics in, and I " hae my doots " about the Episcopalians. But with them, or without them, we must go on. I feel inclined to go on the stump and address half a dozen great meetings in the great provincial centres. More than ever I am convinced it's the provinces which move things and not London. London has no soul. I think I could get the Archbishop of York to go with me to these meetings, and that in itself would be a demonstration of something. . . . But I don't think I am made for running about. Perhaps as I get stronger I shall like it better."

Jowett had found in Sir Ernest Hodder-Williams an enthusiastic and resourceful coadjutor in his *British Weekly* Campaign. Sir Ernest exerted all his skill and deployed all his resources to make the bugle call heard round the world, and Jowett's gratitude for his colleague's efforts was frankly acknowledged :

Croydon,
November 23 1922.

To Sir Ernest Hodder-Williams, C.V.O.

You were altogether magnificent and I shall never forget it. You have done something that can never be undone, and, whether we succeed or not at the present time in formulating definite proposals, we have been able to focus the sentiment of peace throughout the Protestant world.

The idea of a national campaign in the great cities of England and Scotland soon took tangible shape. The Archbishop of York agreed to join Jowett in a series of meetings designed to prepare the Churches for a solemn dedication of Christendom to the cause of peace. Jowett organised the whole campaign himself, at an incredible expenditure of nervous and physical energy. At a time when he needed to conserve whatever strength he possessed he overstrained his depleted powers in preparing for this " last fight and the best," and he wore himself out by the travelling and desk work his campaign involved. In a letter to Rev. David Young, on November 1st, Jowett described the movement which he had inaugurated as " the strangest of all things " that had come his way.

If I were to judge myself I should conclude that I was the last of all men to be any sort of a leader in it. I have been much at Lambeth Palace lately in conference with the two Archbishops, and I am glad to say we have come to an agreement which will carry us a long way. One of our first arrangements is that the Archbishop of York and I should go to half a dozen great centres and hold big meetings of Church people of every order. That in itself will be a striking act of unity. Of course we shall wait until the election is over, and the meetings will be held between the election and Christmas. A definite scheme is also being devised for some corporate act, either

on Christmas Sunday or the first Sunday in the
New Year. The details of this have not yet been
formulated.

Immediately the turmoil of the election had subsided
Jowett launched his campaign. All the provincial
meetings had to be compressed into about a month,
and Jowett, who was still preaching regularly at
Westminster on Sunday mornings, showed signs of
acute strain under the effort. One or two meetings
which were planned had, indeed, to be abandoned.
However, a series of memorable meetings was held in
the great cities—the Lord Mayor in every case presiding. The Archbishop of York declared that he had
" rarely seen gatherings so large, so representative, so
intelligent, so enthusiastic." At the meeting at
Bristol the Archbishop said he was proud to stand
by the side of his friend Dr. Jowett as a humble
lieutenant, and he added that " when a Jowett was
carrying an Archbishop about England as his lieutenant
something was going to happen." Everywhere Jowett
had a rapturous hearing for his challenging speeches.

There was (wrote the Archbishop of York) no
mere rhetoric, no sentimentality. The argument
was clear and well thought out, commended by
incisive phrase, apt illustration, and a delightful
humour; and the appeal both to mind and heart
was enforced by a strong and sincere eloquence.
But what impressed me most was the spirit of the
man—a deep and passionate faith in the Kingdom of
God, the spiritual rule of Truth, Righteousness and
Love as the one supreme cause for the service of
personal, national, and international life; and this
combined with an inner quietness, almost detach-
ment, as of one who, knowing that his cause was
right, left the issue of his own striving for it in
God's hands.*

* *The British Weekly*, January 30, 1924.

The campaign reached its climax in a gigantic meeting in Queen's Hall, London, when Viscount Grey, Lord Robert Cecil and Mr. Philip Snowden spoke along with Jowett. " We need," Viscount Grey said, " the moral basis without which nothing prospers in human affairs, and it is men like Dr. Jowett who will give us that moral basis." Jowett's speech that night was his last public utterance as it was one of his happiest, most eloquent and most forceful. But he was obviously worn out by sheer fatigue and by the mysterious malady that was sapping his life blood. A few days later came a startling collapse.

After many consultations at Lambeth Palace between the Archbishops and Jowett it had been decided that the Peace Campaign should culminate in a " common act of worship " in all the churches on the Sunday before Christmas, which for many years has been set apart in Free Churches as " Peace Sunday." This custom is not so prevalent in Anglican churches; but the Archbishops made an urgent appeal to the parish clergy to dedicate Sunday, December 24th, 1922, to the cause of Peace. With this in view a uniform form of special prayer for peace was issued to all the churches, Anglican and Free, for use on that day. Since the Act of Uniformity was passed, just 260 years before, there had never been an occasion when a common form of prayer had been used in all the churches, and the issue of this special petition is consequently a point of peculiar moment and interest. At the request of the Archbishops Jowett wrote the prayer and, in view of its historical significance, it may be well to quote it here.

O God, our Father, who as at this time didst send Thy Son to be the Saviour of all men and the Prince of Peace, look, we pray Thee, in mercy upon the nations of the world, and prosper all counsels which make for righteousness and peace; forgive what Thou hast seen in us of selfishness and pride; remove far from us the tempers which provoke the spirit of strife; and grant us such a measure of the gentleness and patience of Thy Son, that we may live peaceably with all men and be by Thy blessing the makers of peace, through the same Jesus Christ our Lord. Amen.

In a joint manifesto the Archbishops of Canterbury and York, Dr. J. D. Jones, as Moderator of the Federal Council of the Free Churches, Rev. Samuel Chadwick as President of the National Free Church Council, and Jowett commended the use of this prayer to all the Churches, and further suggested that after joining in the prayer the individual worshippers in each church should solemnly and devoutly make an act of dedication or resolve, bracing themselves by the help of God against the things which make for war.

To Jowett's intense disappointment he was too ill to preach at Westminster Chapel on the Sunday set apart for the culmination of his own Peace Campaign. On the Saturday morning he was in good spirits, enjoying the company of old friends who were guests in his Croydon home for the Christmas season. But in the afternoon he was seized with pain, and his doctor, summoned early next morning, ordered him to stay in bed. A lay neighbour, Mr. David Williamson, was, at an hour or two's notice, secured to supply the pulpit at Westminster, where a vast congregation had gathered. Nowhere, perhaps, did the prayer and dedication have so solemn a response as in Jowett's own church. His unseen presence was felt, though it was not realised that in bodily presence he would not be seen again in the pulpit. The observance of Peace Campaign Sunday was general throughout the country— a fact which brought to Jowett, racked by pain, a rewarding sense that his arduous labours of the previous three months had, indeed, not been in vain. " I look

back upon the past year," he wrote to Sir Ernest
Hodder-Williams, "as one of the great times of my
life. *I think we did something together that will never
be undone. The impact of it has been felt round the
world.*"

One permanent outcome of Jowett's call to the
Churches to realise their responsibility for promoting
goodwill between the nations was the reconstruction,
on a representative basis, of the British Council of
the World Alliance for Promoting International Friendship through the Churches. At an informal little
conference, in which Jowett participated, held late one
night in the Bishop of Oxford's bedroom at Copenhagen, the suggestion was thrown out that the British
Council, which had up to then been a more or less self-
constituted body, should become the official organism
of British Christianity in the work of promoting goodwill between the nations. Later in the Autumn this
proposal was seriously considered at another small
Conference, held at Cuddesdon Palace. Jowett unfortunately was prevented by ill health from being
present, though he gave it his most cordial approval.
As a direct result there came into being the present
British Council of the World Alliance composed of
representatives, directly and officially appointed by
all the denominations in Britain, in some rough proportion to their numerical strength and influence. The
Council is the first permanent body in which Anglicans
and Free Churchmen, officially and authoritatively
appointed by their governing Assemblies and Unions,
have co-operated. A symbol of the growing unity of
the Churches for which Jowett worked and pleaded
in his later years, this British Council is, in some senses,
his memorial, since it carries forward the cause of
international goodwill on whose altar he laid the last
dregs of his ebbing vitality.

A PRAYER (1923).

My Father God, the day is breaking. Let the light of thy grace come as a sweet dawn upon my soul. Scatter the darkness of sin & ignorance. Let my eye be glorious with thy light, so that every faculty may be bathed in thy holy grace. Wash out of my soul my secret sin. Wash out my selfishness. Wash out my self-conceit. Wash out my inordinate passion. Wash out my touchiness. Wash out my censoriousness. Wash out any forwarding mood & temper which makes me hard and unsympathetic with others. Create within me a clean heart, O God! Let me be clothed in the robe of righteousness, & the garment of salvation. Let the beauty of the Lord be upon me, — the love of thy word & thy grace in me appear. Let this be a day of welcome into thy love.

[To face p. 272.

CHAPTER XVI

CLOSING DAYS

(*Æt.* 59–60)

" THERE is," said Samuel A. Tipple, " one chapter in the biography of distinguished persons—in the biography of a great genius, an eminent saint or seer —which has for us generally special interest, into which we are often most curious to dip—the chapter entitled ' Closing Days,' curious to learn how he bore himself, or what fell from his lips during those days in the shadow of the approaching end, to see something of the thoughts that then expressed his mind, or to hear something of his latest words. What of his behaviour, his expression, we ask, in his latest hours? The favourite pursuit—was its influence upon him then exemplified? The ruling passion—was it strong with him in death? "

The last year of Jowett's life was spent in the very valley of the shadow of death, but with the Shepherd Psalmist he could still say, " I will fear no evil: for Thou art with me; Thy rod and Thy staff they comfort me." His anchorage in the faith which he had proclaimed so confidently in the days of his strength held firm in the time of his weakness, and when his own life was ebbing away the spiritual comfort he had ministered to others served him and sustained his soul. During the year from the Christmas Eve when the shattering breakdown of his health came upon him until the eve of the following Christmas

T

when he made the " transition into the eternal day "
—to quote his own words about death—he passed
through long days and nights of desolating weakness.
But he bore it with invincible courage and never lost
heart.   There were flows as well as ebbs in the tides
of his waning strength, and with the slightest recovery
of strength came a rebound of spirits, and a recovery
of gaiety and humour.   His letters reflect his hopes
and fears.

Croydon,
5th January, 1923.

To Rev. Thomas Towers.
    I am dictating this from my bed, where I
have been spending Christmas.   I have felt my
strength failing for some time and was not entirely
surprised when the breakdown came.   My doctor
insists on certain limits and I have got to move
guardedly for some time.   All this means a somewhat new road to me and I take to it rather badly.

Baffled by the insidious disease—later diagnosed as
anæmia—the doctors ordered a rest and fresh-air cure
at Matlock.   Dr. Griffith-Jones, who was staying at
Smedleys, writes :—

    It was clear to me when we met at Matlock that
the end was not far off.   Mercifully he did not
realise this, and one of his favourite topics in conversation was his future plans when he got better.
His favourite idea was to take a city pulpit for a
short time each season and preach once a week on
a week day.   Of course I said, " You could get any
Free Church in London with joy and gladness, and
if the Dean of St. Paul's knew his business or was
free to follow his inclinations, you would willingly
get that—and Westminster Abbey too."   " Well,"
he laughingly said, " I must confess that I should
like to preach in the Abbey before I die."   He
returned to this subject more than once, as though

it were very near to his heart, and I encouraged him to talk about it, for it seemed to help him to forget his dire weakness, as he lay on the veranda of the Hydro, wrapped in blankets, fingering his Bible (which was always to hand wherever he was, and whatever he did). And there, on my return home, I left him, with the assurance that I would certainly travel up to town to hear his first sermon as Canon in residence at Whitefields, at which he laughed delightedly.

Matlock worked wonders for a while, and by March Jowett was well enough to accept Sir Arthur Black's hospitality at Sutton-on-Sea, where, again, he gained strength and weight rapidly. A jubilant, school-boyish outburst in a letter to Rev. John Loosmore, shows his responsiveness to new hope.

Sutton-on-Sea,
March 25, 1923.

My dear Loosebox.
        Now for a few correlations! You expert Pelmanisers, doff your guerdons and gaze in silence!
        No. 1.   Loosebox—soap-box—soap—Lever—Port Sunlight. What about that?
        But here's another :—
        No. 2.   Bolton-le-Sands—Bolton—Bolt—Bolt from the Blue—Blue Devils—John Ediwardy.
        Well, then, the next wonder in the process is as to how the sunshine was brought to the one possessed with Blue Devils. Simple as A.B.C. It was just three ha'pennyworth of postal miracle and your letter did it!
        Do you want to make a little money? Advertise in *The Daily Mail* or *The Lancaster Thunderer* —" I cast out Blue Devils! No money if no cure! Expulsion certain. Apply the Rev. etc., etc." And in answer to your applicants (at 5s. each) you would send one of your high explosive

letters, and out would go the blue ones like magic. You have got a fortune, brother.

Meanwhile in sheer gratitude I will put you on the track of another discovery. First of all you must assume that a dog is a tree. You cannot make any headway until that assumption is firmly laid. Everything depends on that. Well, then, a dog is a tree. Now let the tree be represented by the letter R. The third step is to arrange the dog and the tree and the symbolical R in such algebraical formula as will disclose in their issue the secret of the universe! That is as far as I have got, but there is a clear gleam of light on the horizon.

No, you are wrong! It ain't spirits which account for this letter. It is spirit—spirit, sir, without a degrading " S " in its tail. Spirit, sir, high spirit, good report, healthy spirit—of which an extra stone of flesh is the splendid and appropriate symbol! And as for liberty, I can now write with a pencil.* Not yet with a pen! If I try the pen the product is like a railway map of England, or the track of a fly which has just escaped from a pot of ink! My hand mistakes licence for liberty, but I expect that freedom is just a few weeks ahead.

Everything is now settled for the summer. We propose to make a state entry into Bolton-le-Sands † on May 1st. So you must be sure to have a clean collar on, and if you wish to wave a handkerchief, be sure it is a clean one too. Stand well back from the road, as we travel at a good pace! Just a flash and we are gone! I hope you will catch a glimpse of it.

I am looking forward with great delight to spending three months in your neighbourhood. You will give me much; I hope I may give a little in return.

---

* The letter was written in pencil, in almost indecipherable script, quite unlike Jowett's usual caligraphy.

† The Lancashire coast resort where Mr. Loosmore was living.

My wife, who is in boisterous health, sends her love to your missis " hopin' as it is the same with her."

After a month at Sutton-on-Sea he returned to Matlock for a little more treatment before going to Bolton-le-Sands. He was full of hope and cheer, and as usual eagerly interested in religious and political news and movements of the day.

Matlock,
April 20, 1923.

To Arthur Porritt.

. . . I am making decided progress, and though it is slow I am greatly cheered. It now looks as though some day I shall preach again.

So Berry * is going to the Memorial Hall. Frankly I'm sorry. It seems a destructive thing to take a fine preacher and put him in that office. Preachers are too rare for us to use them in that way. And Berry is making such strides in his calling. And then again preaching gifts are not those most required in the office. I would have set a competent layman at the job with business gifts, plus spirituality and vision ! I would have put —— in the office. " But there——"

Hutton for Westminster. . . . I think he will have a mighty ministry.

Please excuse this writing; my hands have been giving me trouble.

A week later he is writing again in cheerful strain to two of his friends.

Matlock,
April 27, 1923.

To Mr. J. G. Hurst, K.C.

. . . Of course I feel rather on a siding and it is good to know something of the movements on the main track.

* Rev. Sidney M. Berry, M.A., who succeeded Jowett at Carr's Lane, Birmingham, had been nominated for the Secretaryship of the Congregational Union.

Croydon,
Oct. 17, 1923.

To Rev. A. A. Lee.

Many thanks for your kindness in sending me the information about the dear old church. I think your programme of service for next winter is most attractive. You are fishing in many waters, you are using many baits, and I am sure there will be a wonderful reward to your toil. And best of all, and back of all, there is the evangelical gospel of the love of Christ, which is as broad as human need. That is the inspiration of your work, and that is why the sunshine of grace rests upon it.

Another letter shows his continued concern about the forms of public worship and the growth of his inclination towards liturgical services.

Croydon,
30th October, 1923.

To Arthur Porritt.

I wonder if I may interest you in the enclosed.* In the early part of the year, when we were staying at Matlock, we were greatly impressed with the devotional services at the little Congregational Church. Mr. Russell, the Minister, is a spiritual genius, and there was something about the Services which was quite unique. Every Sunday cards were distributed throughout the pews on which the Services for the day were printed, and they were exceedingly beautiful, and I know nothing quite like them. At my suggestion Mr. Russell has gathered these separate Services into a little book, and at his request I have written a short introduction. That is the whole of my interest in the matter. I am wondering if you will notice the little book in *The Christian World.* I think it is well worth recognition, and

* " Intercession Services—for Congregational use in Public Worship," by Rev. H. G. Russell.

if it were in general use it would greatly enrich the Free Church Services.

If I may just add a word about myself, my progress is very slow. Sometimes I get a bit discouraged, although the doctors tell me that with much patience I shall get out again.

New hopes were born out of a suggestion from the doctors that the removal of his home from Croydon to the crest of one of the Surrey Hills might prove reinvigorating. A house was found at Belmont, on the Epsom ridge—a house with a pretty garden on the edge of a noble down. The prospect buoyed his flagging spirits, but before the removal could be effected he had a relapse and came nigh unto death itself.

Croydon,
November 12, 1923.

To Rev. John Loosmore.

I am sending you a very short letter. I have been very ill and have not the power to send you more than a few words. I became suddenly worse a few weeks ago and I have had a hard fight. Indeed I thought the fight was over a fortnight ago. But I have turned the corner : and my old powers of recuperation are showing themselves. The doctors say by next Spring I may find myself a little freer.

We are soon leaving this house for a smaller house, just above Sutton, and I think the air up there will help me to get back my strength.

Mrs. Jowett read your letter to me to-day : I heard it with affectionate interest. I wish you could just look in and see me. I wish I could send you a letter to help you, but I am afraid I cannot dictate any more just now. I send my love. . . .

Save for a few short intervals when his flesh and blood cried out in weariness, Jowett had kept up his

" Meditations " in the columns of *The British Weekly*
during this period of bodily weakness. One of the
last he wrote closed with a *Nunc Dimittis*.

> If then, the " curfew tolls the knell of parting
> day," if the fair-day landscape is fading on the
> light, let the startled soul turn its face toward
> home. And home is not far away, for home is
> God, and God is as near as our glance, and vastly
> nearer than our cry. In trust and quietness let
> the darkened soul breathe these familiar words :—
>
> > Sun of my soul, Thou Saviour dear,
> > It is not night if Thou be near !
>
> or these words :—
>
> > Abide with me; fast falls the eventide;
> > The darkness deepens; Lord with me abide !
>
> or these words : " And lo ! it shall be found that
> the desolate hour becomes the hour of the Lord's
> visitation, and the night shall shine as the day."

When the time came for removal to the new home
at Belmont Jowett's physical force was clean forspent.
He had to remain in bed and he had not strength
sufficient to bear visits save from his dearest friends
and nearest relations. Three days before his death
he was visited by his friend from his Airedale College
days, Rev. John Loosmore, and he was able to talk
a little with him. " After my recent experience of
God," he said, " I have great things to tell men—
things men want to hear."

Happily as the end neared he experienced no pain
—he felt nothing but abject weariness and utter
weakness. But his cheerfulness never forsook him,
nor his sense of humour. Soon after he began his
ministry at Newcastle, one of his senior elders, " a
noble and stately figure who had done his Maker's
work in a great way," was stricken by mortal illness.
Jowett visited him when it was known that the old

man's end might come at any moment and found him reading "The Pickwick Papers." The dying man told his minister very simply that he had always been fond of Pickwick and he would not be ashamed when his Master came if He found him deep in the enjoyment of such innocent humour. Jowett never forgot it—he said it broadened all his conceptions of matured piety—and he faced his own end in the spirit of his old elder.

His last day was an epitome of his whole manner of life. The night had been broken, followed by extreme drowsiness, and when Mrs. Jowett went to him in the early morning for their accustomed family prayers she suggested that, as he was so weak, she should only read him a few verses of Scripture and not have prayer that morning. He assented, but when Mrs. Jowett had read the Beatitudes he quietly prayed in one sentence that the spirit of the words that had been read might sink into both their hearts and enrich their souls. An early afternoon sleep refreshed him. He chatted cheerfully, cracked a little joke or two with Mrs. Jowett with a flicker of his old merry humour, and laughed cheerily. Later he inquired if the evening paper had arrived. He wanted to see it. The Asquithian Liberals and the Lloyd George Liberals were meeting that day to try to compose their differences, and he said he was eager to know the result of the Conference. Mrs. Jowett brought the newspaper and was searching its columns for the report. But he could not wait. "Give me the paper," he said, "I shall find it quicker than you can." A typical day of his life—prayer, humour, public affairs—such was his last day.

> E'en as he trod that day to God, so walked he from his birth,
> In simpleness and gentleness and honour and clean mirth.

Night brought with it swiftly increasing weakness, and

at about 10 o'clock on Wednesday morning, December 19th, he passed quietly and painlessly to his rest.

Tributes such as have rarely—if, indeed, ever—been paid to a Free Church minister were rendered to Jowett—from the Throne, the pulpit, the platform and the Press. His Majesty the King sent Mrs. Jowett the following message by telegram :—

> The King has heard of your grievous loss with sincere regret, and I am commanded to express His Majesty's sympathy with you in your sorrow. The King, through his personal acquaintance with Dr. Jowett, can well realise how deeply his loss will be mourned by all who experienced the power of his great spiritual influence and guidance.
>
> STAMFORDHAM.

Bishops, Deans and clergy in all parts of the country publicly spoke of the loss inflicted on the Christian pulpit by the death of such an illustrious preacher. A General Election was in progress, and from the political platform prominent statesmen referred sympathetically to Jowett, acknowledging his services to the causes of national righteousness and international peace. In the Free Churches, and especially in the Congregational Churches, honour and praise were everywhere paid to his memory. With the passing of a great man, differences of creed and conflicts of opinion are forgotten. Jowett had aroused no sectarian animosities; his words had been a solace and an inspiration to men of all creeds and Churches. So, in his case, the obliterating charity, born in the awe of death's cold touch, was unnecessary. He had won the respect of his age and earned the guerdon of universal esteem, and in the days that followed his death tributes of affection and admiration came from all four quarters of the world.

The funeral took place on the Saturday (December 22nd) at Westminster Chapel and cremation followed at Golder's Green, where Rev. John Loosmore spoke the committal words. In the congregation at the service all the Churches were represented and almost all phases of English public life. The utmost simplicity marked the occasion. By special request no flowers were sent save by family friends—the one exception being a wreath of Los Angeles roses from Fifth Avenue Presbyterian Church, New York. Jowett's successor at Westminster, Dr. John A. Hutton, conducted the service, and his successors at Newcastle-on-Tyne (Rev. A. A. Lee) and at Carr's Lane Church, Birmingham (Rev. Sidney Berry, M.A.), read the Scriptures and gave an address. Jowett's friend and former neighbour, Rev. W. E. Daniels, Vicar of St. Matthew's, Croydon, offered prayer. Mr. Sidney Berry, in his tender tribute, spoke of Jowett's world-wide influence, his singleness of purpose as a preacher of the Gospel of Christ, his fidelity to the central verities, the penetrating beauty of his great language, the vividness of his arresting words and the ardour of his unwavering yearning to bring the things of Christ to the minds and hearts of all sorts and conditions of men. On Jowett's humility, his true spirit of friendship, his generosity of judgment, and his encouragement of young men Mr. Berry dwelt with loving simplicity. " A Greatheart indeed," was his final epitome and epitaph.

One vivid memory, recalled by Mr. Berry, left an indelible impression upon all who paid homage to Jowett by their presence at his funeral.

> I can see him now (said Mr. Berry) standing in the pulpit of my old home church preaching the memorial sermon of my father hardly a week after

his death. I was a boy then, but a boy whose heart knew that his biggest friend and hero had been taken away from him; but before the end of that sermon on the text " A man shall be a hiding place from the wind and a covert from the tempest " the sorrow in the heart of a boy had been transformed into a strange blending of pride and glory and joy. In the mysterious unfolding of life new and more intimate associations were to follow in the course of time, but somehow it is that first memory which returns to-day. To take the wounded heart of a boy, and to turn it from a passionate anguish to the glow of pride and the desire to go on—of how much in Dr. Jowett's ministry is that grateful memory the fitting symbol?

CHAPTER XVII

CHARACTERISTICS

An ingenious American professor invented a mathematical formula to express, relatively, Jowett's qualities as a man and a preacher. For Christlike character he gave him 38 A.A. marks : 30 A.A. marks were awarded him for talents : 20 A.A. for their training : 10 A. for prestige : 2 B. for personal appearance and 0 F. for " comradery." The formula, if somewhat grotesque, is a suggestive misinterpretation of a temperamentally shy man whose natural reserve and humility were mistaken for aloofness. Humility was a fundamental trait in Jowett's character. On the eve of leaving for America in 1911, after a sequence of overwhelming farewells, he wrote :—

> I feel like one who has been in the devouring glare of some furnace but has now passed into God's sweet sunshine. Surely I was never meant for glare and limelight, and yet it seems as though my path led through Vanity Fair. . . . One thing at any rate God has done for me. He has made me graciously numb to it all. I have felt no exciting response to all the garish curiosity of these latter days and to the publicity which has accompanied it. On that side the Lord has taken away " feeling " and I am unmoved. And this is an answer to prayer.

Five years later, after a surfeit of popularity in America, writing to Miss Alice Slater he said :—

> The older I get the less satisfaction I find in crowds. A crowd is very imposing if it is yielding

disciples for Christ. What would be the use of
a huge mine if we got no ore out of it ? And what
is the use of a multitude if we get no jewels for
Christ ?

Vanity was altogether foreign to him. To be lionised
distressed him and fulsome adulation froze all the
springs in his being. " Of all the difficult things one
has to face," he said, " eulogy is perhaps the most
difficult." For the loyalty of his coadjutors and the
affection of his friends he overflowed with gratitude.
" It just sets my work to music," he said.

Nothing impressed those who came into intimate
touch with Jowett more than this genuine unaffected
humility. The honours piled upon him never stirred
in him the faintest suggestion of conceit or self-conse-
quence. He had not a swagger at his command.

Croydon,
Nov. 24, 1922.

To Miss Alice Slater.
      I am feeling that my pleasure in the Honour *
is greatly enriched in the pleasure it has given to
my friends. I do not know that it has added to
my sleep, or that distinctions of this kind add any
real worth to life except in so far as they may open
doors which have hitherto been closed.
      I have just come back from Manchester, where
I have been preaching in the Free Trade Hall to a
congregation of 4000 listeners. What hymn singing there was, and what power of prayer, and what
spiritual enthusiasm ! Anybody could preach
in such an atmosphere.

Croydon.

To Miss Jessie Spicer.
      I know it is so easy preaching, but I do want
to prove the worth of what I preach in my own
experience. And I always feel that all my

* Companionship of Honour conferred upon him by the King.

privileges have failed and perhaps done me harm, unless they have enabled me to take up humble service and make it beautiful.

Jowett was one of the very rare souls who can " walk with Kings " and " keep the common touch," receive high honours and wear them modestly and walk humbly amid the adulation of the crowd. The publicity that arose naturally out of his work he endured without liking it ; but he went through life without granting a single " personal " interview, and no newspaper or magazine ever secured a " Dr. Jowett at Home " article.

His home life was sheltered from public gaze. Writing to his daughter Monica on her seventeenth birthday, and addressing her as My Dearest Seventeen, he said :

> Phew ! It seems only yesterday that I was teaching you to step off the garden walk on to the lawn. And now you are seventeen and a whopper at that. . . . Well, you have given Mother and me all these years of happiness and it is lovely to see you growing up. . . . I am happiest when we are all together at the fireside. Are you going to see " Peter Pan " to-night ?

His own visits to the theatre were not frequent, but he conceded that the dramatic art has its rightful place in the cultured life. Music he loved. After a classical concert in New York he wrote to his daughter : " . . . The music was a bit above me. I could see that the execution was wonderful, but the sounds did not make much impression upon me. But that is nothing against it."

His piety was innate and central to his character. He lived close to the Eternal Springs, and dwelt constantly in the secret places of the Most High. In

U

Dr. John Watson's famous phrase he was a true mystic—" far ben " in the spiritual realities.

Selsey,
Aug. 27, 1920.

To Miss Alice Slater.

I wish you wouldn't think I am such a saint. You seem to imagine that I have no ups and downs, but just a level and lofty stretch of spiritual attainment with unbroken joy and equanimity. By no means ! I am often perfectly wretched and everything appears most murky. I often feel as though my religious life had only just begun, and that I am in the kindergarten stage. But I can usually trace these miserable seasons to some personal cause, and the first thing to do is to attend to that cause, and get into the sunshine again. Of one thing I am sure . . . we are far too much concerned about " doing " and far too little concerned to " let God do." Isn't that the difference between law and grace ? Law says " do " : grace says " done." (I am going to preach on that some day). . . . That is where we are going to find lightheartedness.

A large part of his life every day was scrupulously reserved for private devotions—" interludes " he called them, " when the soul can correct her conscious and unconscious wanderings by the contemplation of the serene and majestic things of God." This mystical union with Christ did not lead him into fruitless reveries and idle dreams. " There is no one," he said, " so practical, no one so splendidly energetic as the advanced mystic," and a sanctified common sense found expression in his preaching and in his conversation. " Religious life " was always a practical reality to him, and he had no patience with people who flaunt their religious profession but have no religious life. " They constitute the bane of the Kingdom," he said once with unwonted savagery, " for they are the unconscious professionals who make the Christian religion unattractive and repellent."

He could be merry—even hilarious—enough on the right occasion and he would assuredly have conceded that a cheerful Christian is one of the best of apologetics : but the function of the pulpit, as he saw it, was not to amuse but to inspire, and he used to say that it is always a perilous thing when a crusade is led by a jester. Appeals " to the gallery " were alien to him and he believed that people resent them from the pulpit.

One of the secrets of Jowett's capacity to hold the attention of a congregation of uncomfortably crowded people throughout a sermon lay in the conviction carried by the simplicity of his ardent faith. He spoke with the authority of a man inspired by the urgency of his own message. Very little argument entered into the fabric of his sermon. He affirmed, and his affirmations rang with an authoritativeness seldom heard in the pulpit since Spurgeon's silvery voice was silenced. His reasoned optimism also lent a gripping quality to his words. It was the optimism of a man with a long view and a wide horizon. He never doubted right would triumph—in the long run : but, with Robert Browning, he knew that a wide compass round might have to be fetched. Bishop Lightfoot's recipe for curing drooping spirits, the reading of history, had been adopted by Jowett, who was less depressed perhaps by the period of moral declension and worldwide social unrest that followed the war than most preachers of his period.

Croydon,
Jany. 31, 1920.

To Miss Alice Slater.

I am immensely interested in India just now, and I am reading all I can lay hold of. I am

particularly interested in the native papers, especially
in those papers which are not Christian but are im-
bued with a mighty spirit of social reform. Some
of the articles seem to be miles ahead of us. I just
want to broaden my outlook in all directions so that
I may interpret these movements as the marchings
of the Spirit of God.

Fastidiousness about his personal appearance was
a characteristic of Jowett, as it was of Henry Drummond. He dressed well, only just behind the best
Savile Row fashion in the cut of his trim morning
coat. The parsonic collar and the conventional
black tie were outside his scheme of things. Distinctly above the average height, he bore himself with
soldierly uprightness and got the full advantage out
of every inch of his stature. With his small head,
lean face, drooping moustache and all-seeing eyes
gleaming steadily through his glasses, he might well
have passed for a prosperous solicitor, or a medical
specialist in a good Harley Street practice.

Caring nothing for luxuries, he had no personal
extravagances. Travel he regarded as a sort of
post-graduate education, and the money it cost was,
he thought, well spent. " The prices are high," he
wrote to Mr. J. G. Hurst from the Riviera, " but of
course the exchange is in our favour. And it's all in
a life time." He travelled with a seeing eye and an
open mind :—

To Miss Jessie Spicer.
    In the lands to which you are going you will
see many things which will repel you. Pray, and
seek to obtain a spirit of more sensitive sympathy
that you may feel all that is good in faiths and
practices which are not yours. One of the things

which will happen to you is this, that when you return you will have a far more intelligent appreciation of what we call the " heathen " world, and your outlook and your prayers will be correspondingly enriched.

Until middle life he was a non-smoker—he was a lifelong total abstainer—and he only began to smoke with a sick brother who needed a little encouraging company. He always toyed with a cigarette in an unenthusiastic fashion that showed that My Lady Nicotine had no charms for him.

When he was leaving Birmingham for New York his sensitive spirit was sorely bruised by the suggestion, current in some quarters, that he was tempted to Fifth Avenue Church by the large stipend. He resented the imputation deeply and repudiated it hotly. His New York income left him no greater margin than he had in Birmingham, and he told one of his friends that he was always profoundly thankful, while he was in New York, that he had taken that stand, and had refused to accept from Fifth Avenue Church anything more than the American equivalent of his former English income. It had relieved him, he said, of a great bondage. Concerning the stewardship of money he was, in fact, very conscientious. He was generous in his own personal contributions, and he never appealed to his people for money without contributing handsomely himself. His benevolences were many and large—but they were always made unostentatiously. On the first day of each month certain pensioners upon his bounty invariably received a remittance from him, and he subscribed liberally to missions and philanthropies. He came in for some wealth, and had he sought riches he might have amassed them : but he refrained.

A man who lives in the public gaze (he wrote to a friend) as I do, is very tempted to forget the necessity of making his by-ways neat and beautiful. If only we looked after our back streets, the front streets might pretty well be left to look after themselves. Perhaps the angels would take the front streets in hand.

Though keenly alive to all the hectic stirrings of thought in his time, Jowett very rarely digressed from his life work as a preacher. His nature demanded an atmosphere of serenity for his work. He would never have dreamed of having an open conference after one of his services, and the mild heckling after his Lyman Beecher lectures at Yale was not to his liking. Contradiction would have disturbed his habit of mind. His, as someone has said, was a rounded character with no angles to crush into anyone's ribs. He did nothing sensational. His sermons did not provide " copy " for secular newspapers. He stuck to his own last. The heresies of other preachers never tempted him to raise a hue and cry. The same eirenic temperament made him somewhat disdainful of denominational differences. Scientific discoveries and the ascertained results of the Higher critics did not flutter him. He stood between the Fundamentalists and the Modernists, calm and confident, with his faith based on Christian experience, to him the impregnable rock. His was a *via media* mind, typically Yorkshire. He had a spark of the quietist spirit, and often found inspiration in a Quakers' meeting. Nothing in sacramentarianism made any deep appeal to him. He thought of the Lord's Supper as " a permanent memorial of Calvary, purposed to keep a stupendous fact in mind, and prevent it becoming a neglected commonplace." Baptism meant to him " a proclamation of God's covenant of Grace under which all children are born into a world redeemed—an illustration of the doctrine that the Holy Ghost has been given to the world—and an opportunity of solemnly dedicating oneself and one's children, and of openly professing one's faith." The question of immersion or sprinkling he regarded as incidental and unimportant. The regeneration of the individual,—and through the individual the race,—through Jesus Christ was his fundamental belief, and preaching that insistently he was content to treat incidentals as incidental.

His sympathy was quickly aroused and freely expressed. From the consolatory letters written by Jowett to people in sickness, anxiety or bereavement a " Book of Comfort " of infinite solace and assuagement might be compiled. This aspect of his wider ministry was necessarily carried on privately : but he gave himself unsparingly to it, especially in his later years when his own health and the scattered nature of his congregation made pastoral visitation almost impossible. Letters received from Jowett in seasons of pain or sorrow have, I find, been treasured long after the occasion that evoked them, for they conveyed a spirit of tender sympathy and a gracious fragrance that made them an abiding possession. In comforting the bereaved, Jowett, in these letters, almost invariably spoke of death as a natural transition wholly without terrors for him.

He has reached the haven he longed for (he wrote to a son mourning the death of a noble father) : he has met his Lord. I have an almost devouring curiosity to know what such men realise when they stand in the immediate presence of the Lord whom they have served. Their wonder and praise must be overwhelming.

How must your father feel to be young again, and to be for ever young.

This glad assurance of immortality was the constant theme of his consolatory letters. His heart leapt out to people in trouble and he was lavish in little kindnesses to heal their distresses. When the wife of a member of his Carr's Lane congregation was taken seriously ill, and it was necessary to send the little children to stay with a friend in Yorkshire, Jowett at once volunteered for the errand, and he spent a whole day in travelling there and back.

In his personal judgments Jowett was charitable and generous. He gave all men the benefit of the doubt. " I never heard him," writes a friend, " utter an unworthy sentiment, or speak evil of any man, or knew him to do an unkind deed." Ministers who sought his aid, or his counsel, with a view to changes of pastorate found him sympathetic and eager to be helpful, and the encouragement he gave to younger ministers stirred many of them to higher incentives and closer devotion to their ministry. He enjoyed listening to the sermons of other preachers, and always found something to praise. Probably he was too generous in these appreciations, and may have encouraged some geese to imagine that they were swans. But that was an amiable weakness. All that concerned the Christian ministry interested him. He viewed with real anxiety the growing reluctance on the part of Congregational Churches to invite to their pastorates men who have passed their fiftieth milestone in life. Writing to a friend respecting a church which had sought his advice, he said, " I do not know what kind of man they are seeking. It may be that, like so many of our churches, they are wanting a raw, inexperienced man who is just out of College. It is truly tragical the way our churches are ready to throw away the ripe fruit for early blossom." When, later, he heard that the Church barred a minister above the age of fifty he wrote again : " It is amazing how these churches are willing to throw aside the matured and experienced of our best men."

Asceticism made no appeal to Jowett, with all his simplicity of taste. He believed in an ample and symmetrical life, as long as every avenue—as he put it—" was lit up with the light of the supreme relationship to Christ." A letter written to his daughter on the day after she first left home for Boarding School illustrates his ideal of womanhood.

> And now (he wrote) I am sure you will live the life of a noble girl. I have no fear about that. Wherever you are, and whatever you are doing, I am never anxious about your behaviour. I am sure you are a girl of high principle, and Mother and I can trust you implicitly. You will be straight and true and kind and gentle. I really wish nothing better for you than that you should become like Mother. Your mother is a lovely Christian woman and you know how she lives. She keeps up an intimate friendship with Christ, and nothing is allowed to interfere with it. And you will do the same. Be a firm noble friend of the Master and everything will be all right. Keep in communion with Him by prayer and be one of the purest and brightest and jolliest girls in the school.

One of Jowett's cherished but unfulfilled ideas was to write a volume of prayers for public school boys. He felt the need of such a book, embodying prayers natural to youth, and rich in piety without pietism. The opportunity never came to him. One of his devotional books, " Yet Another Day," was carried about by the Archbishop of Canterbury, when he visited America, for use in his private devotions.

Through nearly thirty-five years Jowett brought to the ministry of the Gospel every power and faculty he could command. His work was his passion and he had no other. To few men has it been given to realise their ambitions so completely.

> I want the next ten years (he wrote on his fiftieth birthday) to be full of ripened service. I long to be able to expound the Word with greater power. But, O, the thing is so big, so wonderfully big that I seem as one who lifts a pebble from the shore, or one heather bell from these wide-spreading moors. The Book becomes increasingly wonderful to me. Every added experience in life gives me a new lens and deeper things are unveiled. But I suppose there is no bottom to the sea of grace, and that is the reason why we shall never lose our surprise through all eternity.

The ten years were granted to him and he used them nobly :—

> My future work (he wrote on his sixtieth birthday) is not yet quite clear, but I think it is taking shape and I see something on the horizon. Of course the main work of my life, if God mercifully gives me back some of my strength, will be preaching, and I am looking forward to that with great delight. I have learned a good many things during these many months and I want to tell some of my findings to others. Perhaps God will give me a place where I can tell the story.

His consciousness that he had yet much to say to his day and generation accentuated the pathos of his early death. " I'm not sixty yet," he said wistfully to a brother minister, as he lay, a physical wreck, on a couch under the veranda at Matlock in the last summer of his life, " and I should like a few more years." It was not that he repined, or fretted, or rebelled. " I have had a glorious innings," he constantly repeated during that last year—and he accepted his approaching end with perfect Christian resignation. With Robert Louis Stevenson he would have said " Glad did I live . . . and I laid me down with a will."

I.

One night, when busy day was done,
My spoils all ranged in setting sun,
As I reviewed the race well run,
I heard a knocking at my door,
So faint I scarce could hear it !
Not knowing if my sense were vain,
I looked across the window pane,
And saw a presence with a mien
So deeply reverent and serene,
" A kinsman of the Nazarene "
I thought no one could fear it.

II.

I let him in.   I bade him rest:
I thought he would have been my guest
A single night, and coming day
Would see the pilgrim on his way
Along his mystic journey :
Yet not as guest but settled friend
It seemed as if he meant to spend
His life with me.   I asked his name,
A silence followed, and there came
An air of radiant gentleness,
A warmth of heavenly kindliness,
In height, and depth, and length !
" My name is weakness sent by Love
To change the carnal to the dove,
And clothe thee with the life above
And lead thee into strength."

J. H. J

(*Written at Matlock : January* 1923.)

INDEX